The Infrastructure Oracle

How to Profit from Hidden Government Project Plans

Realty Insider

Realty Insider - MARKET KNOWLEDGE. REAL WEALTH

CONFIDENTIAL INDUSTRY INTELLIGENCE

STRATEGIC KNOWLEDGE DISCLOSURE The property market intelligence, hidden valuation frameworks, and insider tactical knowledge contained within represents closely guarded real estate strategies previously restricted to institutional investors and industry insiders. This intelligence has been made available with the understanding that such market-moving information requires careful and strategic implementation.

MARKET INTELLIGENCE DISCLAIMER This publication reveals sophisticated real estate investment strategies historically known only to industry insiders. While RealtyInsider™ provides accurate market intelligence based on extensive industry research, we are not providing legal, financial, or professional services. For specific investment situations, consult qualified professionals.

The strategic patterns, market indicators, and tactical approaches revealed here are based on analysis of thousands of successful real estate transactions. While these methods have proven effective for institutional investors, individual results will vary based on market conditions and implementation.

LIABILITY LIMITATION The publisher and authors assume no responsibility for investment decisions made using this intelligence. Real estate investments carry inherent risks. Neither RealtyInsider™ nor its contributors shall be liable for any financial losses or damages resulting from use of this information. This content serves educational purposes only and is not personalized investment advice.

STRATEGIC INTELLIGENCE ACCESS By accessing this material, you are receiving proprietary insights into real estate wealth-building frameworks previously restricted to industry insiders. This tactical knowledge must be applied in accordance with all applicable laws and regulations.

Market Knowledge. Real Wealth.

RealtyInsider.io

About Realty Insider

Realty Insider exists at the forefront of a real estate intelligence revolution, shattering the protective walls that have historically kept elite property investment strategies hidden from everyday investors. We specialize in exposing the closely guarded operational secrets of the real estate market – the unwritten rules, market triggers, and procedural opportunities that industry insiders exploit daily but rarely reveal.

What distinguishes Realty Insider is our insider-to-arsenal approach to market knowledge. Our tactical library includes devastating strategies for property acquisition, value-add investing, market timing, and portfolio optimization – all drawn from real deals where informed investors turned market complexity into wealth-building weapons. Through careful study of thousands of successful transactions, we've identified the precise market indicators, psychological triggers, and procedural advantages that consistently create profitable opportunities in an otherwise competitive system.

Our battle-tested guides transform obscure market knowledge into clear, actionable investment plans, revealing not just what to do, but the hidden reasons why it works. Each strategy represents a tactical blueprint drawn from real-world successes, industry whistleblowers, and exposed internal strategies, converting intimidating market dynamics into systematic profit generators. Whether targeting residential investments, navigating commercial acquisitions, or building a passive income empire, our guides give you the same tactical advantage as any major real estate firm.

Join us in exposing the property market's hidden mechanisms as we transform its barriers into weapons for those bold enough to take control of their financial future. Because true wealth creation requires more than just knowing the basics – it requires knowing how to make opportunities untouchable.

Market Knowledge. Real Wealth.

RealtyInsider.io

Your Gateway to AI-Powered Publishing Success

About Exponential Press

Realty Insider is your gateway to mastering the transformative power of AI, automation, and innovation. We empower entrepreneurs, professionals, and leaders to navigate the rapidly evolving digital landscape with confidence and clarity. At the core of our mission is a commitment to delivering actionable strategies that drive measurable success and growth in an AI-powered world.

Our Development Approach

Every book in this collection emerges from rigorous research and collaboration with industry pioneers who share our commitment to ethical innovation. We integrate diverse perspectives, real-world implementation experience, and careful analysis to ensure each volume provides actionable guidance while maintaining focus on human values and societal impact.

Create Your Own Book

Now you can harness this same powerful technology to transform your expertise into a professionally crafted book. Whether you're sharing specialized knowledge or exploring complex topics, our AI-enabled platform helps you create comprehensive, engaging content in just 48 hours.

What You'll Receive

- 60,000+ Words of Expertly Crafted Content: In-depth, thoroughly researched writing tailored to your chosen topic—designed to inform, engage, and inspire your audience
- AI-Driven Insights and Analysis: Fresh perspectives and meaningful connections across complex subjects, ensuring your book stands out
- SEO-Optimized Publishing Tools: Professional book description, carefully selected categories, and keyword optimization for maximum discoverability
- Professional Formatting: Complete guidance ensuring your book meets professional standards on your preferred platforms
- Full Ownership Rights: Retain complete publishing rights, maintaining creative freedom and maximizing profits
- Fast Turnaround: Your polished, professionally crafted book within 48 hours

Quality Commitment

Each book undergoes rigorous review to ensure it meets our standards of excellence while serving your specific needs. We maintain full transparency throughout the development process

Ready to begin your publishing journey? ***RealtyInsider.io/custom-book*** to learn more.

Innovate. Automate. Lead.

RealtyInsider.io

RESTRICTED INTELLIGENCE

Realty Insider

The Property Insider's Arsenal For the first time, RealtyInsider is revealing five of the most closely guarded playbooks used by institutional real estate investors. This comprehensive tactical package exposes profit-generating strategies typically reserved for billion-dollar property portfolios.

Get immediate access to:

- *The Market Prophet Blueprint:* Hidden indicators professional investors use to predict property booms months in advance
- *The Shadow Market Manual:* How to find and secure incredible off-market deals before they hit the MLS
- *The Value Accelerator System:* Proven tactics to force rapid appreciation in any market condition
- *The Risk Eraser Protocol:* Due diligence secrets that institutional investors use to eliminate costly mistakes
- *The Negotiation Dominator:* Psychological triggers that make sellers accept your price, even against higher offers

Regular Value: **$497** Special Access: **FREE**

Contents

Introduction

Think for a moment about the intricate dance of cranes silhouetted against a city skyline. Each one is a testament to the power of human ambition, a visible marker of growth and progress. Yet, beneath this majestic spectacle lies a world of unseen decisions, plans, and opportunities—an intricate web that, if understood, can lead to significant financial gains. Infrastructure projects, often overlooked, hold the key to transformative investment possibilities. As cities expand and evolve, government plans for roads, bridges, public transit, and utilities quietly shape the future. The foresight to interpret these plans before they become public can position an astute investor at the forefront of opportunity. This book, The Infrastructure Oracle: How to Profit from Hidden Government Project Plans, invites you to explore this often-unseen world and harness its potential for success.

Understanding the Opportunity in Infrastructure Projects

The landscape of infrastructure projects teems with potential for those who know where to look. From foundational endeavors like highways and bridges to modern marvels such as high-speed rail networks and smart city grids, these developments are the lifeblood of economic growth and urban vitality. Yet, the true opportunities lie not in the projects themselves but in the ability to anticipate their emergence. By understanding the governmental processes that drive infrastructure planning and execution, one can discern the subtle signals that herald new projects. This knowledge transforms the seemingly mundane details of policy documents and budget reports into a treasure map of investment possibilities. Imagine identifying a new transit hub before the first shovel breaks ground or recognizing the implications of a rezoning plan long before it affects land prices. Such insights can open doors to lucrative real estate investments and business ventures, and this book is your guide to unlocking them.

The Basics of Decoding Government Signals

At the heart of successful infrastructure investing is the ability to decode the complex signals woven into government documents and planning processes. Governments, despite their vast bureaucracies, leave a trail of breadcrumbs for those who know where to look. Capital Improvement Plans (CIPs), budgets, permit applications, and public meetings each contain valuable insights into future projects. The challenge lies in interpreting these signals accurately and timely. Mastery of these skills allows investors to act decisively and confidently. This book demystifies the processes and tools necessary for effective signal decoding, providing a practical framework to analyze and extract actionable intelligence from the layers of governmental planning. Through clear explanations and real-world examples, you will learn to navigate the labyrinth of public records and legislative agendas, turning what was once a daunting task into a strategic advantage.

Why Timing and Research Are Key

Timing, as they say, is everything. In the realm of infrastructure investments, this adage holds especially true. The ability to act on insights before they become common knowledge is what separates the successful investor from the rest. Research-driven investing, grounded in diligent analysis and informed predictions, provides a competitive edge. By honing the skills to anticipate infrastructure developments, investors can position themselves to capitalize on emerging opportunities. This book emphasizes the importance of thorough research and strategic timing, guiding you to make informed decisions that maximize potential returns while minimizing risks. Whether it's choosing the right property, securing advantageous financing, or knowing when to exit, the lessons within these pages are designed to empower you with the tools needed for success. As you journey through the chapters, you'll gain the confidence to navigate the complexities of infrastructure investing, transforming knowledge into wealth.

As you embark on this journey through The Infrastructure Oracle, prepare to uncover a world of hidden potential and untapped possibilities. Each chapter builds upon the last, equipping you with the expertise to identify, analyze, and profit from government project plans before they become public knowledge. This book is not just a guide but a call to action—a blueprint for those who wish to seize the opportunities that lie beneath the surface. With every insight gained, you'll move closer to mastering the art of infrastructure investing, turning foresight into fortune. The path to success is lined with knowledge, and this book invites you to take the first step toward unlocking its secrets.

Chapter One

The Foundations of Government Infrastructure Planning

In a bustling city, a seemingly mundane plot of land lies untouched, surrounded by the hum of daily life. To the untrained eye, it's just another vacant lot. Yet, to those equipped with the knowledge of government planning, it holds the potential to become a hub of transformation—a new public transit station, a state-of-the-art hospital, or a sprawling park that rejuvenates the neighborhood. This hidden narrative of infrastructure is unfolding across cities, states, and nations, offering remarkable opportunities for those who can read between the lines of government documents and plans.

Understanding the intricate dance of infrastructure development requires more than just a knack for numbers or a hunch about future growth. It demands a deep dive into the lifecycle of projects, from the initial spark of an idea to the day the ribbon is cut. This chapter unravels the threads of this complex tapestry, revealing the roles of key agencies and stakeholders who steer these massive undertakings. These entities, with their specific mandates and objectives, act as the architects of progress, shaping the timelines and outcomes that ripple through communities.

But projects don't just leap from blueprints to reality; they weave through a maze of budgets, funding battles, and public discourse. Each stage of the process is marked by critical decisions made in public meetings and hearings, where voices are heard and futures are debated. By navigating these waters, readers will gain the insights needed to anticipate the next big development, positioning themselves to turn foresight into financial gains. As we embark on this journey into the world of government infrastructure planning, the potential to profit from these hidden opportunities becomes not just a possibility, but a tangible strategy.

The Lifecycle of Infrastructure Projects: From Idea to Construction

Imagine a bustling city where the hum of construction fills the air, signaling progress and transformation. Beneath the surface, however, lies a meticulous blueprint, a lifecycle of infrastructure projects that begins long before the first shovel hits the ground. This journey from conception to construction is a complex dance, orchestrated by a myriad of players and shaped by economic realities and community needs. Each project starts as a spark of an idea, a response to identified needs, and a vision for future growth. It is here, at this nascent stage, that opportunities for savvy investors begin to take root. Understanding how these projects evolve, from initial brainstorming sessions to the ribbon-cutting ceremonies, holds the key to unlocking potential financial gains.

As we embark on this exploration, we delve into the stages of planning, where stakeholder engagement becomes the heartbeat of progress. Navigating these waters requires a keen eye for detail and an understanding of the intricate processes that govern approvals and overcome pre-construction hurdles. Each phase, each decision, adds another layer to the tapestry, revealing paths for those perceptive enough to see them. The ability to interpret these signals not only equips investors with foresight but also empowers them to anticipate shifts that others might overlook. The lifecycle of infrastructure projects is more than a sequence of events; it's a window into future landscapes, an opportunity to align investments with impending change.

Conceptualizing Infrastructure Needs and Prioritization

When conceptualizing infrastructure needs, the initial step is to identify the specific demands of a community or region, taking into account both immediate requirements and long-term aspirations. This involves a meticulous analysis of demographic trends, economic forecasts, and environmental considerations. For instance, a rapidly growing suburban area may prioritize expanding transportation networks to accommodate increased traffic, whereas a coastal city might focus on flood defenses in response to climate change projections. Advanced data analytics and predictive modeling play crucial roles in this phase, allowing planners to simulate various scenarios and outcomes. By integrating insights from local stakeholders, including residents, businesses, and civic organizations, planners can ensure that the proposed infrastructure aligns with the community's broader vision and goals.

Prioritization of projects often hinges on a complex interplay of factors, including economic impact, social equity, and political feasibility. Decision-makers must weigh the potential benefits of an infrastructure project against its costs and potential disruptions. For example, a new transit system might offer significant long-term economic and environmental benefits but require substantial upfront investment and temporary inconveniences during construction. Prioritization frameworks, such as cost-benefit analysis and multi-criteria decision analysis, provide structured methodologies for evaluating these trade-offs. Additionally, incorporating cutting-edge technologies, such as artificial intelligence and machine learning, can enhance the prioritization process by offering nuanced insights into potential project impacts and risks.

Navigating the planning stages requires adept stakeholder engagement and strategic foresight. Effective communication and collaboration among various parties—including government agencies, private sector partners, and the public—are essential for fostering a shared understanding of project goals and challenges. Transparent dialogue helps build trust and mitigate opposition, ultimately facilitating smoother project progression. Innovative tools, such as digital platforms for public consultation and virtual reality simulations, can enhance stakeholder involvement by providing interactive and immersive experiences that clarify complex project details. By fostering an inclusive planning process, stakeholders can collaboratively address potential obstacles and devise solutions that reflect diverse perspectives and priorities.

Securing the necessary approvals and overcoming pre-construction challenges demands a proactive approach and a thorough understanding of regulatory landscapes. Navigating the labyrinth of permits, environmental assessments, and legal requirements can be daunting, yet it is a critical component of successful infrastructure development. Establishing early and ongoing communication channels with regulatory bodies can expedite the approval process and preempt potential roadblocks. Moreover, leveraging innovative practices, such as modular construction techniques and sustainable materials, can address environmental concerns and enhance project viability, ultimately gaining favor with both regulators and the community.

The exploration of infrastructure planning raises intriguing questions about the future of societal development. How can emerging technologies further revolutionize the way we conceptualize and prioritize infrastructure projects? What role will public engagement play in shaping the next generation of infrastructure, and how can planners ensure that diverse voices are heard? By contemplating these questions, readers are encouraged to think critically about the evolving landscape of infrastructure development and consider how they might apply these insights in their own contexts. Ultimately, the ability to anticipate and respond to emerging trends and challenges will distinguish successful infrastructure planners and investors from the rest.

Navigating Planning Stages and Stakeholder Engagement

Navigating the planning stages of infrastructure projects requires a nuanced understanding of both procedural dynamics and stakeholder engagement. At the heart of this process lies the intricate dance between governmental agencies, private entities, and the general public. Projects often begin with the identification of infrastructure needs, where government bodies assess demands based on population growth, economic forecasts, and existing deficiencies. This initial stage is crucial, as it sets the groundwork for prioritizing projects that align with strategic development goals. Engaging with stakeholders early on, including community groups and industry experts, can bring diverse perspectives and ensure that projects are not only viable but also beneficial to a wide range of constituents.

Stakeholder engagement is an evolving art form, one that requires project managers to be adept communicators and consensus builders. Effective engagement goes beyond mere consultation; it involves genuine collaboration and transparency. This can be achieved through a variety of platforms, such as public forums, digital surveys, and interactive workshops, which allow stakeholders to voice concerns and provide input. For instance, a city planning a new public transit system might hold town hall meetings to gather feedback from residents, ensuring the project considers local commuting patterns and addresses community needs. By fostering an inclusive dialogue, planners can mitigate resistance and cultivate support, which can be pivotal in propelling projects forward.

The planning stages are not just about gathering input but also about navigating the complex web of regulatory requirements and approvals. This phase often involves conducting environmental impact assessments, securing zoning permits, and adhering to local, state, and federal regulations. Each of these steps demands meticulous documentation and a strategic approach to negotiations. Projects that proactively address potential legal and environmental hurdles tend to progress more smoothly through the approval pipeline. Innovative approaches, such as utilizing predictive analytics to foresee and address community concerns, can streamline this process, ensuring that projects remain on schedule and within budget.

In today's interconnected world, cutting-edge technology offers new avenues for enhancing planning efficiency. Geographic Information Systems (GIS), for instance, provide a powerful tool for visualizing project impacts and optimizing routes and locations. This technology aids planners in making data-driven decisions, balancing technical requirements with community preferences. Concurrently, emerging trends emphasize the integration of sustainable practices, such as incorporating green infrastructure and renewable energy sources, which not only align with environmental goals but also attract investment by demonstrating long-term viability and resilience.

Contemplating the future of infrastructure planning, one might ponder how evolving societal values and technological advancements will reshape stakeholder engagement. Will digital platforms continue to democratize participation, allowing for more nuanced and inclusive planning processes? As we move forward, the challenge lies in transforming these insights into actionable strategies, ensuring that infrastructure projects not only meet immediate needs but also anticipate future demands. By continuously refining engagement techniques and embracing innovation, planners can create infrastructure that serves as a cornerstone for sustainable growth and community well-being.

Securing Approvals and Managing Pre-Construction Challenges

Securing approvals and navigating the pre-construction phase are pivotal steps in transforming infrastructure concepts into tangible projects. This stage demands a keen understanding of regulatory frameworks and a strategic approach to stakeholder engagement. At its core, the approval process involves multiple layers of government oversight, requiring project proponents to meticulously prepare and present detailed proposals to satisfy diverse criteria. Each jurisdiction may have unique regulatory nuances, often involving environmental impact assessments, zoning compliance, and alignment with regional development plans. Successfully navigating these complexities necessitates a robust strategic plan that anticipates potential roadblocks and adapts to evolving regulatory landscapes, ensuring that projects remain on track and within budgetary constraints.

A profound grasp of the intricate dance between public and private interests is crucial for overcoming pre-construction hurdles. This phase often witnesses a confluence of interests, where balancing community concerns, governmental priorities, and economic feasibility becomes paramount. Engaging with local communities and stakeholders early in the process can mitigate opposition and foster a collaborative atmosphere. Innovative approaches, such as public consultations and participatory planning sessions, can transform potential adversaries into advocates, smoothing the path for approvals. Establishing open lines of communication with all parties involved not only builds trust but also provides valuable insights that can be integrated into project designs, enhancing their resilience and societal acceptance.

Advanced project management methodologies are instrumental in managing pre-construction challenges. Employing cutting-edge tools, like Building Information Modeling (BIM) and predictive analytics, enables project teams to simulate various scenarios, identify potential pitfalls, and optimize resource allocation. These technologies offer a proactive approach to risk management, allowing for the refinement of project plans before they are set into motion. By integrating data-driven insights with traditional project management techniques, infrastructure developers can fine-tune timelines and budgets, ensuring that projects proceed smoothly from the drawing board to the construction site. This fusion of technology and strategy not only minimizes unforeseen delays and costs but also positions projects for long-term success.

Incorporating lessons from recent case studies and emerging trends can provide invaluable insights into the approval process. Observing how other projects have successfully navigated regulatory mazes can offer transferable strategies and highlight potential pitfalls. For instance, the adoption of green building standards and sustainable practices has become a compelling factor in gaining regulatory favor. Projects that demonstrate environmental stewardship and social responsibility often enjoy expedited approval processes and enhanced public support. By staying attuned to these evolving standards, project proponents can align their initiatives with broader societal goals, thereby strengthening their case for approval.

Encouraging critical evaluation and strategic foresight, consider scenarios where infrastructure projects face unexpected regulatory challenges or shifts in public opinion. How can project leaders adapt their strategies to accommodate these changes? The key lies in maintaining flexibility and fostering a culture of continuous learning and adaptation. By cultivating relationships with regulatory bodies and staying informed about legislative shifts, project teams can anticipate changes and adjust their strategies accordingly. The journey from concept to construction is fraught with challenges, yet by embracing innovative approaches and maintaining a forward-thinking mindset, infrastructure developers can not only secure approvals but also pave the way for transformative projects that meet the needs of communities and stakeholders alike.

Key Agencies and Stakeholders in Project Development

Imagine waking up one morning to find that the land behind your house, once a quiet expanse of trees, is now buzzing with construction activity. The sound of progress echoes through your neighborhood, signaling the arrival of a new infrastructure project. This transformation, seemingly overnight, is the result of a complex interplay of decisions made by a web of agencies and stakeholders long before a single shovel broke ground. Understanding who these players are and how they influence the process is crucial for anyone looking to anticipate and capitalize on such developments. This section peels back the layers of bureaucracy to reveal the key agencies operating at federal, state, and local levels, each wielding significant power in shaping the urban landscape. These entities, often shrouded in legal jargon and formalities, hold the keys to unlocking future opportunities for savvy investors.

As we navigate this intricate network, the spotlight turns first to the pivotal roles played by federal and state agencies in orchestrating infrastructure plans. Their mandates and objectives often set the stage for large-scale projects, casting long shadows over the planning process. Local governments and municipalities, on the other hand, serve as the boots on the ground, translating grand visions into tangible realities within communities. Their influence is immediate and palpable, bridging the gap between policy and practice. Yet the story wouldn't be complete without acknowledging the private sector stakeholders and interest groups whose vested interests can alter the course of development. These entities bring resources, expertise, and sometimes, opposition, adding another layer of complexity to the infrastructure puzzle. Understanding the motivations and interactions of each group provides a strategic edge, a vantage point from which informed predictions can be made, setting the stage for informed investment decisions.

Navigating the Role of Federal and State Agencies in Infrastructure Planning

Federal and state agencies stand as pivotal players in the realm of infrastructure planning, orchestrating the intricate dance of project development across expansive geographies and diverse sectors. At the federal level, agencies such as the Department of Transportation (DOT) and the Environmental Protection Agency (EPA) lay the groundwork for nationwide infrastructure initiatives that align with overarching policy agendas. These entities wield significant influence, setting regulatory standards and disbursing federal funds that catalyze state and local projects. Meanwhile, state agencies operate as intermediaries, translating federal objectives into localized action, often customizing projects to address regional needs and priorities. This tiered structure not only facilitates coordination across different levels of government but also allows for a nuanced approach to infrastructure planning, accommodating the unique characteristics of various locales.

The interplay between federal and state agencies often hinges on the strategic allocation of funding, a process that embodies both opportunity and complexity. Federal grants and loans serve as crucial lifelines for state-driven projects, yet accessing these resources demands a thorough understanding of the labyrinthine application processes and stringent compliance requirements. Agencies like the Federal Highway Administration (FHWA) and the Federal Transit Administration (FTA) administer competitive funding programs, challenging state entities to articulate compelling project proposals that align with federal priorities such as sustainability, safety, and innovation. This dynamic fosters a landscape where informed and proactive state agencies can leverage federal resources to spearhead transformative infrastructure initiatives, thereby multiplying their impact on regional economic development.

Navigating the regulatory landscape necessitates a keen awareness of the evolving policy frameworks that guide infrastructure planning. Recent shifts towards green infrastructure and resilience in the face of climate change underscore the importance of aligning projects with contemporary priorities. Federal agencies, responding to these shifts, have introduced new guidelines and funding streams aimed at fostering environmentally responsible and climate-resilient infrastructure. State agencies, in turn, must remain agile, adapting to these changes by integrating innovative design principles and sustainable practices into their planning processes. This adaptive capability not only ensures compliance with federal mandates but also positions states at the forefront of the burgeoning green infrastructure movement, unlocking new avenues for funding and development.

A forward-thinking approach also entails recognizing the emerging trends that are reshaping the infrastructure landscape. Technological advancements, such as the integration of smart technologies and data-driven decision-making, are revolutionizing the way infrastructure is planned and managed. Federal and state agencies are increasingly incorporating these innovations into their frameworks, creating opportunities for projects that harness technology to enhance efficiency, safety, and connectivity. By staying attuned to these trends, stakeholders can position themselves to capitalize on the next wave of infrastructure advancements, ensuring that their projects remain relevant and future-proof in an ever-evolving environment.

Strategically engaging with federal and state agencies requires more than just regulatory acumen; it demands a proactive mindset and a commitment to collaboration. Stakeholders who cultivate strong relationships with agency representatives and participate actively in public consultations gain invaluable insights into policy directions and funding opportunities. Such engagement also affords stakeholders the chance to influence project planning and advocate for initiatives that align with community needs and aspirations. By adopting a collaborative approach, stakeholders can transform bureaucratic challenges into opportunities for innovation and growth, paving the way for infrastructure projects that not only meet current demands but also anticipate future challenges.

Understanding the Influence of Local Governments and Municipalities

Local governments and municipalities wield substantial influence over infrastructure projects, often acting as the linchpin between federal initiatives and community needs. Their unique position allows them to tailor large-scale plans to fit the distinct characteristics of their regions, ensuring that projects meet specific local demands. These entities often engage in strategic planning that encompasses zoning laws, land use policies, and community development objectives. By understanding these local dynamics, investors can gain insights into the trajectory of infrastructure developments, revealing opportunities that might otherwise remain obscured by broader national plans. This localized insight often serves as the catalyst for identifying profitable ventures, as local governments frequently prioritize projects that promise to stimulate regional economic growth.

Working closely with local governments, municipalities often collaborate with neighborhood councils and civic organizations to incorporate community feedback, ensuring that projects align with public interests. This collaborative approach not only enhances public support but also streamlines project approval processes, reducing potential bureaucratic delays. For investors, attending municipal meetings and reviewing public records can provide a treasure trove of information about upcoming projects and potential hurdles. By engaging with these local processes, savvy investors can gain advanced notice of infrastructure projects and better assess risk factors, aligning their strategies with municipal priorities well before official announcements are made.

An advanced understanding of municipal finance is equally crucial, as local governments often rely on bonds and other financial instruments to fund infrastructure projects. By scrutinizing these financial tools, investors can discern the fiscal health and priorities of a municipality. For instance, a city issuing bonds for a new transportation hub indicates a commitment to improving regional connectivity, potentially signaling a forthcoming increase in property values around the project area. This financial acumen enables investors to make informed decisions, capitalizing on the economic ripple effects that substantial infrastructure investments can produce.

As municipalities increasingly embrace technology, tools like Geographic Information Systems (GIS) and smart city initiatives are becoming integral to urban planning. These innovations offer deeper insights into demographic trends, traffic patterns, and environmental impacts, providing a rich dataset for evaluating potential infrastructure projects. By leveraging these technological advancements, investors can pinpoint emerging opportunities with remarkable precision, identifying areas poised for growth. Understanding the integration of technology in municipal planning can thus enhance an investor's ability to anticipate and act on infrastructure developments that may not yet be on the federal radar.

While local governments play a pivotal role in shaping infrastructure projects, they are not without challenges. Political shifts, budget constraints, and regulatory changes can all impact project timelines and outcomes. For the astute investor, maintaining an awareness of these variables is paramount. Engaging in continuous dialogue with municipal officials, attending public hearings, and staying informed about local political climates can mitigate risks and provide a clearer picture of the investment landscape. By understanding the complex interplay of factors that influence municipal decisions, investors can position themselves advantageously, ensuring that their strategies align with the ever-evolving tapestry of local infrastructure development.

Identifying the Impact of Private Sector Stakeholders and Interest Groups

Private sector stakeholders and interest groups play a pivotal role in infrastructure project development, often acting as catalysts for innovation and efficiency. Their involvement can range from providing critical funding to introducing advanced technologies that streamline construction processes. For instance, private companies can expedite project timelines by leveraging proprietary construction techniques or materials that reduce costs and enhance sustainability. These stakeholders often bring a wealth of expertise and resources that public entities may lack, enabling a more dynamic and responsive approach to infrastructure challenges. Recognizing the nuanced contributions of private sector participants is essential for anyone aiming to forecast the trajectory of upcoming projects.

The interplay between profit-driven motives and public interest objectives can lead to groundbreaking developments when managed effectively. In many cases, private sector involvement is incentivized through frameworks like public-private partnerships (PPPs), which blend public oversight with the efficiency and innovation typically found in the private sector. This collaboration can result in projects that not only meet public needs but also align with the strategic goals of private enterprises. A prime example is the development of smart cities, where technology firms collaborate with municipalities to create interconnected urban environments. By understanding the motivations and strategies of private stakeholders, investors can gain insights into potential project outcomes and opportunities.

Interest groups, ranging from environmental organizations to trade unions, also wield significant influence over infrastructure projects. These groups can either support or oppose developments based on their specific agendas, often impacting project timelines and scopes. For instance, environmental advocacy groups may push for stricter sustainability standards, which could lead to increased project costs but also open avenues for innovative green technologies. Conversely, trade unions may emphasize labor rights and safety standards, which can affect the choice of contractors and project execution methods. By analyzing the positions and influence of these groups, investors can better anticipate regulatory changes or shifts in public opinion that might affect project viability.

To capitalize on the opportunities presented by private sector stakeholders and interest groups, it's crucial to adopt a forward-thinking approach that anticipates future trends and challenges. Keeping abreast of technological advancements and regulatory shifts can provide a competitive edge. For instance, the increasing emphasis on renewable energy and carbon-neutral construction methods is reshaping the landscape of infrastructure development. Companies investing in these areas are likely to see increased demand from both public and private sectors. By identifying firms and technologies aligned with these emerging trends, investors can position themselves advantageously in the market.

In this complex ecosystem, the ability to synthesize information from diverse sources and perspectives is invaluable. Investors should actively engage with a wide array of stakeholders, attending industry conferences, and participating in public consultations to gather firsthand insights. Developing a network of contacts within both the private sector and interest groups can provide early access to information and help investors navigate potential challenges. This proactive engagement, coupled with a keen understanding of the underlying dynamics at play, allows investors to transform potential roadblocks into opportunities for growth and innovation.

How Budgets and Funding Shape Project Timelines

Let's start with a fundamental question: How do budgets and funding shape the timeline of infrastructure projects? The answer lies at the heart of understanding how government projects evolve from initial concepts to tangible structures. Budgets serve as both the blueprint and the backbone of infrastructure planning. They dictate not just what gets built, but when and how. The allocation of funds establishes priorities, determining which projects move forward and which remain on the drawing board. This interplay between budget allocation and project prioritization becomes a critical factor in predicting future developments. For those aiming to profit from infrastructure plans, understanding these financial undercurrents can reveal where the next big opportunity might lie.

As we delve deeper into this topic, the complexity of funding cycles becomes apparent. These cycles, characterized by their periodic nature, can either propel a project forward or stall it indefinitely. Recognizing how these cycles influence milestones and potential delays offers a strategic advantage. Navigating budgetary constraints, therefore, is not just a bureaucratic challenge but a strategic necessity for successful infrastructure planning. The ability to anticipate and adapt to these financial dynamics allows investors to time their moves effectively, turning potential obstacles into opportunities. As we explore these subtopics, we'll uncover the nuanced role of budgets and funding in shaping the infrastructure landscape, equipping readers with the insights needed to make informed investment decisions.

The Role of Budget Allocation in Project Prioritization

Budget allocation plays a pivotal role in determining which infrastructure projects advance to the forefront of governmental agendas. This process involves a complex interplay of prioritization criteria, stakeholder interests, and strategic planning. Governments often face a myriad of proposals, each vying for limited financial resources, necessitating a meticulous evaluation to determine which projects align most closely with long-term developmental goals and immediate community needs. By understanding the nuances of how funds are allocated, astute investors can anticipate which projects are likely to receive the green light, thus positioning themselves advantageously in the market. Recognizing patterns in previous budget allocations, such as a consistent focus on transportation or renewable energy, can offer predictive clues about future priorities.

In the competitive arena of infrastructure funding, projects are often ranked based on a combination of economic impact, social benefit, and political expediency. Decision-makers must weigh the potential return on investment against the urgency of community needs—a balancing act that requires both foresight and pragmatism. For instance, a project aimed at improving public transportation may be prioritized over a new highway, reflecting a shift towards sustainable urban development. This prioritization process is not static; it evolves with changing political climates and societal values. By analyzing these shifts, investors can gain insights into which sectors are on the cusp of receiving increased funding, allowing them to align their financial strategies accordingly.

Emerging technologies and innovative funding models further complicate the landscape of budget allocation. Public-private partnerships, for example, have become a cornerstone of modern infrastructure financing, where private entities contribute capital in exchange for future revenue streams. This approach not only alleviates the fiscal burden on governments but also accelerates project timelines. Investors knowledgeable in these dynamics can leverage this trend by identifying early-stage opportunities in projects likely to attract such partnerships. Additionally, digital tools like blockchain are being explored to enhance transparency and efficiency in fund allocation, offering new avenues for investors to engage with the infrastructure sector.

The intricacies of budget allocation also encompass the political and bureaucratic processes that govern funding decisions. Understanding the legislative environment and the influence of lobbying groups can provide deeper insights into why certain projects receive funding over others. Political cycles, particularly election years, often see a surge in funding for projects that promise immediate benefits to constituents. Investors who can correlate these political patterns with funding decisions may uncover hidden opportunities that others overlook. By staying attuned to these developments, they can strategically position themselves to benefit from shifts in funding priorities.

A robust grasp of budget allocation mechanics equips investors with the foresight to anticipate and act on infrastructure opportunities before they are publicly announced. By dissecting the layers of decision-making that contribute to project funding, investors are able to construct a predictive framework that identifies which projects are not only feasible but also imminent. This foresight is invaluable in a landscape where timing can significantly impact financial outcomes. By cultivating this expertise, investors can transform potential uncertainties into actionable strategies, ensuring they remain at the forefront of the infrastructure investment frontier.

How Funding Cycles Influence Project Milestones and Delays

Funding cycles serve as the heartbeat of infrastructure projects, dictating the rhythm of progress through financial infusions at critical junctures. The cyclical nature of funding, often aligned with fiscal budgets, necessitates strategic planning to anticipate both cash flow availability and potential bottlenecks. Projects frequently depend on multi-year appropriations, requiring foresight to align milestones with funding releases. This temporal alignment ensures that each phase of development, from preliminary design to final construction, progresses without unnecessary interruptions. For instance, an infrastructure project might secure initial funds for planning and design, but delays in subsequent appropriations can stall construction, leading to cost overruns and extended timelines. Understanding this ebb and flow allows stakeholders to adeptly navigate the complexities of project timelines, ensuring that each phase is both financially supported and strategically timed.

In recent years, innovative funding mechanisms have emerged to mitigate the impacts of funding cycle misalignments. Public-private partnerships, for instance, have gained traction as a means to inject private capital into public projects, bridging gaps that traditional funding might leave unaddressed. These partnerships not only expedite project timelines but also introduce accountability measures that can reduce the risks associated with governmental delays. Additionally, the use of revolving funds—where money is continuously replenished as projects generate revenue—offers a dynamic approach to maintaining financial fluidity. By leveraging these contemporary funding strategies, project managers can circumvent traditional delays, ensuring that infrastructure advancements proceed with alacrity.

The influence of funding cycles on project timelines extends beyond mere financial considerations, impacting stakeholder engagement and public perception. Delays due to funding shortfalls can erode public trust, especially when expectations for timely completion are unmet. To counteract this, transparent communication regarding funding status and anticipated timelines is paramount. Engaging the community through regular updates and participatory budgeting sessions can foster a sense of ownership and patience among stakeholders. This proactive approach not only mitigates dissatisfaction but also galvanizes community support, which can be pivotal in securing additional funding or overcoming bureaucratic hurdles.

Amidst these financial intricacies, a deep understanding of legislative processes becomes crucial. Legislative sessions often dictate the timing and availability of funds, especially in jurisdictions where budget approvals coincide with political cycles. Savvy investors and project managers can glean insights from legislative calendars, predicting potential delays or accelerations in funding disbursements. By staying attuned to these legislative rhythms, stakeholders can preemptively adjust project timelines, thereby optimizing resource allocation and maintaining momentum. This foresight transforms potential impediments into strategic opportunities, ensuring that infrastructure projects remain on course.

Readers are encouraged to adopt a proactive stance towards funding cycles, utilizing predictive analytics and scenario planning to forecast funding trends and their potential impacts. By employing a data-driven approach, stakeholders can simulate various funding scenarios, identifying optimal strategies for resource allocation and risk mitigation. This forward-thinking methodology not only augments decision-making but also enhances the resilience of project timelines against fiscal uncertainties. Through this lens, funding cycles become not merely a challenge to be managed, but a strategic lever to be harnessed, propelling infrastructure projects towards their envisioned futures.

Strategies for Navigating Budgetary Constraints in Infrastructure Planning

Navigating budgetary constraints in infrastructure planning requires a nuanced understanding of financial ecosystems and innovative approaches that transcend traditional practices. Successful navigation begins with a robust financial analysis that identifies potential bottlenecks early in the planning process. This involves scrutinizing budget allocations at the federal, state, and local levels, understanding their implications, and anticipating potential shifts in funding priorities. By dissecting funding cycles, stakeholders can forecast periods of financial scarcity and abundance, allowing for strategic planning and resource optimization. A proactive approach to budgetary analysis not only mitigates the impact of fiscal limitations but also reveals opportunities for reallocating resources to more critical phases of a project.

A critical strategy in overcoming budget-related hurdles is the cultivation of diverse funding streams. Infrastructure projects often depend on a combination of public funds, private investments, and alternative financing methods such as bonds or grants. By diversifying the financial portfolio, planners can reduce reliance on a single source and enhance resilience against economic fluctuations. The rise of public-private partnerships (PPPs) exemplifies this approach, offering a collaborative framework that aligns private sector efficiency with public sector goals. These partnerships can unlock new capital while fostering innovation and risk-sharing, ultimately enabling projects to advance even in financially constrained climates.

Adopting a phased implementation plan can be another effective strategy. Breaking a project into manageable segments allows for incremental development aligned with available funding. This method not only ensures continuous progress but also provides opportunities for reassessment and realignment as financial conditions evolve. Advanced prioritization tactics can be employed to identify which segments deliver the highest value or are most feasible within the existing budget, ensuring that the most critical components of the project are completed first. This approach can be particularly effective when coupled with rigorous cost-benefit analyses, which help to justify expenditures and secure additional funding from stakeholders.

Harnessing technology and data analytics offers innovative solutions to budgetary constraints. Leveraging Geographic Information Systems (GIS) and predictive modeling can streamline project planning by optimizing routing, reducing material costs, and minimizing environmental impact, all of which contribute to cost savings. Additionally, data analytics can enhance decision-making by providing real-time insights into budget performance and resource allocation. These tools empower planners to make informed adjustments, ensuring that projects remain on schedule and within budget despite financial challenges. The integration of cutting-edge technology not only enhances efficiency but also positions infrastructure projects to adapt to future fiscal landscapes.

Incorporating stakeholder engagement throughout the planning process can further alleviate budgetary pressures. By fostering open communication with community members, governmental agencies, and financial partners, planners can build a coalition of support that advocates for the project's value and necessity. Active stakeholder involvement can also uncover alternative funding opportunities, such as community fundraising or local sponsorships, and enhance the project's adaptability to budgetary changes. Engaging stakeholders in meaningful dialogue ensures that the project aligns with community needs and priorities, thereby increasing the likelihood of sustained financial backing and successful completion.

The Role of Public Meetings and Hearings

Public meetings and hearings are often overlooked goldmines of information, hiding in plain sight. These gatherings serve as the intersection where government intentions meet public scrutiny, creating a dynamic arena for uncovering potential investment opportunities. Governed by rules and procedures, these meetings offer a wealth of insights into the lifecycle of infrastructure projects, from inception to execution. They reveal more than just plans; they expose the nuances of stakeholder priorities, budget constraints, and community interests. For the astute observer, public meetings are not merely bureaucratic formalities but are instead vibrant stages where the future of infrastructure projects is debated, shaped, and, most importantly, unveiled.

The immediacy of these meetings provides a unique opportunity for investors to gather actionable intelligence. Engaging with these forums allows for the early detection of both opportunities and obstacles, offering a competitive edge in the investment landscape. Stakeholders, ranging from government officials to local citizens, interact openly, often revealing critical insights that are not documented in official project plans. By keenly observing and interpreting these interactions, one can anticipate project outcomes and adjust investment strategies accordingly. As we explore the structure and purpose of these meetings, along with techniques to extract valuable signals, the significance of public hearings as a strategic tool in predicting and profiting from infrastructure developments becomes evident. Each subtopic that follows will equip you with the knowledge to navigate this rich informational territory, transforming public discourse into private gain.

Understanding the Structure and Purpose of Public Meetings

Public meetings serve as a critical junction in the infrastructure planning process, bringing together diverse stakeholders to discuss, deliberate, and, at times, dissent. While these gatherings are often perceived as mere formalities, they offer an unparalleled opportunity for investors to glean insights into the dynamics and potential trajectories of upcoming projects. Understanding the format and function of these meetings can unlock a wealth of information. Typically structured to include presentations by project proponents, followed by public commentary and Q&A sessions, these meetings provide a transparent window into the priorities and concerns of both the planners and the community. By attending or reviewing the minutes of these meetings, savvy investors can identify key project milestones and potential roadblocks that might impact timelines and outcomes.

A less obvious yet equally valuable aspect of public meetings is the informal interactions they facilitate. Observing the body language and tone of the participants, such as representatives from governmental agencies, private contractors, and community leaders, can offer nuanced signals about the likelihood of a project's advancement or modification. For instance, a cautiously optimistic tone from a city planner might indicate confidence in funding approval, whereas hesitation or defensiveness could suggest underlying challenges. These subtle cues are often missed in official documentation but can be pivotal in forming a comprehensive understanding of the project's future.

With the advent of digital tools and platforms, the accessibility of public meetings has increased exponentially. Many municipalities now livestream these meetings or archive them online, providing broader access to critical information. This digital shift not only democratizes the data but also enables interested parties to conduct more thorough analyses of stakeholder sentiments and priorities. Advanced sentiment analysis algorithms, for example, can be employed to assess the tone and content of public comments, offering insights into community support or opposition. For those equipped with the right analytical tools, these digital archives can serve as a treasure trove of actionable intelligence.

The global push towards transparent governance has also led to innovative practices in how public input is gathered and utilized in infrastructure planning. Some jurisdictions employ participatory budgeting or use digital platforms to crowdsource ideas and feedback, providing additional layers of data for analysis. While these trends may not yet be widespread, they represent a growing shift in how public input is valued and integrated into project planning. For investors, keeping abreast of these innovations can provide a competitive edge, allowing for a deeper understanding of how public sentiment might shape project outcomes.

In navigating the intricate landscape of public meetings, investors should cultivate a mindset that values both the explicit and implicit information these forums provide. By expanding their focus beyond the formal agenda to include the human elements at play, investors can develop a more robust predictive framework that accounts for the complexities and uncertainties inherent in any large-scale infrastructure project. This holistic approach not only enhances the accuracy of their investment predictions but also positions them to act decisively when opportunities arise.

Leveraging Public Hearings for Early Investment Signals

Public hearings are an invaluable resource for discerning early investment signals, often serving as the crucible where abstract plans begin to take tangible form. By attending these meetings, investors can gather nuanced insights into the trajectory of infrastructure projects long before they reach the public domain. These gatherings provide a rare glimpse into the details of proposed projects, budget allocations, and potential hurdles. Attendees can assess the enthusiasm or resistance from various stakeholders, offering a predictive gauge of the project's likelihood of success. Savvy investors recognize these cues as precursors to investment opportunities, allowing them to position themselves advantageously while the broader market remains oblivious.

The structure of public hearings often includes presentations from project leaders, feedback from community members, and discussions with government officials. This multifaceted dialogue opens a window into the priorities and concerns that may shape a project's evolution. Investors can extract valuable signals by observing which aspects of a project are emphasized, which are challenged, and how these discussions might sway future decisions. For instance, a project that garners strong community support but faces logistical challenges might still be a viable investment, as public backing can often catalyze problem-solving and resource allocation.

Analyzing the interactions between stakeholders at these meetings provides a deeper understanding of the project's potential trajectory. The dynamics between government agencies, private companies, and community representatives can reveal underlying tensions or alliances that may influence project outcomes.

For example, a collaborative relationship between a local council and a private developer could expedite project timelines, providing an early indicator of investment viability. Conversely, visible conflicts or opposition might signal delays or the need for strategic adjustments, allowing investors to recalibrate their strategies accordingly.

Emerging trends in digital technology have further enriched the analysis of public hearings. Many municipalities now stream these meetings online, providing broader access and enabling investors to engage with the content asynchronously. Advanced data analytics tools can be employed to parse sentiment and identify patterns in stakeholder interactions, offering a more sophisticated understanding of potential project trajectories. These tools can highlight key phrases, recurring themes, and shifts in tone, equipping investors with a refined dataset from which to draw predictive insights.

To capitalize on the insights gained from public hearings, investors should adopt a systematic approach that includes diligent record-keeping, hypothesis testing, and strategic networking. By maintaining detailed notes on project discussions and stakeholder positions, investors can track the evolution of projects over time, identifying trends and turning points. Engaging with other attendees, such as local business leaders or government officials, can also provide additional context and intelligence, enriching the investor's perspective. This proactive engagement not only sharpens predictive acumen but also builds a network of contacts that can be invaluable for future investment endeavors.

Analyzing Stakeholder Interactions to Anticipate Project Outcomes

Stakeholder interactions at public meetings and hearings are more than just discussions; they are a goldmine of strategic insights for those keen on anticipating infrastructure project outcomes. Every participant, from government officials to local residents, brings a unique perspective and agenda. Recognizing these dynamics requires a keen eye and a strategic mindset. By examining the language and tone used by stakeholders, one can identify underlying motivations, potential conflicts, and alliances, all of which can influence the direction and success of a project. This is particularly valuable for investors seeking early signals. Dissecting comments and questions raised during these interactions can reveal whether a project is likely to face delays, undergo modifications, or proceed as planned. These nuances, often overlooked by the untrained observer, can provide a competitive edge when timing investments.

Focusing on the subtleties of stakeholder dynamics can further enrich this analysis. Consider the power balance between various groups: elected officials, regulatory bodies, environmental activists, and local businesses, each with their own priorities. A savvy investor might notice, for instance, that a project with strong support from influential stakeholders is more likely to advance without significant hurdles. Conversely, vocal opposition from a well-organized community group could signal potential roadblocks. Documenting these dynamics over time can help investors build a predictive model that anticipates project trajectories based on historical stakeholder behavior. This approach, grounded in pattern recognition and trend analysis, aligns with cutting-edge research in behavioral finance, offering a sophisticated method for forecasting project viability.

Incorporating advanced tools like sentiment analysis software can further refine this process. By quantifying the sentiment of stakeholder statements, investors can detect shifts in support or opposition that may not be immediately evident. This technology, which utilizes natural language processing, provides a data-driven approach to understanding stakeholder interactions. For instance, a noticeable increase in negative sentiment across multiple public hearings might indicate growing dissatisfaction with a project's impact, potentially leading to delays or redesigns. By staying attuned to these shifts, investors can adjust their strategies proactively, minimizing risk and maximizing potential returns. This innovative use of technology in investment decision-making underscores the importance of integrating modern techniques with traditional analysis.

Imagining scenarios where stakeholder interactions might pivot project outcomes can also enhance strategic planning. Suppose a community's concern over environmental impacts prompts a sudden redesign of a proposed highway. In this case, an investor aware of these dynamics might opt to invest in companies specializing in sustainable construction materials, anticipating a shift in project requirements. Such forward-thinking approaches demonstrate how understanding stakeholder interactions not only aids in predicting project outcomes but also in identifying broader market trends. By considering various potential scenarios and their implications, investors can refine their strategies, ensuring they are well-positioned to capitalize on evolving opportunities.

Actionable insights gleaned from stakeholder interactions are invaluable for investors aiming to stay ahead of the curve. Attending public meetings, reviewing transcripts, and engaging with local communities can provide firsthand knowledge of stakeholder perspectives. Investors are encouraged to develop a systematic approach to tracking these interactions, using tools like stakeholder mapping to visualize relationships and influence. This proactive engagement allows investors to make informed decisions, leveraging their understanding of stakeholder dynamics to anticipate project shifts and align their strategies accordingly. By building a robust framework for analyzing stakeholder interactions, investors can transform what may seem like inconsequential discussions into powerful predictors of infrastructure project success, ultimately leading to more informed and profitable investment decisions.

Reflecting on the core concepts explored in this chapter, readers gain a foundational understanding of the intricate web of government infrastructure planning. The journey from project conception to construction unveils a complex lifecycle where key agencies and stakeholders wield significant influence. Budgets and funding emerge as powerful forces that dictate timelines and priorities, while public meetings and hearings offer transparency and insight into the decision-making process. Recognizing these elements not only demystifies the bureaucracy but also empowers readers to anticipate future developments with precision. This knowledge serves as the cornerstone for identifying early signals of emerging opportunities. The insights gleaned here lay a robust groundwork for the more technical analysis to follow, equipping readers with the necessary tools to transform understanding into actionable investment strategies. As we transition to the next chapter, consider how this newfound comprehension can be honed to identify patterns and predict trends, ultimately paving the way for strategic investment decisions. What untapped opportunities might lie hidden within the plans discussed openly yet often overlooked?

Chapter Two

Mastering Government Budgets as Predictive Tools

You stand at the edge of a vast construction site, with the hum of machinery and the clatter of tools filling the air. Now, imagine knowing about this project months or even years before the first shovel broke ground. The secret to this foresight lies within the seemingly dull pages of government budgets, a treasure trove of information for those with the eyes to see. As we embark on this exploration, consider the budget not as a bureaucratic formality but as a roadmap to future opportunities. These documents, often dismissed as tedious and inscrutable, hold the key to understanding where cities, states, and nations are heading.

This chapter unlocks the potential of government budgets, transforming them into powerful predictive tools. By delving into the intricacies of capital improvement plans and tracing the flow of budget allocations, we uncover patterns and signals that can guide savvy investors toward profitable ventures. Recognizing early shifts in funding trends allows us to see beyond the present, spotting red flags and opportunities before they become apparent to the masses. The ability to interpret legislative appropriations becomes a skill akin to reading the stars—a way to predict the moves of governments and, consequently, the markets.

As we navigate this terrain, each topic we cover builds upon the last, creating a comprehensive framework for anticipating infrastructure developments. We aim to demystify these processes, empowering you to convert complex data into clear, actionable insights. By the end of this chapter, you'll be equipped with the tools needed to turn government budgets from dry documents into a rich source of investment intelligence, aligning perfectly with our broader mission of transforming the arcane into the accessible.

Deciphering Capital Improvement Plans (CIPs)

Let's start with a fundamental question: How can understanding government budgets lead to profitable insights into future infrastructure projects? At the heart of this inquiry lies the Capital Improvement Plan (CIP), a crucial document that, when deciphered skillfully, reveals the hidden language of fiscal priorities and strategic development. CIPs are more than just dry lists of proposed expenditures; they are blueprints of a community's ambitions and a government's intentions. They lay out the roadmap for public investment, detailing everything from new highways to revitalized parks, and understanding their structure is key to unlocking a treasure trove of investment opportunities. By dissecting the components of a CIP, one gains the ability to foresee where resources will flow, and perhaps more importantly, where they might not. This knowledge is invaluable for those who wish to position themselves advantageously before the crowd catches on.

As we journey through the intricacies of these plans, attention turns to the nuances of project timelines and funding allocations. These elements are not just numbers on a page; they are signals of growth and potential. Recognizing shifts in budget priorities or unexplained delays can be early indicators of broader economic trends. The ability to spot these trends sets the savvy investor apart, providing an edge in an ever-competitive market. By closely examining and understanding these signals, one can identify growth indicators and investment opportunities long before they become apparent to the untrained eye. The ensuing sections will equip you with the tools needed to interpret these signals, enabling you to anticipate opportunities and make informed investment decisions.

Understanding the Structure and Components of CIPs

Capital Improvement Plans (CIPs) represent a cornerstone in understanding governmental infrastructure planning, serving as a roadmap for future public projects. These documents, often dense and technical, outline the strategic allocation of resources towards various initiatives. A thorough comprehension of CIPs begins with recognizing their multifaceted structure. They typically encompass sections detailing project descriptions, funding sources, timelines, and prioritization criteria. Each element offers distinct insights into governmental priorities and potential investment opportunities. For instance, the inclusion of detailed timelines and funding sources can illustrate the trajectory of a project, signaling when financial commitments might translate into tangible developments. By dissecting each component, investors can gauge the feasibility and political backing of projects, offering a glimpse into the likelihood of their progression.

Analyzing project timelines within CIPs provides an essential vantage point for discerning both short-term and long-term investment prospects. These timelines often detail phases from initial planning to project completion, offering a chronological framework that investors can utilize to align their strategies. Early stages of a project, such as feasibility studies or environmental assessments, may signal nascent opportunities where entry costs are lower, while later stages could indicate imminent construction phases ripe for investment in ancillary services or real estate. By correlating these timelines with funding allocations, investors can pinpoint periods of substantial fiscal input, which often coincide with accelerated development activities. This strategic alignment allows investors to synchronize their actions with governmental schedules, maximizing their potential returns.

Identifying growth indicators within CIPs requires a keen eye for patterns that transcend the explicit information provided. One effective method is to scrutinize the geographical distribution of projects, which often mirrors anticipated demographic shifts or economic growth areas. Projects clustered in specific regions may indicate a governmental push to stimulate local economies or accommodate population increases. Additionally, the frequency and scale of proposed projects in a sector, such as transportation or renewable energy, can reflect broader policy priorities and technological advancements. By recognizing these patterns, investors can anticipate the ripple effects on related industries and position themselves accordingly, whether through direct investments in affected companies or by exploring emerging markets that stand to benefit from the infrastructure improvements.

Innovative perspectives on CIPs involve integrating advanced technologies and data analytics to enhance predictive accuracy. Geographic Information Systems (GIS), for example, offer powerful tools for visualizing CIP data in spatial contexts, revealing hidden correlations between infrastructure projects and socio-economic variables. By overlaying CIP data with demographic, environmental, and market data, investors can uncover nuanced insights into project impacts. Machine learning algorithms further augment this analysis by identifying subtle trends and predicting future developments with greater precision. This fusion of technology and traditional analysis equips investors with a robust toolkit to navigate the complexities of CIPs, transforming abstract data into actionable intelligence.

Engaging with CIPs as predictive instruments requires a proactive stance, inviting investors to apply critical thinking and strategic foresight. Consider a scenario where a CIP outlines ambitious plans for expanding public transit in a growing metropolitan area. An investor might question how this expansion will affect residential and commercial property values, or which industries might emerge to support increased transit usage. By exploring these questions, investors can develop a nuanced understanding of potential opportunities and risks. This proactive approach not only enhances the investor's ability to capitalize on infrastructure developments but also fosters a mindset attuned to the dynamic interplay between public planning and private enterprise.

Analyzing Project Timelines and Funding Allocations

Analyzing project timelines and funding allocations within Capital Improvement Plans (CIPs) requires a nuanced understanding of the intricacies involved in government budgeting. A CIP serves as a roadmap for infrastructure development, delineating the projected phases of a project alongside the financial resources earmarked for each stage. By scrutinizing these timelines, investors can gain foresight into when a project might begin and when it might face financial hurdles or accelerate towards completion. This insight is invaluable for predicting market movements and making strategic financial decisions. Timelines often reveal not only the intended pace of progress but also potential roadblocks—such as delays in funding disbursements or shifts in political priorities—that can impact project execution.

Examining funding allocations demands an astute analysis of how resources are apportioned across different projects and phases within a CIP. This involves assessing both the initial budgetary commitments and any subsequent reallocations that may occur. A keen observer will note patterns indicating priority projects, which are typically allocated larger or more consistent funding streams. Conversely, projects with fluctuating or minimal allocations may signal potential risk or lack of governmental focus. Understanding these nuances allows investors to gauge which projects are likely to proceed smoothly and which may encounter obstacles, thereby informing investment strategies.

In addition to examining historical allocation patterns, it is crucial to incorporate recent trends and innovative funding mechanisms that are reshaping infrastructure financing. The rise of green bonds, for instance, reflects a growing emphasis on sustainable projects, signaling lucrative opportunities for those poised to align their investments with environmental priorities. Furthermore, the integration of technology in project management and funding oversight introduces a new layer of transparency and efficiency, allowing for more accurate predictions of project viability and timeline adherence. Staying abreast of such trends provides a competitive edge, enabling investors to anticipate shifts in funding priorities and adapt their strategies accordingly.

Beyond the numbers, understanding the socio-political context surrounding funding decisions can yield deeper insights. Political agendas, economic conditions, and public opinion often influence how and when funds are allocated. For example, a sudden increase in funding for public transportation might correlate with a government's commitment to reducing urban congestion or carbon emissions. Recognizing these underlying drivers not only enhances predictive accuracy but also broadens the scope of potential investment opportunities. By considering these factors, investors can craft a more comprehensive and robust framework for evaluating CIPs.

To fully capitalize on the insights gleaned from analyzing project timelines and funding allocations, investors should develop a systematic approach to monitoring CIPs. This involves setting up alerts for updates to key documents, regularly attending public budget meetings, and leveraging data analytics tools to synthesize and interpret information. Engaging in scenario planning can also be beneficial, allowing investors to explore different outcomes based on various funding and timeline scenarios. By employing these strategies, readers can transform their understanding of CIPs from mere observation to actionable intelligence, positioning themselves advantageously in the marketplace.

Identifying Growth Indicators and Investment Opportunities

Capital Improvement Plans (CIPs) serve as a treasure trove of information for discerning investors, offering a glimpse into the development priorities and future growth trajectories of municipalities. To identify growth indicators within these plans, one must first understand the nuanced interplay of project timelines, budget allocations, and strategic visions set forth by governing bodies. These elements collectively signal where and when substantial investments are likely to occur, providing a roadmap for potential financial ventures. By scrutinizing the detailed allocations in CIPs, investors can pinpoint neighborhoods or sectors ripe for expansion, guiding them to align their investment portfolios with regions poised for significant development.

A keen analysis of timelines within CIPs reveals much about the urgency and scale of a project. Projects with accelerated timelines often indicate areas of immediate need or strategic importance, suggesting a higher likelihood of near-term economic activity and development. Conversely, projects with extended timelines might denote long-term city planning goals, offering opportunities for patient investors willing to capitalize on gradual growth. Understanding these temporal dynamics enables investors to tailor their strategies effectively, seizing opportunities aligned with their risk tolerance and investment horizons.

Budget allocations provide another vital layer of insight, revealing the financial commitment and priority assigned to various projects. By examining shifts in funding or sudden increases in budgetary provisions, investors can infer which projects are gaining momentum and which are losing favor. This financial data acts as a barometer for political and economic priorities, helping investors anticipate where government support—and by extension, economic activity—will concentrate. Notably, allocations in sectors such as transportation, housing, and technology often serve as harbingers of broader economic transformations, suggesting fertile ground for investment.

Identifying investment opportunities also involves discerning the less obvious growth indicators embedded within CIPs. These might include plans for infrastructure enhancements in underserved areas, which could signify upcoming revitalization efforts and potential property value increases. By recognizing patterns such as increased connectivity infrastructure, one can forecast a rise in business activity and population inflows, both of which contribute to economic vitality. Such insights require a blend of data analysis and intuition, allowing investors to draw connections between governmental intentions and market realities.

To translate these insights into actionable strategies, investors should consider crafting a diversified portfolio that accounts for both immediate opportunities and longer-term prospects. By systematically monitoring CIPs and related documents, investors can remain agile, ready to pivot as new information emerges. Treating CIPs as living documents rather than static reports enables proactive investment decisions, ensuring that one's financial strategies evolve in tandem with infrastructural developments and governmental shifts. Through diligent analysis and strategic foresight, the potential of CIPs as predictive tools can be fully harnessed, empowering investors to thrive in an ever-changing landscape.

Tracking Budget Allocations and Reallocations

Imagine unlocking a treasure map, not of hidden gold, but of untapped financial potential buried within the dense language of government budgets. As you track allocations and reallocations, you're not just following numbers; you're tracing the flow of priorities and intentions of those who shape infrastructure's future. What makes this intriguing is the chance to glimpse tomorrow's opportunities today. Budget allocations reveal much more than mere financial plans—they are the whispers of forthcoming transformations and the silent markers of strategic shifts. By understanding how funds are distributed and, more importantly, how they are reshuffled, you can start to see patterns that hint at larger trends, emerging priorities, and the direction of future developments. This insight empowers you to anticipate where the next wave of infrastructure investment will crest, placing you ahead of the curve and ready to seize opportunities before they surface in the public eye.

As you dive into this exploration, consider each line item as a clue, each reallocation a hint of change. Analyzing budget line items offers a window into the strategic priorities of the present and the potential pivots of the future. Identifying patterns in reallocations unveils shifts in focus, whether due to changing political winds or emerging societal needs. By tapping into historical budget data, you can construct a predictive model that not only reflects past decisions but forecasts future possibilities. These skills, once honed, transform budget documents from bureaucratic paperwork into strategic tools that guide informed investment decisions. In the chapters that follow, we will uncover the nuances of these techniques and delve deeper into how they can be harnessed to craft a predictive framework that is both robust and insightful.

Analyzing Budget Line Items for Emerging Trends

Analyzing budget line items requires a meticulous approach akin to piecing together a complex puzzle. Each line item, essentially a financial breadcrumb, can unravel the trajectory of a government's infrastructure priorities. By scrutinizing these items, one can discern subtle patterns that might indicate an impending shift in project focus or resource allocation. For instance, incremental increases in budget allocations for transportation infrastructure might suggest the groundwork for more extensive urban transit development. The key lies in identifying these seemingly minor adjustments early on, as they often foreshadow larger strategic initiatives. This foresight enables investors to position themselves advantageously, ready to capitalize on emerging trends before they become broadly apparent.

A deep dive into budget line items also entails understanding the context and rationale behind each allocation. It's not merely about numbers; it's about what those numbers signify in terms of policy direction and economic priorities. Consider a scenario where funding for renewable energy projects sees a substantial uptick over consecutive fiscal periods. Such a trend might reflect a governmental pivot towards sustainable infrastructure, driven by policy changes or international agreements. By continuously scanning these line items over time, investors can construct a narrative that informs their predictive modeling, allowing them to anticipate future market demands and align their investment strategies accordingly.

The interplay between different budget line items can also yield strategic insights. For example, a rise in allocations for technology infrastructure coupled with cuts in traditional manufacturing might indicate a broader digital transformation strategy. This shift could have cascading effects on related industries, from software development to logistics, offering a broader spectrum of investment opportunities. Understanding these interdependencies requires not just a keen eye for detail but also a holistic view of how different sectors may interact and evolve in response to budgetary changes. By fostering a comprehensive understanding of these dynamics, investors can make more informed decisions that go beyond the superficial analysis of numbers.

Harnessing the power of budget line item analysis also involves incorporating advanced data analytics and visualization tools. Techniques such as machine learning and predictive analytics can sift through vast amounts of budgetary data, highlighting patterns and anomalies that might elude manual scrutiny. These cutting-edge tools can transform raw data into actionable insights, enabling investors to predict infrastructure developments with a higher degree of accuracy. By integrating these technologies into their analytical framework, readers can elevate their capacity to forecast future trends, thereby gaining a competitive edge in the rapidly evolving economic landscape.

Consider the broader implications of budget line item analysis in terms of strategic investment planning. It's not just about predicting where the government will spend money; it's about understanding the ripple effects of these decisions across the economy. Thought-provoking questions such as "What secondary industries will benefit from increased infrastructure spending?" or "How might reallocations in budget priorities influence local economies?" can guide readers in refining their investment strategies. By constantly questioning and refining their assumptions, investors can stay ahead of the curve, continuously adapting to the ever-changing landscape of government infrastructure projects. This proactive approach is essential for transforming budgetary insights into tangible financial gains, ensuring that investors are not merely reacting to changes but anticipating them with strategic foresight.

Identifying Strategic Shifts Through Reallocation Patterns

The art of discerning strategic shifts through reallocation patterns within government budgets is an invaluable skill for the astute investor. In the labyrinth of fiscal documents, reallocations often signal priorities that are subtly evolving, revealing where future opportunities may lie. These shifts are not merely administrative adjustments; they are reflective of strategic realignments that can indicate emerging areas of governmental focus. For instance, a consistent increase in funds reallocated towards renewable energy infrastructure might suggest an impending wave of projects in green technologies. By meticulously tracking these movements, investors can glean insights into the evolving landscape of public investment and position themselves accordingly.

Understanding the nuances of budget reallocations requires a keen eye for detail and a robust analytical framework. This involves scrutinizing line items and discerning patterns that may not immediately stand out. A reallocation of funds from traditional transportation projects, like road maintenance, to more innovative solutions such as smart city infrastructure, may suggest a broader policy shift towards technological modernization. These subtleties can often go unnoticed by those not trained to look beyond the surface, but they hold the key to uncovering profitable ventures before they become mainstream.

To master this skill, one must develop a methodology that combines historical data analysis with current fiscal decisions. By comparing past reallocations with subsequent project announcements, investors can build a predictive model that anticipates future allocations. This approach not only sharpens one's ability to predict governmental priorities but also enhances the capacity to make informed investment choices. For instance, analyzing shifts in budget allocations over time can reveal a pattern of increased funding towards broadband expansion, highlighting potential growth in digital infrastructure investments.

Incorporating diverse perspectives can further refine this predictive model. Engaging with independent research, industry insights, and global trends offers a broader view, allowing investors to contextualize domestic reallocations within a larger framework. For instance, if international trends indicate a surge in electric vehicle infrastructure funding, a similar reallocation within domestic budgets could confirm a strategic alignment with global priorities. This multifaceted approach not only strengthens predictive accuracy but also provides a competitive edge in identifying lucrative opportunities.

Envisioning a scenario where these reallocations become apparent can prompt strategic foresight. Suppose a local government's budget reveals a reallocation of funds towards water management infrastructure, possibly indicating an upcoming series of projects focused on sustainability and climate resilience. By recognizing and acting on these reallocations early, investors can strategically acquire related assets, ensuring they are well-positioned when these projects are officially announced. This proactive approach transforms budget reallocation analysis from a passive observation into an active strategy, enabling investors to seize opportunities ahead of the curve, thus maximizing their financial outcomes.

Leveraging Historical Budget Data for Predictive Modeling

Dissecting historical budget data can unlock a treasure trove of insights for those keen on predicting future infrastructure initiatives. A thorough examination of past financial allocations reveals patterns and rhythms in government spending, enabling investors to anticipate the direction of upcoming projects. By scrutinizing previous budgetary decisions, one can identify trends that hint at the priorities and strategic shifts within governmental planning. This approach requires more than a superficial glance at numbers; it demands a nuanced understanding of the context surrounding each line item and the ability to discern the subtle shifts that signal a change in focus or intent. One might consider analyzing data from multiple years to detect cyclical spending behaviors or pinpoint anomalies that suggest a significant shift in priorities.

A key aspect of utilizing historical budget data is identifying patterns in reallocations. These shifts often reflect a strategic pivot or re-prioritization that can be pivotal for investors seeking to anticipate future infrastructure endeavors. For instance, if funds consistently move from one sector to another, it may indicate emerging areas of interest or the government's response to evolving societal needs. By mapping these reallocations, investors can construct a predictive model that reflects not only where money has been spent but, more importantly, where it is likely to flow next. This analytical approach transforms static historical data into dynamic predictive tools, offering a competitive edge to those who can master it.

Historical budget data serves as a foundation for predictive modeling, which can be significantly enhanced by incorporating advanced analytics and machine learning techniques. These tools allow for more sophisticated data interpretation, uncovering hidden correlations and forecasting future allocations with greater precision. By feeding historical data into predictive algorithms, investors can simulate various scenarios and evaluate the potential outcomes of different budgetary decisions. This forward-thinking approach enables a proactive stance, empowering investors to position themselves advantageously ahead of formal announcements or public disclosures. The application of such cutting-edge technology in budget analysis represents a paradigm shift in how financial opportunities in infrastructure are uncovered.

Beyond merely analyzing the numbers, investing in infrastructure demands an understanding of the societal and political contexts that drive budgetary decisions. By integrating qualitative insights—such as public sentiment, political agendas, and legislative shifts—into their analyses, investors can enhance the accuracy of their predictive models. This holistic approach acknowledges that budgets are not just financial documents but reflections of broader societal goals and challenges. For instance, a sudden increase in funding for renewable energy projects might not only reflect technological advancements but also a political commitment to sustainability. Thus, investors who can interpret these signals in conjunction with quantitative data stand to gain a deeper understanding of future investment landscapes.

To harness the full potential of historical budget data, investors must cultivate a mindset of continuous learning and adaptation. As government priorities evolve, so too must the strategies employed to decipher them. This requires staying abreast of the latest research and methodologies in data analysis, as well as remaining vigilant to shifts in political, economic, and societal landscapes. By fostering a culture of curiosity and innovation, investors can refine their predictive frameworks and maintain a competitive edge in identifying lucrative opportunities before they become apparent to the broader market. This proactive approach not only enhances investment returns but also contributes to a more nuanced understanding of the complex interplay between government policy and infrastructure development.

Spotting Early Red Flags in Funding Trends

This topic explores the intricate dance of numbers and priorities that unfolds within government budgets, offering a keen lens through which to glimpse the often-hidden narratives that signal shifts in infrastructure funding. At first glance, budget documents might appear as dry collections of figures and jargon, yet they hold the power to reveal stories of changing priorities and strategic shifts. Understanding these hidden cues is akin to reading between the lines of a complex novel, where the plot twists are not always immediately apparent. The ability to spot early red flags in funding trends is a skill that can elevate one's investment strategies, providing foresight into projects that may face hurdles or those that are poised for unexpected acceleration. As you navigate through this topic, you will develop an eye for detecting these subtle signals, transforming raw data into insightful predictions.

Identifying discrepancies between budget proposals and historical allocations is the first step in this journey, as it uncovers anomalies that may hint at deeper shifts in focus. Recognizing shifts in priority through unexpected budget cuts or additions further sharpens this perspective, revealing areas where government attention is either waning or intensifying. Lastly, analyzing legislative amendments for potential impacts on funding stability offers a deeper understanding of how political dynamics can alter the financial landscape. This chapter equips you with the tools to interpret these signals with precision, positioning you to anticipate changes before they materialize in the public domain. As you engage with the following subtopics, envision yourself as a detective, piecing together clues that others might overlook, crafting a narrative that guides your investment decisions with confidence and clarity.

Identifying Discrepancies Between Budget Proposals and Historical Allocations

In the realm of government budgeting, identifying discrepancies between proposed budgets and historical allocations can reveal telling insights into future infrastructure developments. Such deviations often serve as indicators of shifting priorities or impending policy changes. By meticulously comparing current budget proposals with the historical record, one can unearth patterns that suggest new directions in governmental planning. For instance, a sudden increase in funding for renewable energy projects, when compared to previous years, might indicate a strategic move towards sustainable infrastructure. Conversely, a significant reduction in allocations for a long-standing initiative can be a harbinger of its impending phase-out, paving the way for alternative projects. This analytical approach requires not only a keen eye for detail but also an understanding of the broader socio-economic context that informs these fiscal decisions.

The art of spotting budgetary anomalies involves more than mere number-crunching; it necessitates a nuanced appreciation of political dynamics and strategic objectives. Legislative bodies often shift funds in response to emerging needs, political agendas, or external pressures, reflecting a complex interplay of factors beyond the surface-level figures. A savvy investor must therefore cultivate the skill to discern these underlying motivations. For example, a government facing public pressure to improve public transportation might be inclined to reallocate funds from less urgent sectors to expedite such projects. Recognizing these shifts allows investors to anticipate where public money will flow, offering a head start on potential investment opportunities that align with these newly prioritized areas.

Beyond the immediate fiscal year, long-term budgetary trends offer a treasure trove of predictive insights. Analyzing multi-year budget plans can uncover gradual shifts that signal changing governmental focus, often before they are widely publicized. This foresight is particularly valuable in sectors with prolonged gestation periods, such as large-scale infrastructure projects. For instance, incremental increases in funding for smart city technologies over several budget cycles may point to a burgeoning commitment to urban modernization. This foresight offers investors the chance to position themselves advantageously in markets poised for growth, turning early investment into substantial returns.

Advanced tools and methodologies can further enhance the accuracy of such budgetary analyses. Data visualization software, predictive modeling, and machine learning algorithms are increasingly being harnessed to sift through voluminous budget documents efficiently. These technologies can highlight anomalies and trends that might be overlooked in manual reviews, providing a more sophisticated understanding of financial trajectories. By integrating these cutting-edge tools into their analytical arsenal, investors can uncover hidden gems within government budgets, gaining a competitive edge in identifying nascent opportunities.

While budgetary analysis offers a powerful predictive tool, it is essential to maintain a balanced perspective by considering diverse viewpoints and potential pitfalls. Not all discrepancies herald significant changes; some may simply reflect temporary adjustments or bureaucratic inefficiencies. Engaging with a variety of sources, consulting experts, and participating in public forums can provide a more holistic view, enriching the interpretation of budget data. Through this multi-faceted approach, investors can transform raw data into actionable insights, harnessing the latent potential of government budgets to anticipate and capitalize on future infrastructure initiatives.

Recognizing Shifts in Priority Through Unexpected Budget Cuts or Additions

Diving into the intricacies of budget allocations reveals a world where unexpected shifts can be both warning signals and opportunities. Budget cuts or additions that deviate from established patterns often indicate a change in governmental priorities. Recognizing these shifts involves a keen eye for patterns and an understanding of historical allocations. When a project suddenly receives a substantial funding boost, it may suggest an emergent focus or a strategic pivot, while unexpected cuts could hint at a deprioritization or reallocation of resources to more urgent needs. For the astute investor, these changes can be a goldmine of information, providing clues about where future infrastructure growth or contraction might occur.

Historically, infrastructure investments have been closely tied to political and economic climates. For instance, consider a scenario where an unexpected budgetary increase is allocated to renewable energy projects. This could be indicative of a governmental shift towards sustainable infrastructure, possibly driven by new environmental policies or international agreements. Conversely, a sudden reduction in funding for highway expansions might suggest that resources are being redirected to more pressing concerns, such as public transit systems or tech-driven transportation solutions. These movements are not always explicitly stated in public documents, requiring a sophisticated approach to decipher the underlying motivations and implications.

The ability to anticipate these changes extends beyond merely observing the numbers. Analysts must engage with the broader socio-political context, examining legislative discussions, public opinion, and technological advancements that may influence budgetary decisions. For instance, the rise of smart city technologies might spur unexpected investments in digital infrastructure, diverting funds from traditional projects. By staying informed of such trends, investors can align their strategies with the evolving landscape, making informed decisions that others might overlook until it's too late.

An advanced technique involves analyzing legislative amendments that accompany budget proposals. These amendments often contain critical insights into the stability and longevity of funding allocations. For example, if an amendment proposes a temporary reallocation of funds with a clear sunset clause, it might suggest a short-term priority rather than a long-term strategic shift. On the other hand, amendments that embed funding into multi-year plans could indicate a more entrenched commitment to a particular sector or project. Understanding these nuances allows investors to differentiate between transient opportunities and enduring trends, refining their approach to align with sustainable growth.

To harness these insights effectively, investors should develop a systematic approach to tracking and analyzing budgetary changes. This can include creating a database of historical allocations, employing visualization tools to identify anomalies quickly, and cultivating relationships with insiders who can provide context beyond what is publicly available. By adopting a proactive stance, investors can transform unexpected budgetary shifts from mere curiosities into powerful predictive tools, leveraging their insights to outpace competitors in identifying lucrative opportunities in infrastructure development.

Analyzing Legislative Amendments for Potential Impact on Funding Stability

Navigating the intricate world of legislative amendments requires a discerning eye, especially when assessing their potential impact on funding stability for infrastructure projects. Legislative amendments often serve as the linchpins for budgetary changes, introducing modifications that can either stabilize or destabilize project financing. These amendments can be subtle, yet they frequently harbor significant implications for the allocation of financial resources. By meticulously analyzing these legislative shifts, one can discern patterns and predict future outcomes that may not be immediately apparent to the casual observer. This calls for a nuanced understanding of legislative language, as well as the ability to interpret the intentions behind such changes.

Consider a scenario where an amendment introduces a reallocation of funds from one infrastructure project to another. This could indicate a shift in governmental priorities, suggesting that the project losing funding may face delays or cancellations, while the project gaining support is likely to advance more swiftly. Spotting these shifts early can provide investors with a competitive edge, enabling them to adjust their strategies accordingly. Analyzing the context and stakeholders involved in these amendments further enriches this insight, revealing underlying political or economic motivations that drive such decisions.

The impact of legislative amendments extends beyond mere budgetary allocations, influencing the long-term stability and viability of infrastructure projects. Certain amendments may introduce new regulatory requirements, alter project scopes, or even redefine project timelines. For instance, an amendment mandating additional environmental assessments could delay a project, impacting its projected completion date and financial outlook. Understanding these nuances enables investors to anticipate potential disruptions and recalibrate their risk assessments, ensuring that their investment strategies remain resilient and adaptive to changing circumstances.

Despite the challenges posed by the complexity of legislative language, there are practical strategies for effectively scrutinizing these amendments. One approach involves maintaining a vigilant watch on legislative sessions and committee meetings where such amendments are often discussed and debated. Engaging with policy analysts or legal experts can provide further clarity, offering insights into the potential ramifications of specific amendments. Additionally, leveraging technology and data analytics can streamline the process of tracking amendments, identifying trends, and predicting their implications on project funding.

This proactive analysis of legislative amendments not only enhances investment strategies but also fosters a broader understanding of the political landscape shaping infrastructure development. It encourages critical thinking and prompts investors to question not only what changes are being made but also why they are occurring. By adopting a multifaceted approach that integrates legislative analysis with other predictive tools covered in this book, investors can develop a robust framework for identifying and capitalizing on infrastructure opportunities, ultimately transforming complex legislative data into actionable insights.

How to Use Legislative Appropriations to Predict Projects

Visualize a future where you possess the foresight to predict the next wave of infrastructure projects before they even break ground. The key to unlocking this potential lies in understanding the intricate world of legislative appropriations. These appropriations are not just dry numbers on a page; they are dynamic indicators of governmental priorities and economic shifts. By mastering the art of interpreting legislative language, one can uncover hidden signals that reveal the trajectory of public investments. This chapter transforms the seemingly impenetrable language of government budgets into a powerful tool for forecasting, offering a strategic advantage to those who seek to align their investments with forthcoming public projects.

The ebb and flow of funding allocations offer a narrative of emerging opportunities. Legislative appropriations act as both compass and map, guiding investors through the complex landscape of government decision-making. By identifying key trends in how funds are distributed, you gain insight into the priorities that will shape future development. The patterns hidden within these financial forecasts are crucial for making informed, strategic investment decisions. As you explore the nuances of legislative appropriations, you'll discover how to read between the lines, recognizing funding patterns that signal promising ventures. With this knowledge, you can position yourself ahead of the curve, anticipating the projects that will not only transform communities but also offer substantial financial returns.

Interpreting Legislative Language for Financial Forecasting

Understanding legislative language is akin to learning a new dialect, one that reveals the financial intentions and priorities of government bodies. This specialized lexicon, often dense with jargon, contains critical clues that can forecast future infrastructure developments. For the informed reader, dissecting phrases like "subject to appropriation" or "contingent upon funding" can shed light on the certainty and timing of a project. By delving into the nuances of legislative documents, investors can identify where governmental focus lies, potentially signaling lucrative opportunities. This process involves recognizing not just the allocation of funds but also the context in which these decisions are made, allowing for a comprehensive understanding of future financial landscapes.

A key to mastering this language lies in identifying patterns and trends within legislative appropriations. By tracking how funds have been historically allocated, one can discern the priorities that drive government action. For instance, a consistent increase in budgetary allocations towards renewable energy infrastructure might indicate a significant policy shift. Such insights can be invaluable for investors seeking to align their portfolios with emerging trends. By examining the continuity or abrupt changes in funding, one can gauge the steadfastness of governmental commitment to specific projects, thereby making more informed investment decisions.

Connecting the dots between legislative language and financial outcomes requires a strategic approach. It's essential to not only interpret the language but also to contextualize it within broader economic and political environments. For instance, understanding the interplay between federal and state appropriations can enhance forecasting accuracy. Recent studies suggest that projects with bipartisan support are more likely to receive consistent funding. Investors can leverage this insight by focusing on projects that enjoy cross-party backing, thereby reducing risk and enhancing the potential for profit. By developing an analytical framework that incorporates these variables, investors can predict which projects are likely to materialize and thrive.

Critical thinking is further enriched by considering alternative perspectives and potential challenges inherent in legislative appropriations. While certain projects may seem promising based on funding alone, external factors such as political shifts or economic downturns can alter their trajectory. Engaging with diverse viewpoints and scenarios can provide a more robust predictive model. For instance, what if a sudden economic contraction leads to budget cuts? How might a change in administration impact previously funded projects? By contemplating these possibilities, investors are better equipped to anticipate and navigate the complexities of government-driven financial landscapes.

Acting upon these insights requires a proactive stance. Investors should cultivate relationships with key stakeholders and stay informed about legislative sessions and budget meetings. Networking with policymakers and attending public forums can provide firsthand information and early indicators of shifts in funding priorities. Additionally, employing technologies such as data analytics and machine learning can enhance the ability to process and interpret legislative language efficiently. By integrating these strategies, investors can transform legislative insights into actionable financial strategies, positioning themselves at the forefront of infrastructure investment opportunities.

Identifying Key Appropriation Trends and Their Implications

Navigating the landscape of legislative appropriations offers a treasure trove of insights for those keen on predicting future infrastructure projects. By meticulously examining appropriation bills, astute investors can discern patterns and priorities that may not be immediately apparent to the untrained eye. Legislative appropriations often follow certain trends that signal shifts in governmental focus or emerging areas of interest, such as renewable energy projects or smart city initiatives. These trends can serve as precursors to large-scale infrastructure investments. For instance, a sudden increase in appropriations for green technology may precede investments in sustainable public transport systems. Recognizing these signals allows investors to position themselves advantageously, anticipating market movements before they become widely recognized.

Identifying appropriation trends requires a keen understanding of both the language used in legislative documents and the broader political landscape. The nuanced wording in these documents can often reveal intentions and priorities that are not explicitly stated. For example, recurring phrases or terms like "pilot program" or "strategic initiative" might indicate a long-term commitment to specific projects or sectors. By decoding these phrases, one can gain a deeper understanding of the government's strategic direction. Furthermore, understanding the political motivations behind appropriations—such as regional development goals or responses to lobbying efforts—can provide additional context that enhances predictive accuracy.

In analyzing appropriation trends, it is crucial to differentiate between short-term allocations and long-term commitments. Short-term funding might address immediate needs, like disaster recovery, whereas long-term appropriations often align with strategic projects that can reshape a region's infrastructure. By focusing on these enduring commitments, investors can identify sustainable investment opportunities that promise more stable returns. This requires not only an analysis of current appropriations but also a historical perspective to understand past trends and predict future directions. Continually refining this knowledge allows investors to anticipate which sectors will receive sustained financial support and which may face cuts or reallocations.

The intricacies of legislative appropriations also invite a broader examination of their implications on regional and national scales. Understanding how appropriations influence local economies, job creation, and technological advancement can provide a more comprehensive view of potential investment landscapes. For instance, increased funding for rural broadband could signal opportunities in telecommunications and related sectors. By examining appropriations through this multifaceted lens, investors can identify multiple layers of impact, leveraging these insights to craft a diversified investment strategy that captures both direct and ancillary benefits.

Critical thinking remains a vital skill in this endeavor. Investors should constantly question and reassess their interpretations of appropriation trends, considering alternative scenarios and potential disruptions. What might a sudden increase in funding for electric vehicle infrastructure suggest about future transportation networks? How could shifts in defense spending impact regional economies? Encouraging these thought-provoking questions not only sharpens predictive skills but also fosters a mindset open to innovation and adaptation. Equipping oneself with this analytical toolkit empowers investors to transform legislative appropriations from mere documents into dynamic maps guiding them toward profitable ventures.

Analyzing Funding Patterns for Strategic Investment Decisions

In the intricate world of government budgets, discerning the nuances of funding patterns can provide astute investors with a strategic advantage. Understanding the ebb and flow of financial allocations is akin to reading a map of future infrastructure developments. By examining multi-year funding allocations, one can identify consistent investment trends that signal burgeoning opportunities. For instance, a subtle yet steady increase in transportation budget allocations over several fiscal years might indicate an impending expansion of public transit systems, opening avenues for strategic property investments or startups catering to commuters. Such patterns, when viewed through a lens of strategic foresight, can transform an ambiguous budget line into a beacon of potential profit.

Advanced analytical techniques can further refine this predictive capability. Harnessing data analytics and machine learning to sift through vast troves of budgetary data can reveal correlations and patterns invisible to the untrained eye. Research on predictive analytics underscores its efficacy in identifying these patterns, offering investors tools to anticipate shifts with remarkable accuracy. Imagine utilizing an algorithm that tracks fluctuations in municipal budgets across various sectors, pinpointing which are poised for exponential growth. By leveraging these insights, investors can position themselves ahead of market shifts, capitalizing on opportunities before they become apparent to the wider public.

Strategic decision-making benefits immensely from a keen understanding of how funding patterns align with broader governmental priorities. Consider the implications of a government suddenly reallocating funds from traditional infrastructure to green energy initiatives. Such a pivot not only signals a shift in policy but also heralds a plethora of investment prospects in renewable energy sectors. By recognizing these shifts early and understanding their broader context, investors can make informed decisions, aligning their portfolios with future trends. This alignment not only mitigates risk but amplifies the potential for substantial returns in emerging markets.

Exploring diverse perspectives within funding patterns can also yield valuable insights. While mainstream analysis may focus on established sectors, innovative investors might explore niche markets or less obvious sectors that receive increased funding. For instance, an uptick in budget allocations for cybersecurity infrastructure could be overlooked by those fixated on physical infrastructure. However, this trend might present lucrative opportunities for investors willing to explore the burgeoning intersection of technology and public safety. By considering such less conventional avenues, investors can cultivate a diverse portfolio that balances risk with the promise of high returns.

Thought-provoking scenarios can further illuminate the potential within funding pattern analysis. Picture a scenario where a sudden increase in government funding for disaster resilience projects arises in response to climate change predictions. An investor attuned to this signal might invest in companies innovating in flood defenses or sustainable building materials, anticipating these sectors' growth as they align with governmental priorities. Readers are encouraged to continuously refine their analytical frameworks, testing new hypotheses and exploring varied funding patterns to uncover untapped opportunities. This proactive approach not only enhances investment acumen but fosters a dynamic understanding of an ever-evolving fiscal landscape.

Mastering government budgets as predictive tools unlocks a treasure trove of insights for those looking to anticipate infrastructure projects and capitalize on them. By deciphering capital improvement plans, tracking budget allocations, and identifying early funding trends, readers gain a powerful edge in understanding where government priorities lie. Legislative appropriations further reveal the nuanced dance of financial commitments that precede public announcements. Together, these elements form the bedrock of a predictive framework that transforms technical budgetary data into actionable investment intelligence. As readers hone these skills, they are not just learning to read numbers; they are learning to foresee the future of infrastructure landscapes. Embracing this knowledge offers the potential for significant financial returns and positions one at the forefront of strategic investment opportunities. As we transition to exploring how other facets of government planning inform investment strategies, consider how these budgeting insights can be integrated into a broader predictive approach, continually refining your skills to stay ahead of the curve.

Chapter Three

The Hidden Clues in Permit Applications

In the bustling corridors of urban development, there's a quiet rhythm that many overlook—a rhythm that, when listened to carefully, can reveal the future skyline of a city and the fortunes that come with it. Picture a world where a single piece of paper holds the power to transform an empty lot into a thriving community hub or a sleepy neighborhood into a bustling commercial center. This is the world of permit applications, where hidden clues lie in wait for those with the eyes to see them. It's a world where the careful observer can become a step ahead of the market, armed with insights that others only grasp too late.

Permit applications are more than mere bureaucratic necessities; they are the whispers of transformation, hinting at the next wave of growth and opportunity. These documents, often buried in government offices, hold the secrets of tomorrow's developments. Understanding how to interpret these permits can be the key to unlocking the potential of untapped markets. In this chapter, we dive into the art of reading between the lines, exploring how each application paints a picture of future change. From the impact of environmental considerations to the subtle shifts in zoning laws, every detail offers a piece of the puzzle.

As we embark on this exploration, imagine the possibilities that unfold when you can predict the next big change before it happens. This chapter is your guide to turning the complex language of permits into a treasure map. By the end, you'll be equipped with the tools to uncover actionable insights, ready to seize the opportunities that lie just beneath the surface. The road to becoming an infrastructure oracle begins here, where the hidden becomes visible and the future takes shape one permit at a time.

How Development Permits Signal Future Growth

Ponder for a moment about the untapped potential hidden within stacks of development permits, often overlooked yet brimming with insights. These seemingly mundane documents are the whispers of future landscapes, quietly foreshadowing the direction of urban growth and economic vitality. Just as a seasoned detective uncovers clues in the smallest details, an astute investor can decipher the language of permits to predict where the next wave of opportunity will emerge. Each permit application tells a story, revealing intentions of expansion, transformation, and innovation. For those who know where to look, development permits are not just bureaucratic necessities; they are a window into tomorrow's prosperity.

Examining the intricacies of these permits unveils a treasure trove of information. Zoning changes and land use modifications offer glimpses into how areas may evolve, potentially transforming sleepy neighborhoods into bustling hubs. Analyzing trends in permit applications can uncover market signals that point toward burgeoning sectors or geographic hotspots. With a keen eye, one can even forecast economic impacts by connecting the dots within infrastructure permit data. As we navigate through the subtopics, the knowledge required to harness these insights becomes clearer, crafting a roadmap for strategic investments rooted in foresight and precision.

Interpreting Zoning Changes and Land Use Modifications

Zoning changes and land use modifications are pivotal indicators of potential growth and development, acting as the harbingers of economic transformation in a given area. As municipalities and local governments adjust zoning laws, they essentially redefine the landscape, paving the way for new residential, commercial, or industrial projects. This reclassification of land use can offer a treasure trove of insights for the astute investor. By carefully examining zoning amendments, one can anticipate shifts in property values and the potential for increased demand in specific sectors. For instance, a change from agricultural to residential zoning often signals impending suburban expansion, while an adjustment to mixed-use zoning can herald the rise of vibrant, multifunctional neighborhoods.

Deciphering these zoning shifts requires more than just surface-level scrutiny. It involves a nuanced understanding of local government agendas, community feedback, and broader urban development trends. Governmental planning documents and public meeting minutes can offer clues about the rationale behind land use changes. These documents might reveal a strategic push for economic rejuvenation or an effort to accommodate population growth. By piecing together these elements, investors can forecast the types of businesses or housing that will likely thrive, allowing them to position themselves advantageously in the market.

Analyzing historical data on zoning changes can provide a rich context for understanding current trends. Patterns often emerge when one looks at past modifications and their subsequent economic impacts. For example, the rezoning of a district to allow for tech parks might have led to a boom in local employment and infrastructure development. By comparing these past case studies with current zoning proposals, investors can gauge the potential success of new projects. This historical perspective not only enhances predictive accuracy but also equips investors with a framework for assessing risk and opportunity.

Emerging tools and technologies also play a significant role in interpreting zoning changes. Geographic Information Systems (GIS) and data analytics platforms can visualize and analyze spatial data, offering dynamic insights into how land use modifications might affect property values or demographics. These technologies can highlight trends that might be invisible to the naked eye, such as the gradual encroachment of urban sprawl or the clustering of commercial activities in newly rezoned areas. By leveraging these tools, investors can refine their strategies, making informed decisions based on robust data.

The art of interpreting zoning changes isn't just about understanding the present; it's about forecasting the future. Investors should constantly question how these modifications align with broader societal shifts, such as the move towards sustainable living or the increase in remote work. What kinds of developments will support these trends? How might zoning changes cater to an environmentally conscious population? By considering these questions, investors can not only anticipate future demand but also align their investments with societal values, ensuring long-term relevance and success.

Analyzing Permit Application Trends for Market Signals

Recognizing patterns in permit application trends offers invaluable insights for discerning market signals that might otherwise remain obscured. As government entities and private developers initiate permit applications, they often unwittingly signal impending waves of development. By systematically tracking these applications over time, investors can anticipate shifts in market dynamics and potential areas of growth. This approach requires a keen understanding of the nuances within permit data, such as identifying which sectors are submitting a surge of applications and analyzing the geographical locations most affected. For instance, a noticeable increase in residential building permits in a particular suburb could presage a broader trend of urban expansion, suggesting a ripe opportunity for investment in related infrastructure or services.

A sophisticated analysis involves not just tallying applications but also discerning the intent behind them. By examining the specifics of each permit—be it the type of construction, the scale of the project, or the proposed timeline—investors can gauge the economic vitality of an area. A surge in commercial permits, for example, can indicate burgeoning business prospects and potential job creation, which often lead to increased demand for housing and amenities. Tracking these trends requires access to reliable data sources and tools that can parse large datasets effectively. Advanced data analytics platforms can assist in visualizing trends and identifying outliers, providing a clearer picture of where the market is headed.

Equally crucial is understanding the external factors that influence permit applications. Economic conditions, demographic shifts, and technological advancements all play pivotal roles in shaping these trends. For example, a region experiencing rapid population growth or an influx of tech companies might see a corresponding spike in permits for multi-family housing and commercial spaces. By correlating these external indicators with permit data, investors can refine their understanding of future market trajectories. The interplay between these factors underscores the complexity of the market, necessitating a multi-faceted approach to analysis that goes beyond surface-level observations.

Innovative perspectives can further enhance this analysis. Considering how emerging technologies like artificial intelligence and machine learning can be utilized to predict permit trends opens new avenues for investment strategy. These technologies can analyze vast amounts of data with precision, identifying patterns and correlations that might elude human analysts. Furthermore, engaging with diverse sources of information, such as local government reports, industry publications, and community feedback, can provide a more nuanced view of permit trends. By synthesizing information from varied perspectives, investors can mitigate biases and make more informed decisions.

Thoughtful application of these insights is paramount. Investors must not only identify trends but also devise actionable strategies to capitalize on them. This involves determining the optimal timing for investment, balancing risk with potential reward, and devising exit strategies to maximize returns. By staying attuned to permit application trends and integrating this knowledge into a broader investment framework, readers can position themselves advantageously in the marketplace. Consider, for instance, the scenario of a region anticipating the construction of a major transportation hub; savvy investors could explore opportunities in adjacent sectors such as real estate, retail, and logistics, capitalizing on the ripple effects of such a development.

Predicting Economic Impact Through Infrastructure Permit Data

Infrastructure permit data often reveals intricate details about upcoming projects, serving as a powerful tool for forecasting economic impact. By scrutinizing permit documentation, one can discern the magnitude of proposed developments, which provides an indication of the potential economic ripple effects. For instance, a substantial increase in permits for new commercial buildings in a particular area may signal a forthcoming surge in employment opportunities, increased demand for local services, and a rise in property values. This data, when meticulously analyzed, can thus guide investors in pinpointing regions poised for economic expansion, allowing them to make astute investment decisions in real estate, business ventures, or local enterprises.

The sophistication of permit data analysis lies in recognizing patterns that are not immediately evident. A deeper dive into these patterns can uncover trends linked to infrastructure growth, such as the clustering of permits related to technology hubs or renewable energy projects. These clusters often indicate regions that are becoming innovation centers, drawing in talent and investments. By identifying these clusters early, investors can capitalize on the economic upswings that typically follow. This anticipatory approach not only minimizes risks but also maximizes potential returns, as investments are made before the broader market catches on.

Beyond straightforward economic indicators, permit data can also reveal shifts in demographic and social dynamics. For example, an uptick in residential permits in suburban areas could suggest a trend towards remote work and a desire for more spacious living environments. This trend might lead to increased demand for nearby amenities, schools, and healthcare facilities, prompting further infrastructure development. By understanding these nuanced shifts, investors can tailor their strategies to align with evolving consumer preferences and societal changes, thereby staying ahead of the curve in a rapidly transforming market landscape.

Incorporating advanced data analytics and geographic information systems (GIS) can enhance the precision of economic impact predictions. By mapping permit data against existing infrastructure, investors can visualize potential growth corridors and strategically position themselves in prospective hotspots. This method not only highlights opportunities but also helps in identifying potential challenges, such as inadequate infrastructure or regulatory hurdles, which could impede growth. Such a comprehensive approach ensures that investment strategies are robust, adaptable, and aligned with both current realities and future possibilities.

Exploring the potential effects of infrastructure permits on local economies encourages a broader understanding of how these developments interconnect with other sectors. Investors are urged to consider scenarios where a single permit could trigger a cascade of developments across related industries, such as transportation, education, and retail. Engaging with this thought process fosters a holistic view, prompting investors to ask critical questions: How will these permits affect local job markets? What are the potential environmental considerations? By contemplating these questions, investors refine their strategies, ensuring they are not only profitable but also sustainable and socially responsible.

Understanding Environmental Impact Statements

In recent years, we've seen a surge in the importance of Environmental Impact Statements (EIS) as a crucial component of infrastructure planning. These documents, often dense and complex, hold the keys to understanding the potential effects a project might have on both the environment and the surrounding community. For investors seeking to unearth hidden opportunities, EISs offer a treasure trove of insights that can reveal not only the feasibility of a project but also the nuanced risks and benefits associated with it. By dissecting the structure and content of these reports, one can uncover indicators that significantly influence project viability, helping to make informed decisions well before the public catches wind. Understanding how to navigate these environmental assessments transforms what might seem like bureaucratic jargon into a strategic advantage, setting the stage for a more profound comprehension of the development landscape.

Analyzing Environmental Impact Statements isn't just about grasping ecological consequences; it delves deeper into the social and economic ripple effects a project might generate. These multifaceted documents can illuminate how a project aligns with wider community goals or poses challenges, offering a broader lens through which to evaluate potential investments. By identifying key indicators within these statements, investors can gauge the project's long-term sustainability and the community's reception, both of which are vital for anticipating future growth and profitability. As we explore the intricacies of EISs, from their structural components to the socioeconomic implications, you'll gain the tools needed to extract actionable insights. This knowledge not only enhances predictive capabilities but also strengthens your strategic framework, ensuring that your investment decisions are rooted in a comprehensive understanding of all possible outcomes.

Deciphering the Structure and Content of Environmental Impact Statements

Environmental Impact Statements (EIS) serve as a comprehensive tool in assessing the potential consequences of proposed infrastructure projects on the environment. Their structure is meticulously crafted to provide a detailed overview of the anticipated effects and the steps developers plan to take to mitigate negative outcomes. Typically, an EIS begins with an executive summary, offering a high-level view of the project's objectives, scope, and potential environmental impacts. This section is crucial for investors as it encapsulates the project's overall viability and potential red flags at a glance. The body of the statement dives deeper, delineating the environmental baseline conditions, potential impact scenarios, and alternatives to the proposed action. This structure not only aims to inform policymakers and the public but also serves as a rich resource for those with a keen eye for investment opportunities, as it reveals both the challenges and advantages inherent in the proposed developments.

A sophisticated understanding of the content within an EIS can uncover subtle indicators of project viability and associated risks. For instance, a project with extensive mitigation measures outlined might indicate significant environmental challenges, which could delay permitting processes or increase costs. Conversely, projects demonstrating minimal adverse impacts and robust community engagement strategies often face fewer hurdles and can proceed more smoothly. Analyzing these nuances requires an ability to discern between regulatory language and genuine project feasibility, demanding both critical thinking and an understanding of environmental law. Investors should pay attention to the discussions surrounding cumulative effects, as these can offer insights into long-term sustainability and the project's alignment with regional growth plans. Thus, mastering the art of interpreting EIS content is a valuable skill, providing a competitive edge in predicting the success of infrastructure endeavors.

Delving into the socioeconomic ramifications embedded within Environmental Impact Statements can reveal significant insights into a project's broader implications. Often, these documents will assess how a development might alter local economies, demographics, and employment landscapes. A project promising substantial economic benefits such as job creation or infrastructure improvements can signal lucrative investment potential. However, projects that might lead to displacement or significant demographic shifts could face opposition, influencing the project's timeline and ultimate success. By rigorously evaluating these socioeconomic factors, investors can anticipate community responses and regulatory challenges that may not be immediately apparent, effectively enabling them to make more informed investment decisions.

The ability to mine Environmental Impact Statements for actionable insights often involves examining the less obvious components, such as appendices and technical reports. These sections frequently house detailed studies and data that may not be highlighted in the main document but can offer critical information about the project's feasibility and environmental compatibility. For example, hydrological studies within an appendix might reveal potential water resource conflicts, while biodiversity assessments could highlight endangered species concerns. Investors who meticulously comb through these details can uncover hidden opportunities or risks that others might overlook, allowing for a more nuanced understanding of the project's potential trajectory.

Engaging with EIS content requires not only analytical skills but also a proactive approach to applying insights gained from such analyses. Investors should consider building a framework for systematically evaluating these documents, focusing on key indicators of project success and potential pitfalls. This framework might include creating a checklist of critical elements to assess, such as mitigation strategies, community impact analyses, and regulatory compliance challenges. By refining this approach over time and integrating new research findings, investors can continuously enhance their predictive capabilities, ensuring they remain ahead of market trends and ready to capitalize on emerging opportunities in the infrastructure sector.

Identifying Key Indicators of Project Viability and Risk

In the realm of infrastructure project analysis, Environmental Impact Statements (EIS) serve as a treasure trove of information, offering a nuanced glimpse into the potential viability and risk associated with future developments. These documents are not merely a bureaucratic formality; they encapsulate critical data points that can signal the trajectory of a project. To effectively harness this information, an adept reader must identify and interpret key indicators that reflect both opportunity and caution. For instance, a comprehensive review of the anticipated environmental repercussions and mitigation strategies can reveal much about the project's feasibility. High costs or complex mitigation measures may indicate potential hurdles, while streamlined processes suggest a smoother path forward.

Beyond the environmental aspects, an EIS often provides insights into broader project impacts, including economic and social dimensions. Delving into these sections can unearth indicators of community support or opposition, which can significantly influence a project's success. A project with strong backing is more likely to proceed without delays, whereas those facing resistance may encounter prolonged permitting processes. This understanding is vital for investors seeking to assess the likelihood of timely project execution. Moreover, analyzing stakeholder comments and responses can offer clues about public sentiment and potential legal challenges, both of which are crucial factors in evaluating risk.

Cutting-edge research has increasingly focused on the integration of advanced technologies, like Geographic Information Systems (GIS), to enhance the predictive power of EIS analysis. By layering EIS data with spatial analytics, investors can visualize patterns and trends that might not be immediately apparent through text alone. This approach can uncover correlations between environmental factors and project success rates, providing a competitive edge in forecasting outcomes. Additionally, emerging artificial intelligence tools are beginning to automate the extraction and interpretation of complex data sets from EIS documents, streamlining the identification of key indicators.

The evolving landscape of regulatory frameworks also plays a critical role in shaping the risk profile of infrastructure projects. Keeping abreast of legislative changes and policy shifts can offer foresight into potential obstacles or accelerators for project approval. For instance, new environmental regulations might impose stricter standards, thus altering the risk landscape for certain developments. Savvy investors can stay ahead by monitoring these shifts and adjusting their strategies accordingly, ensuring they remain aligned with regulatory trends and maximize their investment potential.

One must cultivate a holistic perspective, considering not only the environmental factors but also the interconnected socio-political and economic variables that influence project viability. Engaging with environmental consultants or specialists can further enhance one's ability to parse through the intricacies of EIS documents, transforming raw data into strategic insights. By honing these analytical skills, investors can navigate the complexities of infrastructure projects with confidence, turning potential risks into informed opportunities.

Analyzing the Socioeconomic Implications of Environmental Impact Findings

Environmental Impact Statements (EIS) are vital documents that unravel the intricate tapestry of a project's potential effects on both the environment and surrounding communities. These statements are treasure troves of information waiting to be harnessed by astute investors and analysts. By dissecting the socioeconomic layers embedded within an EIS, one can glean insights that extend beyond mere compliance with regulatory frameworks. For instance, a proposed infrastructure project might promise economic revitalization in a stagnant region. Yet, a deeper dive into the EIS could reveal underlying tensions, such as community displacement or strain on local resources, which could alter the anticipated economic trajectory. Understanding these nuances requires a keen eye for detail and a comprehensive grasp of both the immediate and long-term impacts on local economies.

A skilled analysis of Environmental Impact Statements often involves identifying pivotal indicators that signal project viability and risk. These indicators include projected changes in employment rates, shifts in demographic patterns, and alterations in local business ecosystems. For example, a proposed highway expansion might promise to improve traffic flow and increase accessibility, potentially boosting local businesses. However, if the EIS points to significant disruption to existing transport networks during construction, or a potential increase in pollution, these could be red flags indicating risks that investors must weigh carefully. Recognizing the balance between economic opportunity and environmental cost can empower investors to make informed decisions, potentially leading to more sustainable and profitable outcomes.

Socioeconomic implications outlined in an EIS also shed light on broader community impacts that might not be immediately apparent. A new industrial facility, for instance, could bring much-needed jobs but might also lead to increased housing demand, driving up property prices and altering the socioeconomic fabric of the area. This dual-edged sword presents both challenges and opportunities for investors, prompting them to consider how infrastructure growth can catalyze changes in local real estate markets. By anticipating these shifts, savvy investors can position themselves advantageously, aligning their strategies with both community needs and economic trends.

Beyond the immediate economic impacts, emerging trends in EIS analysis emphasize the importance of considering long-term sustainability and resilience. The shift towards more sustainable infrastructure projects, influenced by global environmental goals and local regulatory pressures, is increasingly reflected in modern EIS documentation. Projects that integrate green technology or prioritize minimal environmental disruption often receive favorable assessments, signaling reduced long-term risks and aligning with growing investor interest in sustainable ventures. By staying attuned to these trends, investors can align their portfolios with projects that not only promise economic returns but also contribute positively to environmental objectives.

Thoughtfully analyzing the socioeconomic dimensions of an EIS requires a blend of quantitative and qualitative assessment skills. Investors should not only focus on the data presented but also question underlying assumptions and potential biases within the report. Engaging with diverse perspectives, such as community stakeholders or environmental advocates, can provide a more holistic view of a project's potential impacts. This approach not only enhances the accuracy of predictions but also fosters deeper engagement with the communities involved. By cultivating this level of insight, investors not only strengthen their decision-making framework but also contribute to more equitable and sustainable infrastructure development.

Zoning Changes and Their Implications

Let's start by examining the transformative power of zoning changes, a subtle yet potent force that can reshape entire neighborhoods and redefine property landscapes. Zoning regulations, often hidden in the labyrinth of government documents, play a pivotal role in laying the groundwork for urban development. They determine what can be built and where, influencing everything from residential expanses to commercial hubs. In the realm of strategic investing, understanding zoning changes becomes a crucial skill. They are not just bureaucratic formalities; they are harbingers of growth, capable of elevating property values or redirecting the flow of capital. With each amendment and reclassification, zoning changes leave a trail of clues about future development that, when decoded, can offer investors a distinct advantage. This section will unravel the mysteries behind zoning regulations, guiding you to see beyond the surface and into the emerging trends that shape tomorrow's investment landscapes.

As we journey through this topic, the first step is to comprehend how zoning regulations impact property values. Recognizing these effects equips you with the ability to anticipate shifts in the market. Next, we explore the art of identifying key indicators of upcoming zoning changes hidden within government documents. Mastering this skill transforms complex bureaucratic language into insightful predictions for the savvy investor. Finally, we delve into the strategic opportunities that zoning changes present, offering a roadmap for transforming regulatory shifts into profitable ventures. By the end of this exploration, you will possess a sharper vision for identifying and capitalizing on the hidden potentials within zoning changes, turning them into a cornerstone of your investment strategy.

Understanding the Impact of Zoning Regulations on Property Values

Zoning regulations play a pivotal role in shaping urban landscapes and directly influencing property values. At their core, these regulations dictate land use, building heights, and density, which can dramatically affect the desirability and utility of a location. For instance, a shift from residential to commercial zoning can significantly escalate land value due to heightened demand for business premises. Conversely, a downzoning from commercial to residential might lower property value but increase neighborhood livability, attracting different types of investors. Understanding these dynamics allows investors to anticipate changes in property value based on zoning trends, positioning themselves strategically in the market.

In the intricate world of urban planning, zoning changes often emerge as subtle signals within government documents, offering a glimpse into future developmental priorities. Identifying these indicators requires a keen eye for detail and an ability to interpret bureaucratic language. Planners might hint at upcoming zoning modifications in public meeting minutes, city council agendas, or comprehensive plans. These documents may reveal intentions to create mixed-use districts or green spaces, which often precede zoning adjustments. By meticulously analyzing these sources, investors can gain an edge, recognizing opportunities before they become widely acknowledged.

Strategically aligning property investments with zoning trends can unlock lucrative opportunities. When a zoning change is anticipated, savvy investors might acquire properties in transitional zones, banking on future demand and appreciation. For instance, acquiring land on the outskirts of a city poised for zoning reclassification can yield substantial returns as the area urbanizes. The key lies in synthesizing zoning intelligence with broader market trends, ensuring that investment choices are both informed and forward-thinking. By doing so, investors can effectively mitigate risks and capitalize on growth potential.

Zoning regulations not only shape economic outcomes but also reflect broader societal and environmental objectives. Recent research underscores how zoning can be leveraged to promote sustainable urban development, incorporating green building codes and encouraging pedestrian-friendly areas. These progressive zoning practices align with global trends toward sustainability, providing investors with opportunities to support eco-friendly projects while still reaping financial rewards. By embracing these innovative zoning frameworks, investors can contribute to a more sustainable future, aligning profit motives with environmental stewardship.

Exploring the multifaceted nature of zoning regulations invites thought-provoking questions about the future of urban development. How might zoning evolve to accommodate increasing urban populations, or to counteract climate change? What role will technology play in reshaping zoning practices? For investors, these considerations are not merely academic; they represent the frontier of strategic property investment. By staying informed and adaptable, investors can harness the transformative power of zoning changes, turning municipal policies into profitable ventures. Through critical engagement with zoning trends, investors not only secure financial benefits but also influence the direction of urban growth.

Identifying Key Indicators of Upcoming Zoning Changes in Government Documents

Scrutinizing government documents to discern impending zoning changes can be an invaluable skill for those looking to capitalize on future opportunities. Key indicators often lie in the subtleties of language used within city council minutes, planning commission reports, and proposed amendments to local ordinances. These documents can unveil intentions long before they materialize, offering a glimpse into the future landscape of development. By paying attention to phrases such as "rezoning application," "land-use amendment," or "proposed district change," savvy investors can identify potential shifts in zoning that could dramatically alter property values. Understanding the legislative process behind these changes is crucial, as it often involves multiple readings, public consultations, and revisions that can provide further insight into the likelihood and timing of the adjustments.

Detecting the nuances within these documents requires a keen eye and an understanding of bureaucratic jargon. For instance, a proposed zoning change from residential to mixed-use can signal an upcoming boom in commercial activity, potentially increasing demand for adjacent properties. It's not just about identifying the changes themselves but also understanding the broader implications—how they align with regional development goals, transportation plans, or economic incentives. Advanced tools such as natural language processing algorithms can assist in parsing large volumes of text to unearth these clues more efficiently, turning what once was a labor-intensive process into a more streamlined, data-driven approach.

In addition to direct references to zoning changes, indirect signals can also point towards future development. The announcement of infrastructure projects, such as new transit lines or highway expansions, often precedes zoning amendments as cities look to accommodate increased accessibility and growth. Similarly, shifts in demographic data or economic forecasts within government reports can provide context for likely zoning adjustments. These indirect indicators, when combined with explicit signals, create a more comprehensive picture of anticipated changes, allowing investors to make informed decisions grounded in a deep understanding of multifaceted trends.

Arming oneself with the ability to discern these signals also means staying abreast of legislative calendars and attending public hearings or workshops where zoning changes are discussed. These venues offer a platform for direct engagement with policymakers and can provide additional context, such as community sentiment or potential objections that might delay or alter proposed changes. This proactive approach not only enhances one's predictive accuracy but also fosters a network of contacts that can yield further insights into the zoning process.

The true art of leveraging zoning changes lies in synthesizing this information to identify strategic investment opportunities. By correlating zoning amendments with market trends and economic indicators, investors can pinpoint properties poised for appreciation or redevelopment potential. This requires not only a reactive approach to the data but also a proactive mindset that anticipates and adapts to evolving urban landscapes. Critical thinking and strategic foresight thus transform raw data into actionable insights, offering a competitive edge in the dynamic realm of property investment.

Leveraging Zoning Changes for Strategic Property Investment Opportunities

Zoning changes can drastically alter the landscape for strategic property investments, often creating opportunities where none previously existed. By understanding the potential ripple effects of zoning decisions, investors can anticipate shifts in property values and capitalize on upcoming market trends. The process begins with a thorough examination of municipal zoning plans and proposed amendments. These documents, while sometimes dense and technical, hold the keys to future development possibilities. For instance, a reclassification from agricultural to residential zoning could signal an impending surge in housing demand, offering a preemptive opportunity to acquire land at a lower price before the market responds.

To unlock the profit potential hidden within zoning changes, investors must develop a keen eye for specific indicators that hint at future real estate transformations. These indicators often reside in the minutiae of city council meeting minutes, planning commission reports, and neighborhood development proposals. A seemingly innocuous mention of increased infrastructure funding in a particular area, for example, might imply future zoning modifications aimed at supporting new commercial or residential projects. By connecting these seemingly disparate dots, astute investors can position themselves to benefit from the consequent upswing in property value or rental income.

Embracing innovative technologies can further enhance an investor's ability to interpret zoning changes for strategic advantage. Geographic Information Systems (GIS) and data analytics provide unprecedented capabilities to visualize and analyze zoning data, offering a more comprehensive understanding of spatial relationships and market dynamics. These tools can help identify underutilized parcels of land that, due to zoning changes, may soon become prime real estate. By leveraging data-driven insights, investors can minimize risk and maximize returns, making informed decisions based on the most current and relevant information available.

While zoning changes present lucrative opportunities, they are not without risks. Investors must remain vigilant about potential challenges, such as community opposition or political shifts that could stall or alter proposed changes. Engaging with local stakeholders and participating in public forums can provide valuable insights into the community's reception of planned developments. Additionally, understanding the regulatory landscape and potential legal hurdles is crucial for mitigating risks and ensuring that investments remain viable as projects progress.

Ultimately, the ability to synthesize zoning data into actionable investment strategies hinges on continuous learning and adaptation. Investors should cultivate a mindset of curiosity and resilience, constantly seeking new information and perspectives to refine their approach. This could involve subscribing to industry publications, attending seminars on urban planning, or collaborating with local real estate experts. By staying informed and proactive, investors can not only anticipate zoning changes but also align their strategies with broader market trends, ensuring sustained success in the ever-evolving realm of property investment.

Mining Permit Databases for Actionable Insights

One of the most challenging aspects of turning permit applications into investment gold is navigating the labyrinth of databases where these permits reside. These repositories, teeming with raw information, hold the subtle whispers of future growth and transformation. Each record, each application, paints a fragment of a larger picture—an emerging horizon of infrastructure evolution. Within these digital vaults, the astute investor can unearth early signals of governmental intent, often hidden beneath layers of procedural jargon. The task is not just to find these signals, but to interpret them with precision, drawing connections between seemingly disparate data points. This is where the true art of mining permit databases lies: discerning the patterns that herald the dawn of new projects and developments.

As you begin to explore these databases, the potential for identifying trends becomes evident. Patterns emerge from the chaos, waiting for those with a practiced eye to recognize them. Perhaps it's the frequency of applications in a particular area or the sudden spike in permits of a specific type that draws your attention. Understanding these data patterns is akin to deciphering a complex code, one that can lead to substantial financial gain. Advanced analytical techniques provide the tools needed to unlock these insights, transforming raw data into a strategic advantage. As the journey through permit databases unfolds, each subtopic will guide you through the intricacies of this process, equipping you with the skills to turn information into opportunity.

Navigating Permit Databases for Early Project Signals

In the labyrinth of permit databases, early indicators of potential infrastructure developments lie hidden, waiting to be unearthed by those equipped with the knowledge and tools to interpret them. These databases, often dismissed as mere bureaucratic repositories, contain a wealth of information that can signal forthcoming growth and investment opportunities. A discerning eye can spot the subtle patterns and trends within permit applications that herald the onset of major projects. By identifying specific types of permits, such as those related to major construction or environmental impact assessments, investors can gain a head start in recognizing areas poised for expansion. This foresight enables strategic positioning ahead of the market curve, capitalizing on opportunities before they become common knowledge.

To effectively navigate these databases, one must adopt a methodical approach. Begin by understanding the structure and categorization of information within these repositories. Many databases segment data by project type, geographic location, or agency involved, allowing for targeted searches. Employing keyword strategies or filters can help refine searches, isolating the most pertinent permits from a sea of information. Utilizing advanced search techniques, such as Boolean operators, enhances the efficiency of data retrieval, ensuring that only the most actionable signals are identified. This granular approach not only saves time but also sharpens the focus on opportunities with the highest potential return on investment.

Industry-specific tools and software can further augment the process of sifting through permit databases. Programs designed for big data analysis or geographic information system (GIS) applications can streamline the interpretation of complex datasets. These technologies can visualize data trends over time or space, offering a dynamic perspective on how infrastructure developments are likely to evolve. For instance, GIS tools can map out permit concentrations, revealing hotspots of upcoming activity that might be missed through manual analysis alone. By integrating these technological solutions, investors can transform raw data into a visual narrative that guides their decision-making process.

While technology plays a critical role, human intuition and expertise remain indispensable. Cross-referencing permit data with other sources, such as industry reports or demographic studies, can provide a fuller picture of a region's growth prospects. Experts often emphasize the importance of considering socio-economic factors alongside permit data. For example, a surge in residential construction permits in a previously underdeveloped area could signal an influx of population and demand for commercial infrastructure. By synthesizing various data points, investors can develop a nuanced understanding of potential growth trajectories and refine their investment strategies accordingly.

Engagement with permit databases is not merely a passive exercise in data collection; it is an active pursuit of insights that requires both analytical acumen and strategic foresight. As the landscape of infrastructure evolves, staying attuned to the signals within permit applications can mean the difference between seizing an opportunity and missing out. Encouragingly, this proactive approach empowers investors to shape their own destinies, transforming what might appear as mundane bureaucratic filings into a roadmap for future success. By continually honing their skills and adapting to new trends, readers can remain at the forefront of infrastructure investment, consistently uncovering the hidden clues that lead to profitable ventures.

Data Patterns and Trends in Permit Applications

Data within permit applications often conceal invaluable insights that can signal the trajectory of future development projects. These applications, submitted by developers and entities seeking approval for construction or modification of infrastructure, offer a treasure trove of information about potential growth areas. By scrutinizing the specifics of these permits, astute investors can discern patterns that hint at impending economic booms. This requires a keen eye for detail and an ability to synthesize disparate pieces of information into a coherent picture of future developments. For example, a surge in permit requests for a particular area may suggest upcoming residential or commercial expansion, presenting a prime opportunity for early investment.

Identifying trends within permit applications involves more than simply noting an increase in submissions. It entails examining the types of projects being proposed, their geographical locations, and the stakeholders involved. A rise in permits for energy-efficient buildings, for example, could indicate a regional shift towards sustainable development, attracting businesses and residents interested in green alternatives. Furthermore, cross-referencing these data points with current economic indicators and regional development plans can provide a more comprehensive understanding of where and why these trends are occurring. This multifaceted approach helps investors predict not just the 'what' but the 'when' and 'where' of future growth.

Advanced analytical techniques can significantly enhance the ability to interpret permit data, transforming raw numbers into strategic insights. Data mining and machine learning algorithms offer sophisticated methods to detect hidden patterns and correlations that might elude traditional analysis. By employing these technologies, investors can predict infrastructure trends with greater accuracy and speed. For instance, machine learning models could identify recurring themes or commonalities among successful permit applications, providing a predictive edge. This not only improves the precision of forecasts but also enables investors to adapt quickly to shifts in development priorities.

Engaging with diverse perspectives can enrich the analysis of permit data. While mainstream narratives may focus on conventional growth indicators, alternative viewpoints can uncover overlooked opportunities. This might involve considering socio-economic factors, such as demographic shifts or cultural trends, that could influence the desirability of certain projects. By integrating these factors into their analysis, investors can develop a more nuanced understanding of market dynamics. Additionally, exploring non-traditional sources of information, such as community forums or local news outlets, can provide early warning signs of upcoming developments that are not yet reflected in permit data.

To transform insights into action, investors must develop a strategic framework that aligns their findings with tangible investment opportunities. This involves not only identifying promising projects but also evaluating the potential risks and rewards associated with each investment. By establishing clear criteria for decision-making, such as return on investment thresholds and risk tolerance levels, investors can prioritize opportunities that align with their financial goals. Additionally, maintaining an adaptive investment strategy allows for flexibility in response to new data or changes in market conditions. A proactive approach, combined with rigorous analysis and strategic planning, can turn hidden clues in permit applications into substantial financial gains.

Advanced Analytical Techniques for Permit Data Interpretation

Interpreting permit data requires a level of analytical sophistication that allows investors to glean insights beyond the surface information. Advanced analytical techniques open doors to understanding the intricacies of permit applications, offering a competitive edge in predicting future infrastructure growth. Machine learning models, for instance, can sift through vast datasets to identify patterns and anomalies that might elude manual analysis. By training algorithms on historical data, these models can predict future trends and uncover correlations between permit approvals and subsequent development activities. Additionally, employing network analysis helps in visualizing connections between various stakeholders involved in the permit process, revealing potential alliances or conflicts that could influence project outcomes.

Beyond machine learning, natural language processing (NLP) serves as a powerful tool for extracting meaningful information from permit documents. NLP can analyze the language used in applications, identifying key phrases and terminologies that signal project scope changes or potential environmental impacts. Sentiment analysis, a facet of NLP, can further gauge the tone of public comments attached to permit applications, offering insights into community support or opposition. This linguistic insight can be crucial for investors looking to assess the likelihood of project delays due to public resistance or regulatory hurdles. By combining these techniques, investors can construct a nuanced understanding of the permit landscape, positioning themselves to act swiftly on emerging opportunities.

Visual analytics also plays a vital role in interpreting permit data. Advanced visualization tools can transform raw data into intuitive graphs and heatmaps, highlighting regional hotspots of developmental activity. By layering this data with geographic and demographic information, investors can pinpoint areas of accelerated growth and anticipate ripple effects on local economies. These visualizations enable a more comprehensive assessment of potential investment sites, ensuring that decisions are backed by a multi-dimensional view of the data. As the complexity of infrastructure projects increases, such visual tools become indispensable in distilling insights from multifaceted datasets.

In the realm of predictive analytics, scenario modeling stands out as an essential technique. By creating simulations based on varying permit approval timelines and project conditions, investors can anticipate a range of potential outcomes. This foresight allows for the development of robust investment strategies that account for different contingencies. Moreover, scenario modeling can highlight the sensitivity of projects to external variables such as policy changes or economic shifts, enabling investors to adjust their positions proactively. Engaging with these predictive tools not only enhances strategic planning but also fosters a culture of adaptability and informed decision-making.

Finally, the integration of cross-disciplinary research enriches the analytical framework. By incorporating insights from urban planning, environmental science, and economics, investors can approach permit data with a holistic perspective. This interdisciplinary approach ensures that interpretations are grounded in a broad understanding of the multifactorial influences on infrastructure development. It encourages readers to consider diverse angles and question conventional wisdom, fostering innovative thinking and proactive investment strategies. In this ever-evolving landscape, staying informed and adaptable is key to capitalizing on the hidden signals within permit databases.

Permit applications serve as a treasure trove of insights for those seeking to uncover future infrastructure developments. Recognizing the signals embedded in development permits provides a glimpse into areas poised for growth, while mastering the nuances of environmental impact statements offers a deeper understanding of potential project challenges and timelines. Zoning changes reveal the shifting landscape of urban planning, highlighting regions where opportunities may soon flourish. By diligently mining permit databases, investors can extract actionable insights, transforming complex bureaucratic processes into clear investment signals. Collectively, these tools empower readers to anticipate where and when to invest, ensuring they remain steps ahead of the general market. The ability to decode these hidden clues not only enhances the predictive framework but also solidifies the foundation for strategic investment decisions. As readers continue this journey, they are encouraged to refine their analytical skills, preparing to harness even more sophisticated tools in subsequent chapters, ultimately leading to informed and profitable investment choices.

Chapter Four

Long Term Planning Documents and Their Signals

Visualize standing on the precipice of a vast construction site, a place where the future of a city begins to take shape long before the first brick is laid. This is the realm of long-term planning documents, where whispers of tomorrow's urban landscapes echo through the pages of meticulously drafted blueprints. These documents are more than mere bureaucratic formalities; they are treasure maps, leading the astute investor to opportunities hidden in plain sight. As governments chart the course for infrastructure that will shape communities for decades, the discerning eye can spot signals that reveal not just what is planned, but where and when these projects will unfold.

In this chapter, we venture into the intricate world of municipal and regional strategies, deciphering the language of transportation plans and urban growth strategies. These documents hold the keys to understanding the evolution of cities, indicating where new hubs of activity will emerge, and which neighborhoods will transform. By examining utility blueprints and comprehensive land-use plans, we unlock insights into the infrastructure that sustains and propels urban life. The delicate dance between necessity and innovation plays out in these plans, offering clues to the future contours of urban development.

Throughout this exploration, we equip ourselves with the tools to read between the lines, transforming dense bureaucratic prose into actionable intelligence. These signals are the lifeblood of strategic investment, guiding us toward decisions that capitalize on the momentum of progress. As we peel back the layers of these planning documents, we embrace the opportunity to not only predict the future but to invest in it with confidence. This journey into the heart of infrastructure planning is not just about foresight; it's about seizing the moment to create lasting value.

Transportation Master Plans and What They Reveal

Transportation master plans hold a treasure trove of insights for those keen on anticipating future infrastructure developments. These documents are not just a collection of roadmaps and transit lines; they are blueprints that reveal a city's long-term vision, outlining how transportation networks will evolve to meet the demands of tomorrow. At the core, they encapsulate a narrative driven by projected growth patterns, technological advancements, and policy imperatives. By understanding the nuances of these plans, investors can pinpoint where tomorrow's connectivity improvements will spark today's investment opportunities. Envision a bustling new transit corridor; these master plans are the crystal ball that identifies the future hubs of activity and growth. They whisper of where property values may rise, where businesses might thrive, and where the public sector's next big moves are likely to unfold.

Engaging with these plans requires more than just a cursory glance. It demands a strategic approach to decode the subtle signals embedded within. Recognizing potential investment hotspots involves sifting through layers of data to uncover areas poised for transformation. Policy shifts often act as the catalysts for these changes, altering the trajectory of infrastructure investments and reshaping urban landscapes. By meticulously analyzing these shifts, investors can align themselves with government priorities, positioning themselves advantageously in the market. The ensuing discussion will guide you through the intricate process of interpreting transport master plans, identifying promising locations, and understanding the profound impact of policy changes on infrastructure investments. As we explore these subtopics, the aim is to equip you with the foresight and acumen necessary to transform these comprehensive documents into a wellspring of financial opportunity.

Decoding Future Transportation Trends Through Master Plans

Master plans for transportation offer a treasure trove of insights into forthcoming trends in infrastructure development. These comprehensive documents, often spanning years or even decades, provide a glimpse into the evolving dynamics of urban and regional mobility. By examining these plans, one can discern patterns and priorities that signal future opportunities. For instance, a shift towards sustainable transportation modes such as electric vehicles or bike lanes not only highlights societal values but also indicates potential investment areas. Savvy investors can identify these trends early, positioning themselves to capitalize on changes that are still on the horizon. The ability to extract such insights necessitates a keen understanding of the language and structure of these plans, as well as the socio-political contexts that shape them.

An essential aspect of deciphering these master plans is recognizing the interplay between policy objectives and economic realities. Transportation plans are not merely technical documents; they are strategic blueprints reflecting broader policy goals like reducing carbon emissions, improving public health, or stimulating economic growth. These goals often translate into specific projects or investments, such as new transit corridors or infrastructure upgrades. By aligning investment strategies with these policy-driven projects, one can identify 'hotspots' that promise significant returns. This requires not only a close reading of the plans themselves but also an awareness of the legislative and budgetary processes that will ultimately determine which projects come to fruition.

Understanding the impact of technological advancements on transportation planning is also crucial. As cities and regions adopt smart city technologies, master plans increasingly incorporate innovations like autonomous vehicles, real-time data analytics, and integrated mobility platforms. These technologies can transform the transportation landscape, creating new markets and disrupting existing ones. Investors who stay abreast of technological developments and understand their potential impact on infrastructure planning can position themselves advantageously. For example, the integration of ride-sharing platforms with public transport systems might indicate a future reduction in personal vehicle ownership, influencing real estate values and development patterns in urban areas.

Beyond technology, demographic and social trends are vital components of transportation planning. Changing population dynamics, such as urbanization or aging populations, influence how transportation networks are designed and prioritized. Analyzing these trends enables investors to anticipate shifts in demand for different types of infrastructure, from high-speed rail to pedestrian-friendly urban centers. By connecting these demographic insights with transportation master plans, one can better predict where and when infrastructure investments will yield the most substantial returns. These insights are critical for developing a nuanced and forward-looking investment strategy that accounts for both current realities and future possibilities.

Engaging with transportation master plans as part of an investment strategy also involves a degree of speculation and risk management. While these plans provide a roadmap, they are subject to change due to political shifts, economic fluctuations, or unforeseen events. Therefore, it's important for investors to develop a flexible approach, continuously monitoring developments and adjusting their strategies as needed. This adaptability, coupled with a deep understanding of the plans themselves, can transform the inherent uncertainties of infrastructure investing into opportunities for substantial financial gain. By fostering a mindset that embraces complexity and change, investors can not only decode future trends but actively shape their outcomes.

Identifying Investment Hotspots with Transportation Planning Data

Transportation planning data holds the key to unveiling lucrative investment opportunities in emerging hotspots. As cities evolve and expand, transportation infrastructure serves as a backbone for economic development, dictating where future growth is likely to occur. By scrutinizing transportation master plans, one can identify regions poised for increased accessibility and connectivity, which often translate into high-demand real estate and business prospects. Notably, these plans often outline proposed routes for new transit lines, highway expansions, and other critical infrastructure projects. These elements serve as valuable indicators for potential investment zones, allowing investors to position themselves strategically ahead of market shifts.

Uncovering investment hotspots requires a deep understanding of the interplay between transportation planning and urban development. Master plans not only map out future transport routes but also highlight areas targeted for densification and revitalization. These zones often attract complementary developments, such as residential complexes, commercial hubs, and industrial parks, which can significantly enhance property values. Investors can gain a competitive edge by analyzing how transportation improvements align with broader urban initiatives, thereby identifying synergy-rich areas. This approach calls for a synthesis of data, where insights from transportation planning are integrated with regional growth strategies and zoning adjustments, offering a holistic view of future investment landscapes.

Going beyond conventional analysis, cutting-edge methodologies such as Geographic Information Systems (GIS) and predictive analytics offer sophisticated tools for pinpointing investment hotspots. GIS technology, in particular, allows investors to visualize and analyze spatial data, revealing patterns and trends that might not be immediately apparent. By overlaying transportation data with demographic and economic indicators, investors can gain nuanced insights into potential growth areas. This advanced level of analysis not only uncovers hidden opportunities but also provides a robust framework for making informed decisions, minimizing risk while maximizing returns. Harnessing such technologies equips investors with the foresight needed to capitalize on transportation-driven growth.

While transportation plans provide a roadmap to future developments, understanding the nuances of policy shifts is equally crucial for identifying hotspots. Policies related to sustainable transport, for instance, can drastically reshape investment potential by prioritizing eco-friendly transit options and pedestrian-friendly zones. These shifts often lead to the creation of green corridors and urban renewal projects, which can become focal points for investment. Savvy investors keep a close watch on evolving policy landscapes, leveraging them to anticipate market movements and position themselves advantageously. By aligning investment strategies with policy trajectories, they can navigate the complexities of infrastructure investments with confidence.

Complex scenarios emerge when considering the diverse factors that influence transportation planning. Political dynamics, community input, and environmental considerations often intersect, leading to unexpected shifts in project priorities. Investors need to remain agile, continuously updating their analyses to reflect these changes. Thought-provoking questions, such as how emerging technologies like autonomous vehicles might affect transportation infrastructure, can spark critical thinking and innovation. By staying informed and adaptable, investors can cultivate a keen sense of anticipation, ready to seize opportunities as they arise. Through a proactive and research-driven approach, they can transform transportation planning data into a powerful tool for unlocking investment potential.

Analyzing Policy Shifts and Their Impact on Infrastructure Investments

Policy shifts are pivotal in reshaping the landscape of infrastructure investments, often serving as catalysts for transformative projects. Understanding these shifts requires more than a cursory glance at policy documents; it demands a nuanced appreciation of legislative intent and strategic priorities. By scrutinizing the language and context of transportation master plans, investors can discern subtle yet impactful changes that signal future investment opportunities. For instance, a policy pivot towards sustainable transportation may suggest imminent investments in electric vehicle infrastructure or expanded public transit networks. Such shifts not only indicate direct investment prospects but also provide insight into ancillary markets likely to experience growth, such as renewable energy or smart city technologies.

Examining policy shifts through a multi-faceted lens unveils the interplay between government priorities and market dynamics. An unexpected adjustment in transportation policy, like a renewed focus on pedestrian-friendly urban spaces, can catalyze a ripple effect across related sectors. Investors who recognize these interconnected outcomes stand to benefit by positioning themselves in industries that may initially seem peripheral. This holistic approach transforms policy shifts from isolated events into strategic opportunities, allowing investors to anticipate and respond proactively to emerging trends. It's this ability to connect disparate dots that sets astute investors apart from the rest, enabling them to capitalize on shifts long before they materialize into concrete projects.

The challenge lies in deciphering the implications of policy changes amidst a barrage of information. A discerning reader will look beyond the headlines, digging into the broader socio-economic context and the strategic objectives behind policy amendments. For example, a government's commitment to reducing carbon emissions through enhanced rail infrastructure might initially seem straightforward. However, a deeper analysis could reveal opportunities in sectors like construction materials, where demand for sustainable alternatives might surge. By appreciating these nuanced dimensions, investors can craft a diversified portfolio that not only aligns with current policy trajectories but also anticipates future policy developments.

Innovation in data analytics and modeling tools offers a powerful means to dissect policy shifts with unprecedented precision. Advanced algorithms and machine learning techniques can process vast datasets, uncovering patterns and correlations that might elude the human eye. These technological advancements empower investors to simulate various policy scenarios, assessing their potential impact on infrastructure investments. By leveraging these tools, investors can refine their strategies with greater accuracy, ensuring they remain agile in a rapidly evolving policy landscape. This data-driven approach enhances the ability to predict how policy shifts will unfold, providing a competitive edge in navigating the complexities of infrastructure investment.

Imagining the myriad possibilities of policy shifts encourages a forward-thinking mindset. Consider the effect of a government prioritizing autonomous vehicle infrastructure; the implications extend far beyond the automotive sector. Envision how real estate markets might adapt, with properties near autonomous transit hubs appreciating significantly. By asking such probing questions and exploring alternative scenarios, investors can develop strategic foresight that informs more resilient investment decisions. This proactive stance not only mitigates risks associated with policy volatility but also positions investors to seize opportunities arising from unforeseen policy developments. Through these insights, readers are equipped to transform policy shifts from abstract concepts into tangible investment strategies.

Regional Growth Strategies and Urban Expansion

In recent years, we've seen a surge in the complexity and scale of regional growth strategies, which serve as blueprints for shaping the future of our cities and towns. These strategies are not mere bureaucratic exercises; they are the pulse of urban expansion, hinting at where the next economic hubs will emerge and which areas are poised for transformation. As cities grapple with increasing populations and evolving economic landscapes, regional plans provide a roadmap for sustainable development, balancing the needs of today with the demands of tomorrow. By understanding these plans, investors can gain insights into future hotspots for development, making it possible to anticipate where infrastructure investments will be most impactful and lucrative.

This understanding becomes particularly significant when analyzing economic drivers that fuel urban expansion. From identifying industries likely to spur job growth to recognizing regions with untapped potential, these strategies illuminate the forces shaping the urban skyline. They also highlight infrastructure gaps that present both challenges and opportunities in growing regions. As we navigate these documents, we can predict demographic shifts that will influence housing markets, transportation needs, and public services. With each subtopic, we unlock a layer of understanding about how regional growth strategies can signal where to direct our focus and resources.

Analyzing Economic Drivers for Urban Expansion

Urban expansion is often fueled by a myriad of economic catalysts that, when understood, can offer profound insights into future growth trajectories. These economic drivers include factors like employment opportunities, technological advancements, and shifts in industry focus. For instance, the emergence of tech hubs or the establishment of manufacturing plants can significantly influence urban growth patterns. A city witnessing an influx of tech companies may experience rapid expansion in its infrastructure to accommodate a growing workforce, while regions centered around manufacturing might see developments in logistics and transportation facilities. Understanding these dynamics requires a keen eye on local economic trends and a comprehensive analysis of labor markets. By identifying these economic signals early, investors can strategically position themselves to benefit from the cascading developments that follow.

In rapidly evolving urban landscapes, the relationship between economic forces and urban expansion is multifaceted. It is crucial to consider how public policy can either accelerate or hinder growth. Tax incentives, for example, can attract new businesses, igniting a construction boom and an uptick in housing demand. On the other hand, stringent regulations might slow down development, offering a different set of investment opportunities, such as in renovation and adaptive reuse projects. A nuanced understanding of the interplay between policy and economic drivers enables stakeholders to forecast the direction of urban expansion and align their investment strategies accordingly. This predictive insight is not just about following the current but anticipating where the tide will shift next.

As cities grow and evolve, demographic patterns offer another layer of complexity and opportunity. These shifts can be influenced by economic factors such as job prospects, living costs, and quality of life offerings. For example, an area known for its burgeoning job market may attract younger professionals, leading to increased demand for modern housing and lifestyle amenities. Conversely, regions with a higher cost of living might witness a demographic shift as families move to more affordable suburbs. Recognizing these patterns and their economic underpinnings allows investors to target specific markets and sectors poised for growth, making informed decisions about property acquisitions or developments.

Incorporating cutting-edge research and advanced methodologies can further enhance the understanding of economic drivers behind urban expansion. Techniques such as data analytics and GIS mapping provide sophisticated tools for visualizing growth patterns and forecasting future developments. By leveraging these technologies, investors and planners can gain a competitive edge, identifying opportunities that might not be immediately apparent through traditional analysis. For instance, GIS mapping can reveal underdeveloped areas with high growth potential, allowing for strategic investment before these regions become hotspots. This approach underscores the importance of continually evolving one's toolkit to better anticipate and capitalize on emerging urban trends.

Engaging with the complexities of urban expansion requires not just analysis but also foresight and adaptability. Considering diverse perspectives enriches the understanding of how economic drivers interact with urban dynamics. By questioning conventional narratives and exploring alternative scenarios, such as the potential impact of remote work on urban sprawl, practitioners can better navigate the unpredictable nature of urban growth. This proactive stance ensures that investment strategies remain robust and responsive to changing conditions. As readers digest these insights, they are encouraged to think critically about the potential applications of this knowledge in their investment endeavors, transforming theoretical understanding into tangible success.

Identifying Infrastructure Gaps in Growing Regions

Infrastructure gaps in burgeoning regions present both challenges and opportunities for astute investors. As cities expand and evolve, identifying these gaps provides a roadmap to where future development is likely headed. These gaps often manifest in the form of inadequate transportation networks, insufficient public utilities, or the absence of essential services like schools and hospitals. By scrutinizing regional planning documents and conducting on-the-ground assessments, investors can pinpoint areas where the current infrastructure fails to meet the burgeoning demands of a growing population. This foresight allows for strategic investments in sectors poised for growth, ensuring a competitive edge in the market.

Recent studies have shown that regions experiencing rapid urbanization frequently encounter significant disparities in infrastructure development. For instance, many suburban areas may lack efficient public transportation systems, leading to increased traffic congestion and longer commute times. Investors who recognize these deficiencies can capitalize on the potential for transportation projects, whether through public-private partnerships or by investing in real estate near planned transit routes. Furthermore, the rise of smart city technologies offers innovative solutions to bridge these gaps, such as employing data analytics to optimize traffic flow or investing in electric vehicle charging infrastructure to support the transition to sustainable transport.

The intricacies of utility infrastructure also demand attention. As populations swell, so does the demand for water, electricity, and waste management services. In many cases, existing systems may be outdated or stretched to their limits, indicating a pressing need for modernization and expansion. By analyzing utility blueprints and engaging with local stakeholders, investors can gain insights into upcoming projects aimed at enhancing these essential services. For instance, regions investing in renewable energy sources or modernized water treatment facilities often signal an impending shift in infrastructure priorities, opening the door to lucrative investment prospects.

Demographic trends further illuminate where infrastructure investments are most needed. Population growth, age distribution, and migration patterns can significantly impact the infrastructure landscape. Regions with a rapidly aging population, for example, may require expanded healthcare facilities and senior living accommodations. Conversely, areas attracting younger demographics might prioritize educational institutions and recreational amenities. Understanding these dynamics enables investors to tailor their strategies to the specific needs of a region, ensuring their investments align with the evolving demands of the community.

Consider the scenario of a city projected to double its population over the next decade. While this growth presents numerous opportunities, it also highlights potential areas of concern, such as housing shortages, overcrowded schools, and strained public services. By proactively identifying and addressing these gaps through strategic investments, stakeholders can not only profit but also contribute to the sustainable development of the region. This approach not only enhances the quality of life for residents but also ensures that investments are robust and resilient, capable of weathering the inevitable ebbs and flows of market cycles.

Predicting Demographic Shifts Through Regional Plans

Predicting demographic shifts through regional plans involves a nuanced understanding of socio-economic patterns, migration trends, and urban development strategies. A thorough examination of regional plans reveals invaluable data, often hidden in plain sight, that can forecast population changes. By scrutinizing elements such as housing allocations, transportation networks, and employment hubs, one can discern potential shifts in population density and distribution. These plans often highlight future residential zones, commercial areas, and infrastructure projects, offering clues about where populations might concentrate or disperse.

Consider the intricate relationship between economic drivers and demographic transitions. For instance, the announcement of a new tech park or industrial zone in regional plans often preludes an influx of job seekers and, consequently, a surge in housing demand. This domino effect can transform an area, turning sleepy suburbs into bustling communities. By recognizing these signals early, investors can identify real estate opportunities that capitalize on increased demand. Additionally, examining school district expansions or adjustments can indicate an anticipated growth in young families, signaling a burgeoning community ripe for retail and service investments.

Innovative techniques in data analysis further enhance the ability to predict demographic shifts. Geographic Information Systems (GIS) offer powerful tools to visualize and interpret regional plans, allowing users to spot trends and anomalies with precision. By layering demographic data over planned infrastructure developments, GIS provides a comprehensive view of how future growth will unfold. This sophisticated approach, combined with traditional document analysis, equips investors with a competitive edge in anticipating demographic changes. Embracing such advanced methodologies ensures that predictions are backed by robust, multi-faceted insights.

The dynamic nature of demographic trends also necessitates consideration of global factors and cultural shifts. Remote work, for instance, has altered traditional commuting patterns, prompting regional plans to adapt by accommodating decentralized workforces. This shift opens opportunities in previously overlooked areas, as people seek residences with more space and amenities, away from urban centers. Understanding these evolving preferences allows stakeholders to anticipate shifts that might not be immediately evident in static documents, thus expanding the scope of potential investment areas.

Critical thinking and strategic foresight are paramount in transforming insights from regional plans into actionable investment strategies. One might ask: How will climate change policies affect migration patterns? Or, how might a shift in public transportation focus influence urban sprawl? These questions encourage a deeper exploration of the factors influencing demographic shifts, promoting a proactive rather than reactive approach. By continuously refining their understanding and adapting to new information, investors can effectively position themselves to benefit from emerging demographic trends, securing opportunities that align with long-term growth trajectories.

Utility and Public Works Blueprints

At the core of a thriving society lies the intricate network of utilities and public works that quietly sustain our daily lives. Imagine the bustling energy of a city, powered by carefully orchestrated systems, each a crucial thread in the urban tapestry. While these infrastructures often go unnoticed by the general public, they hold a treasure trove of insights for the astute investor. Utility and public works blueprints, often perceived as mundane details, are in fact strategic roadmaps that reveal the hidden currents of economic growth and development. By examining these plans, one can gain foresight into transformative changes that shape communities and, in turn, present lucrative investment prospects.

Picture a world where understanding the nuances of utility expansion plans becomes a gateway to identifying areas primed for growth. Each blueprint, whether it's for water, electricity, or waste management, outlines the trajectory of services that underpin urban expansion. Public works project schedules, with their detailed timelines and funding allocations, offer a glimpse into the priorities of government and the potential impact on local markets. Meanwhile, emerging technology trends within public works can signal shifts in industry standards, presenting unique opportunities for the informed investor. Together, these elements form a comprehensive guide for decoding the signals embedded within public works strategies, paving the way for strategic investments and financial success.

Analyzing Utility Expansion Plans for Investment Opportunities

Utility expansion plans offer a rich tapestry of information for those looking to identify strategic investment opportunities. As cities grow and populations shift, the demand for utilities such as electricity, water, and gas invariably increases, requiring expansions and upgrades to existing infrastructure. This presents a unique opportunity for savvy investors who can interpret these plans to anticipate areas of growth and development. By examining utility companies' future expansion plans, one can glean insights into where new neighborhoods might emerge or existing ones transform, providing a roadmap for real estate investment and development ventures. Scrutinizing these documents can reveal the specific locations where significant infrastructure investments are planned, signaling likely areas of economic and residential growth.

A deeper understanding of utility expansion plans requires knowledge of key indicators such as projected load growth, capacity enhancements, and strategic partnerships. For instance, a utility's decision to invest in a new substation or water treatment facility in a particular region can indicate upcoming residential or industrial developments. Investors can use this information to their advantage, positioning themselves ahead of market shifts by acquiring properties that will soon benefit from improved utility services. The integration of renewable energy sources into existing grids is another trend reshaping utility expansion strategies. Understanding how utilities are adapting their systems to accommodate solar, wind, and other sustainable energy sources can provide forward-thinking investors with an edge in identifying emerging market opportunities.

Technological advancements play a crucial role in shaping the future of utility expansions. The adoption of smart grids, IoT devices, and advanced metering infrastructure is transforming how utilities operate and plan for future needs. These technologies not only increase operational efficiency but also provide valuable data that can forecast consumption patterns and identify areas requiring infrastructure upgrades. Investors who harness these insights can pinpoint where utilities are most likely to direct future resources and attention, allowing them to make informed decisions regarding property investments or business expansions. Furthermore, the push toward digital transformations within utility companies can signal upcoming partnerships or technology investments, offering additional avenues for strategic financial engagement.

In analyzing utility expansion plans, it's vital to consider the broader context of regional and national policy shifts. Government initiatives aimed at promoting sustainability, reducing carbon footprints, and improving infrastructure resilience can significantly influence utility planning. Policies that encourage the adoption of clean energy or mandate infrastructure improvements to withstand climate change impacts can create new investment opportunities. By staying informed about legislative changes and regulatory trends, investors can better anticipate shifts in utility expansion priorities and align their strategies accordingly. Additionally, understanding how utilities interact with local governments, regulatory bodies, and community stakeholders can provide nuanced insights into the feasibility and timeline of planned expansions.

To turn these insights into actionable strategies, investors should develop a systematic approach to monitoring utility expansion plans. This involves regularly reviewing public records, attending community planning meetings, and engaging with utility representatives. Building relationships with stakeholders in the utility sector can provide access to valuable, often under-the-radar information. Moreover, employing Geographic Information Systems (GIS) technology can help visualize and analyze spatial data related to utility plans, offering a competitive advantage in identifying promising investment zones. By continuously refining these skills and strategies, investors can position themselves at the forefront of infrastructure-driven investment opportunities, ensuring they capitalize on the growth and transformation of urban landscapes.

Decoding Public Works Project Schedules and Funding Priorities

Understanding the intricacies of public works project schedules and funding priorities can transform opaque government initiatives into a treasure trove of investment possibilities. Public works projects, ranging from road repairs to new bridge constructions, follow meticulously outlined schedules that reflect both immediate and future government priorities. These schedules are more than mere timelines; they reveal the strategic intentions of public agencies and the allocation of resources. To interpret these effectively, one must recognize the patterns and indicators that signal shifts in governmental focus and investment. For instance, a sudden acceleration in project timelines often suggests a reallocation of funds, possibly due to policy shifts or emerging public needs. This knowledge can provide investors with a foresight advantage, allowing them to anticipate where government resources—and by extension, economic growth—will be concentrated.

The prioritization of funding within public works projects offers another layer of insight. Budgets are often influenced by political, economic, and social factors, each playing a crucial role in determining project viability and timeline. By scrutinizing funding allocations, investors can gauge which projects are gaining traction and which might face delays. For example, a consistent increase in funding for renewable energy infrastructure may indicate a governmental commitment to sustainable development, signaling potential opportunities for investment in related sectors. Investors who can pinpoint these funding trends are better positioned to align their strategies with governmental priorities, thereby maximizing returns.

Technological advancements are reshaping public works, introducing new elements to project schedules and funding strategies. The integration of cutting-edge technologies like smart infrastructure and digital twins offers a glimpse into the future of public works, where efficiency and precision are paramount. These technologies not only enhance project planning and execution but also serve as indicators of where future investments might yield substantial benefits. For instance, cities investing in smart traffic systems may experience reduced congestion and improved urban mobility, driving demand for related technologies and services. By staying abreast of these technological trends, investors can identify sectors poised for growth and strategically position themselves in emerging markets.

A comprehensive approach to decoding public works schedules and funding priorities involves synthesizing diverse data sources. Investors are encouraged to explore beyond conventional documents, incorporating insights from public hearings, stakeholder interviews, and community feedback. These sources often provide nuanced perspectives that can validate or challenge prevailing assumptions about project timelines and funding. By engaging with a variety of viewpoints, investors can construct a more holistic understanding of the factors influencing public works projects, enabling them to make informed decisions that transcend surface-level analysis.

Critical thinking and strategic application of insights are vital for translating public works data into profitable ventures. Investors should consider scenario planning as a method to explore potential outcomes of various funding and scheduling decisions. By envisioning different scenarios, such as accelerated funding for infrastructure in response to economic stimulus packages, investors can develop adaptable strategies that account for both risks and opportunities. This proactive approach not only mitigates potential pitfalls but also empowers investors to capitalize on the fluid landscape of public works projects, ultimately turning government plans into profitable ventures.

Leveraging Technology Trends in Public Works for Market Insights

Public works have always served as the backbone of urban infrastructure, and in recent years, technological advancements have begun to transform this sector dramatically. Understanding these shifts can provide astute investors with invaluable insights. For instance, the adoption of smart grid technologies in utility management is reshaping how energy is distributed and consumed. Smart grids enable real-time monitoring and management, reducing losses and optimizing efficiency. Savvy investors can identify companies that are pioneering these technologies or those that will benefit from their implementation. This approach not only provides a glimpse into future developments but also highlights potential areas for significant financial returns.

A particularly influential trend is the integration of Internet of Things (IoT) devices in water and waste management systems. These devices facilitate precise resource tracking and predictive maintenance, reducing operational costs and enhancing service delivery. Municipalities investing in IoT solutions for public utilities signal a commitment to modernizing infrastructure, offering strategic points of entry for investors. As IoT adoption increases, opportunities emerge for those who can identify the key players in this market. By focusing on regions where IoT integration is actively being discussed or implemented, investors can position themselves ahead of the curve.

Digital twins, virtual models of physical assets, are another technological advancement gaining traction in public works. These models allow for comprehensive analysis and simulation of infrastructure systems, providing insights into performance and potential issues before they arise. Cities utilizing digital twins can make more informed decisions, leading to smoother project execution and lower costs. Investors recognizing the importance of digital twin technology can seek opportunities with companies supplying these solutions or municipalities committed to their adoption. This strategic foresight not only underscores an understanding of cutting-edge technologies but also highlights an investment's potential for substantial returns.

Renewable energy projects are increasingly embedded within public works initiatives, driven by global sustainability goals and climate action plans. Investment in solar and wind energy infrastructure within public projects is becoming a priority, opening avenues for those interested in green technologies. Projects focusing on sustainable energy alternatives often receive significant funding and public support, offering a stable investment environment. By identifying regions and companies specializing in integrating renewable energy into public works, investors can align their portfolios with long-term environmental trends while capitalizing on government incentives and initiatives.

The future of public works is undeniably intertwined with technological innovation, and discerning investors must remain attuned to these developments. Considering diverse perspectives, such as the ethical implications of data collection in smart cities or the potential for job displacement due to automation, enriches the investment analysis. By asking critical questions about the broader impact of these technologies, investors not only enhance their understanding but also ensure their strategies are comprehensive and forward-thinking. As public works continue to evolve, the ability to interpret these technological signals will be crucial in identifying and maximizing investment opportunities.

Decoding Comprehensive and Land-Use Plans

A closer examination shows that comprehensive and land-use plans are more than just bureaucratic documents—they are blueprints for the future, silently shaping the landscapes we inhabit. These plans, often overlooked in their complexity, hold the keys to understanding where and how cities will transform over the coming decades. They map out the intentions of city planners and government officials, revealing the intricate dance between development aspirations and regulatory frameworks. For the astute investor, these documents are a treasure trove of insights, waiting to be deciphered. They offer a rare glimpse into the future, illuminating paths where infrastructure will burgeon, and development will flourish. By mastering the art of decoding these plans, one gains the ability to foresee changes in the urban fabric, turning potential confusion into clarity and, ultimately, opportunity.

Navigating through zoning regulations and land-use designations uncovers untapped potential in burgeoning growth corridors. These elements signal where the next wave of development might crest, suggesting which neighborhoods will thrive and which will remain static. As cities expand, comprehensive plans detail the infrastructure that will support this growth—roads, utilities, public spaces—all integral to the creation of vibrant, livable communities. By identifying these signals, investors can strategically position themselves to capitalize on emerging trends, ensuring their portfolios align with the pulse of the city's evolution. This chapter invites you to interpret these hidden signals, guiding you to opportunities that lie within planned infrastructure corridors. Prepare to explore the intricate layers of comprehensive planning, where foresight becomes profit and the future unfolds today.

Understanding Zoning Regulations and Their Impact on Development

Zoning regulations serve as the intricate blueprint for urban development, dictating land use and architectural constraints that shape the physical landscape of communities. These regulations, established by local governments, define permissible activities on parcels of land, influencing everything from building height to density and land use types. Understanding these guidelines allows investors to accurately forecast areas poised for transformation or stagnation. For instance, a shift in zoning that permits higher density residential projects could signal a burgeoning neighborhood ripe for real estate investments. Such changes often reflect broader economic shifts or policy initiatives, making them crucial signals for astute investors seeking early-mover advantage.

The impact of zoning extends beyond mere compliance; it unlocks or restricts the potential of an area. By scrutinizing zoning maps and amendments, investors can discern patterns that indicate future development trends. These patterns can highlight potential bottlenecks or opportunities, such as neighborhoods on the cusp of transitioning from industrial to mixed-use residential areas. The ability to anticipate these changes provides a strategic edge, allowing investors to position themselves ahead of market shifts. Consider the case of transit-oriented developments (TODs), where zoning modifications to accommodate increased density and mixed-use projects near transit hubs can significantly boost property values. Recognizing these signals early can lead to substantial financial returns.

Advanced insights into zoning require an appreciation of the nuances involved, such as the interplay between zoning laws and community feedback. Public hearings and stakeholder meetings often precede significant zoning changes, offering a glimpse into the future landscape of an area. By participating in or reviewing the outcomes of these discussions, investors can gauge community sentiment and potential resistance, which can influence the pace and nature of development. This holistic approach to understanding zoning ensures that investors are not only aware of the regulatory framework but also the socio-political dynamics at play. Recognizing the delicate balance between regulatory constraints and community aspirations is key to making informed investment decisions.

Recent research highlights innovative approaches in zoning practices, such as form-based codes that prioritize physical form over land use, granting greater flexibility and aesthetic coherence to urban areas. These codes often encourage sustainable and pedestrian-friendly environments, aligning with contemporary urban planning trends. By embracing these cutting-edge frameworks, investors can identify regions likely to attract demographic groups seeking walkable, environmentally conscious communities. This alignment with modern urban planning philosophies can make certain areas more attractive to developers and residents alike, enhancing their investment potential.

To translate zoning knowledge into actionable investment strategies, investors might consider developing a zoning change monitoring system that tracks amendments, variances, and community feedback in real-time. Utilizing Geographic Information Systems (GIS) can further enhance this system, providing visual insights into spatial patterns and potential growth corridors. Armed with this information, investors can make data-driven decisions, selecting properties in zones with favorable regulations and anticipated development. This proactive approach not only mitigates risk but also maximizes potential returns, transforming zoning regulations from a bureaucratic hurdle into a powerful tool for strategic investment.

Analyzing Future Growth Areas Through Land-Use Designations

Unraveling future growth areas through land-use designations offers a compelling window into the evolving dynamics of urban development. These designations serve as strategic blueprints, guiding the allocation of land for residential, commercial, and industrial purposes. They reveal the anticipated trajectory of urban expansion and highlight potential hotspots for investment. For instance, areas earmarked for mixed-use development often signal a burgeoning demand for diverse facilities, indicating a ripe opportunity for discerning investors. Understanding these designations requires more than a superficial glance; it demands a deep dive into the subtleties of municipal planning documents, where the language of growth is intricately coded.

Advanced geographic information systems (GIS) can be pivotal in analyzing land-use designations, offering a sophisticated lens through which to interpret spatial patterns and trends. By overlaying demographic data with zoning maps, investors can discern intersections of high potential—areas poised for significant growth due to favorable zoning changes. These insights are not merely academic; they translate into actionable intelligence, guiding decisions on property acquisition and development. The ability to anticipate growth corridors, where infrastructure will likely follow, affords investors a strategic advantage, positioning them ahead of the curve before these areas become widely recognized.

Innovative perspectives on land-use designations suggest a shift towards more sustainable and resilient urban planning. As cities grapple with climate change and resource constraints, there is a growing emphasis on eco-friendly developments and green infrastructure. Investors who can identify these trends early, understanding how sustainability is reshaping land-use priorities, are better positioned to capitalize on the next wave of urban evolution. This forward-thinking approach not only aligns with global environmental goals but also taps into a growing market demand for sustainable living solutions.

The interplay between public policy and market dynamics is crucial in understanding land-use designations. Legislative changes can alter zoning laws, influence infrastructure funding, and redirect growth pathways. Staying informed about legislative developments, therefore, becomes essential for investors aiming to navigate the complex landscape of urban planning. This knowledge, combined with an awareness of local community sentiments and stakeholder interests, enables more informed decision-making, ensuring that investments align with both regulatory frameworks and market demands.

In contemplating future growth through land-use designations, one must ask: How might shifts in societal values, technological advancements, or economic conditions reshape the urban fabric? Such questions encourage investors to think beyond conventional paradigms, exploring diverse scenarios that could impact future growth areas. By fostering a mindset attuned to both present realities and future possibilities, investors can craft strategies that are both resilient and adaptive, ensuring long-term success in the ever-evolving realm of infrastructure investment.

Identifying Investment Opportunities in Planned Infrastructure Corridors

Identifying investment opportunities within planned infrastructure corridors requires an astute understanding of how these zones can reshape urban landscapes and drive economic growth. Infrastructure corridors often serve as the backbone of regional development, stimulating both commercial and residential activities. These planned pathways frequently include essential facilities such as roads, railways, and utilities, creating a fertile ground for investment. By examining government documents and land-use plans, investors can pinpoint potential hotspots for development and capitalize on them before they become widely recognized. A keen eye for detail in these documents can unveil the hidden potential of corridors that are poised to become bustling economic hubs.

Investors benefit immensely from understanding zoning regulations and how they interact with infrastructure corridors. For instance, areas designated for mixed-use development can open doors to diverse investment strategies, allowing for the combination of residential, commercial, and recreational spaces. This diversity not only attracts a broad spectrum of businesses and residents but also enhances property values. By identifying these mixed-use zones within infrastructure corridors, investors can position themselves to benefit from the multifaceted growth these areas encourage. It's essential to keep abreast of any amendments to zoning laws, as these can significantly impact the potential returns on investments in these areas.

Technological advancements play a crucial role in enhancing the appeal of infrastructure corridors. Smart infrastructure, for example, integrates technology with urban environments, leading to more efficient transportation systems and utilities. This integration can attract tech-savvy businesses and residents, further driving up property values. Investors should consider the role of technology in planned corridors and seek out opportunities where smart infrastructure is a key component. By aligning investments with technological trends, they can not only capture immediate value but also ensure long-term growth as these innovations become integral to urban living.

The global push towards sustainability also influences infrastructure development, offering another layer of investment insight. Corridors designed with sustainability in mind—such as those incorporating green spaces, energy-efficient buildings, and sustainable transport options—are likely to attract environmentally conscious businesses and residents. These green corridors can lead to higher demand for properties within or around them, as sustainability increasingly becomes a priority for investors and consumers alike. Identifying opportunities within these eco-friendly developments can provide a dual benefit: supporting environmental goals while securing profitable returns.

Critical thinking and strategic foresight are essential when evaluating potential investments in infrastructure corridors. Investors should not only rely on current trends but also anticipate future shifts in urban planning and demographic changes. For example, corridors near expanding urban areas or those linked to major transportation networks might present significant opportunities as cities grow and evolve. By asking thought-provoking questions and considering various scenarios, investors can develop a robust strategy that accounts for both present dynamics and future possibilities. This proactive approach allows them to act decisively and maximize their returns in this ever-evolving landscape.

Unlocking the insights from long-term planning documents marks a pivotal step in identifying infrastructure opportunities that often lie hidden in plain sight. Transportation master plans unveil future transit corridors and expansions, offering clues about areas poised for growth and increased accessibility. Regional growth strategies and urban expansion plans highlight where population and economic activities are expected to concentrate, setting the stage for potential investment hotspots. Utility and public works blueprints reveal essential services that can signal upcoming development zones, while comprehensive and land-use plans provide a broader vision of community transformation over time. By mastering the art of decoding these documents, investors gain a powerful lens through which to anticipate shifts and align their strategies accordingly. This chapter not only arms readers with the tools to decipher these complex signals but also reinforces the importance of foresight in turning seemingly mundane information into a strategic advantage. With these skills in hand, the journey continues towards more sophisticated methods of leveraging government plans, encouraging readers to remain vigilant and proactive in their pursuit of informed investment choices.

Chapter Five

The Role of Public Private Partnerships P3S

Picture yourself standing at the crossroads of opportunity and foresight, where the whispers of future prosperity can be heard if one knows where to listen. Picture a bustling city skyline, where cranes and scaffolding hint at the transformation quietly underway. Behind these visible signs of progress lies a strategic dance between public ambition and private enterprise—a collaboration that often marks the birth of monumental infrastructure projects. In this chapter, we embark on a journey to uncover the secrets of these alliances, which not only shape the urban landscapes but also unlock doors to lucrative opportunities for those with the keen insight to interpret their signals.

Public-private partnerships, or P3s, have emerged as powerful catalysts in the realm of infrastructure development. They are more than just agreements; they are complex symphonies where each stakeholder plays a vital role in bringing grand visions to life. By understanding the dynamics of these partnerships, investors can gain a privileged glimpse into future developments long before they materialize. This chapter delves into the art of identifying key players from the private sector, whose involvement often heralds significant projects on the horizon. Through careful analysis of the intricate structures of P3 agreements, we will learn to read between the lines, extracting valuable insights that can guide profitable decisions.

As we explore these collaborative ventures, we'll uncover methods to track early-stage collaborations that hint at impending opportunities. This is not merely about understanding the mechanics but embracing the strategic foresight that these partnerships offer. By mastering the ability to anticipate the ripple effects of P3s, you'll be equipped to harness their potential, transforming knowledge into tangible financial gain. With each page, we continue to build on the foundation laid in previous chapters, advancing our toolkit for deciphering the hidden language of government projects. Prepare to engage with this powerful concept, where public ambition meets private innovation, and where your ability to predict the future could redefine your investment strategy.

Why P3s Are Often Harbingers of Major Projects

Public-Private Partnerships, or P3s, often serve as the vanguard of transformative infrastructure projects. These collaborative ventures between government entities and private sector partners frequently signal the onset of substantial developments that can reshape entire regions. When governments engage with private firms, it's a strategic move, often indicating a robust commitment to long-term goals that might otherwise remain shrouded in bureaucracy. P3s are more than just contractual arrangements; they are harbingers of significant resource allocation and policy direction, illuminating the path toward expansive public works. This symbiotic relationship not only facilitates the pooling of expertise and resources but also acts as a catalyst for economic vitality and innovation. Recognizing the early signs of these partnerships can offer a window into the future of urban and regional landscapes, providing a competitive edge to those astute enough to interpret these signals.

Understanding why P3s are pivotal involves examining the early indicators of governmental commitment. These partnerships are often the first tangible evidence of a shift in strategic priorities, revealing a government's readiness to invest in infrastructure that aligns with long-term objectives. By dissecting the structure and intricacies of these agreements, one can uncover the underlying motivations and anticipated outcomes. Such insights are invaluable, as they often point to areas ripe for development and collaboration. Moreover, P3s frequently serve as the groundwork for regional economic growth, acting as magnets for further investment and innovation. The journey from concept to execution in these partnerships reveals a complex web of interactions, where each step forward is a signal of future progress and opportunity. As the narrative unfolds, it becomes clear why tracking these early collaborations can unlock untapped potential, offering a glimpse into the trajectory of major projects and the opportunities they present.

Early Indicators of Government Commitment and Resource Allocation

Public-Private Partnerships (P3s) are often the precursors to significant infrastructure undertakings, signaling a deep-rooted governmental commitment to transformative projects. These alliances between government entities and private organizations are frequently early indicators of resource dedication, revealing not just financial backing but also the prioritization of key initiatives. When governments engage in P3s, they typically allocate substantial resources towards planning and execution phases, signifying a high level of commitment. This collaboration often leads to the mobilization of both human and financial capital, setting the stage for projects that have a profound impact on the community and economy. The nuanced understanding of these resource allocations can provide astute investors with a strategic vantage point, allowing them to anticipate and align with forthcoming opportunities.

In examining P3s, it's crucial to recognize their role as conduits for unveiling long-term strategic objectives and infrastructure requirements. These partnerships often emerge as responses to identified needs in transportation, energy, and public utilities, providing a window into governmental priorities. By dissecting the strategic goals outlined within P3 agreements, one can ascertain the infrastructure drawbacks that governments aim to address. This insight empowers investors to position themselves advantageously, anticipating future market shifts and demand surges. For instance, a P3 initiative aimed at modernizing public transportation networks might reveal broader intentions to enhance urban mobility, signaling potential investment opportunities in adjacent sectors like real estate and technology.

Furthermore, P3s serve as catalysts for regional economic growth and collaboration, often spurring ancillary developments that ripple across various sectors. The initiation of a P3 project can attract ancillary business activities, such as construction, supply chain logistics, and technology services, fostering an environment ripe for economic expansion. This, in turn, can lead to job creation, increased local incomes, and a bolstered tax base, all of which contribute to the overall economic health of a region. Understanding the broader economic implications of a P3 can enable investors to predict and capitalize on these secondary benefits, thus multiplying their potential for returns.

The intricate structures of P3 agreements hold a wealth of information that can guide strategic investment decisions. By thoroughly analyzing these agreements, one can discern the allocation of responsibilities, risks, and rewards between public and private sectors. This analysis not only highlights the financial stability and feasibility of a project but also indicates the level of governmental support and oversight involved. A nuanced comprehension of these dynamics enables investors to gauge the project's potential success and longevity. For those skilled in interpreting such documents, P3 agreements can become a treasure trove of insights, revealing hidden opportunities that others might overlook.

To truly harness the potential of P3s, individuals must cultivate a keen eye for early collaborations and stakeholder interactions. Tracking these initial engagements can offer a glimpse into the project's trajectory, providing an opportunity to align with influential partners and stakeholders. Engaging with these entities from the outset can facilitate access to insider knowledge, enhancing the ability to make informed investment choices. By fostering relationships with key players in the P3 landscape, investors can position themselves as integral components of the development process, ensuring they are well-placed to reap the benefits of these transformative projects.

Unveiling Long-Term Strategic Goals and Infrastructure Needs

Public-Private Partnerships (P3s) frequently serve as precursors to significant infrastructure initiatives, offering insights into governmental strategic directions and infrastructure priorities. These collaborations often reveal the government's long-term strategic objectives, as P3s are typically designed to fulfill enduring needs rather than short-term fixes. These partnerships indicate a level of governmental commitment, as they necessitate detailed planning and substantial resource allocation over extended periods. By dissecting P3s, investors can glean insights into the infrastructure goals that government entities prioritize, thereby allowing them to align their investment strategies with these emerging opportunities.

Within the framework of P3s, governments often seek to address expansive infrastructure needs that reflect broader economic and societal objectives. These partnerships can illuminate a strategic vision for regional growth, transportation enhancements, or technological advancements that may not be immediately apparent in traditional public discourse. For instance, a partnership focused on developing a sustainable public transport network might indicate a shift towards greener infrastructure, aligning with global sustainability trends. By interpreting these signals, astute investors can position themselves advantageously, harnessing the foresight into long-term governmental priorities.

The intricate structure of P3 agreements often encompasses several phases and milestones, providing a blueprint of governmental commitment and timelines. By scrutinizing these agreements, investors can discern the granularity of infrastructure needs and the strategic goals underlying these partnerships. Such analysis might reveal not only the immediate infrastructure requirements but also the anticipated evolution of these needs over time. For example, a P3 focused on digital infrastructure might suggest a forthcoming emphasis on smart city developments, hinting at future technological integrations and societal shifts. This level of detail allows investors to tailor their strategies, aligning with anticipated market transformations.

Understanding the role of P3s in regional economic development further underscores their importance as indicators of government planning. These partnerships often act as catalysts for regional collaboration, drawing in multiple stakeholders and resources to achieve common objectives. By tracking the evolution of such partnerships, investors gain insight into the collaborative dynamics and potential economic impacts. A P3 project that engages multiple private sector entities could signal a burgeoning economic hub, indicating areas ripe for ancillary investment opportunities. This proactive approach enables investors to capitalize on regional growth trajectories, maximizing returns as these projects come to fruition.

Envisioning the potential of P3s requires a nuanced perspective that extends beyond conventional analysis. By integrating diverse viewpoints and innovative methodologies, investors can anticipate not only the immediate outcomes but also the transformative potential of these partnerships. Considering scenarios where a P3 might evolve into subsequent phases or spawn additional projects can provide a strategic edge. Investors are encouraged to adopt an inquisitive mindset, questioning how these partnerships might reshape landscapes and economies. This forward-thinking approach, rooted in both current analysis and speculative foresight, empowers investors to align their strategies with the unfolding narrative of governmental infrastructure planning.

Catalysts for Regional Economic Development and Collaboration

Public-private partnerships (P3s) serve as vital catalysts for regional economic development, fostering collaboration that transcends traditional boundaries. These partnerships often mark the beginning of transformative projects, acting as a nexus where government foresight meets private sector innovation. When regions embrace P3s, they open themselves up to a wealth of possibilities, harmonizing diverse resources to address infrastructure needs comprehensively. By pooling resources, expertise, and risk-sharing mechanisms, P3s enable large-scale projects that might otherwise remain beyond reach, thereby stimulating economic growth and regional revitalization. As governments increasingly recognize the benefits of these partnerships, savvy investors can identify regions poised for expansion by observing early P3 formations.

Identifying potential P3s involves scrutinizing regional economic indicators and cross-sector collaborations that hint at forthcoming ventures. For instance, the alignment of local government objectives with corporate social responsibility goals can signal impending infrastructure initiatives. Regions with a history of successful P3s often display a proactive approach to policy-making, incentivizing private sector engagement through tax incentives, streamlined regulatory processes, and robust stakeholder networks. Observing these patterns can provide insightful clues into upcoming projects that will likely drive economic advancement and create investment opportunities.

A nuanced understanding of P3 structures reveals the potential for innovative project financing and risk management strategies. The intricate design of these partnerships often incorporates flexible financial models that adapt to the dynamic needs of a project, thereby mitigating risks and enhancing project viability. Investors who comprehend these complexities can better assess the financial health and sustainability of a P3, positioning themselves to capitalize on these ventures. Innovations in contract structures, such as performance-based incentives and dynamic revenue-sharing frameworks, offer advanced insights into the evolving landscape of public-private collaboration.

The impact of P3s extends beyond immediate project goals, often generating a ripple effect that boosts regional collaboration and economic dynamism. As these partnerships mature, they foster a culture of cooperation between public and private entities, paving the way for future collaborations and reinforcing regional resilience. This cultural shift encourages a shared vision for long-term development, making regions more attractive for both domestic and international investors. Understanding this broader impact allows savvy investors to anticipate areas of sustained growth and potential shifts in market dynamics.

Investors keen on leveraging P3s for profit must cultivate a strategic mindset that looks beyond conventional opportunities. By anticipating and responding to shifts in government policy, regional planning, and industry trends, investors can position themselves at the forefront of emerging infrastructure developments. This involves a proactive approach to research, staying abreast of the latest developments in regional planning, and actively engaging with stakeholders to gain firsthand insights. By honing these skills, investors can transform potential risks into rewarding opportunities, ensuring their strategies are not only reactive but also predictive and adaptive.

How to Identify Key Private Sector Partners

Identifying key private sector partners is akin to discovering the catalysts that propel infrastructure projects from mere blueprints to tangible realities. Private sector partners play a pivotal role in public-private partnerships (P3s), often acting as the engines of innovation and funding that drive large-scale projects forward. Their involvement can indicate a project's potential success and provide early signals of investment opportunities. Understanding how to pinpoint these partners is essential for anyone looking to profit from infrastructure initiatives, as their expertise, financial muscle, and strategic directions can significantly influence the trajectory of a project. As we unravel the complexities of these partnerships, the spotlight shifts to the criteria that distinguish these key players from the rest, revealing insights that can be harnessed for strategic advantage.

The journey begins with evaluating the industry expertise and track records of potential partners, a crucial step in gauging their ability to deliver on ambitious infrastructure projects. Following this, an analysis of their financial stability and investment capacity offers a window into their ability to sustain long-term commitments. Lastly, assessing strategic alignment and long-term goals provides clarity on whether their vision aligns with the broader objectives of the project. Together, these elements form a comprehensive framework that not only identifies the most promising private sector partners but also sets the stage for informed investment decisions. As we explore these subtopics, the path to leveraging P3s for financial gain becomes clearer and more actionable.

Evaluating Industry Expertise and Track Records

Identifying key private sector partners in Public-Private Partnerships (P3s) requires a nuanced understanding of industry expertise and track records. A successful P3 often hinges on the ability of private entities to deliver specialized knowledge and proven capabilities, which can significantly influence the project's outcome. In assessing industry expertise, it's vital to examine the breadth and depth of a partner's experience within the specific sector relevant to the project. This involves scrutinizing past projects of similar scale and complexity, as well as the innovative approaches they have employed. For instance, a company with a robust history in sustainable urban development might bring cutting-edge environmental solutions to an infrastructure project, enhancing its appeal and long-term viability.

Track records offer a concrete measure of a partner's reliability and performance consistency. By analyzing past project outcomes, timelines, and budget adherence, one can gauge the partner's ability to meet commitments. A stellar track record often reflects not only technical prowess but also an adeptness in navigating regulatory landscapes and stakeholder relationships. It's essential to sift through case studies, client testimonials, and industry reviews to gather comprehensive insights into the partner's operational excellence. Consider the example of a technology firm that consistently delivers pioneering smart city solutions; its track record in integrating complex systems efficiently can be a strong indicator of its potential success in future collaborations.

Emerging trends in the evaluation process include the use of advanced analytics and artificial intelligence to assess potential partners. These technologies can parse through vast datasets to identify patterns and predict future performance, offering a more objective lens through which to evaluate partners. Tools like machine learning algorithms can analyze historical data to forecast a firm's ability to innovate and adapt, providing invaluable foresight into their capacity to contribute effectively to a P3. As these tools become more sophisticated, they offer a competitive edge to those who incorporate them into their evaluation processes.

A holistic evaluation also involves understanding the cultural and strategic fit of potential partners. Beyond technical skills, the alignment of values and long-term goals can greatly impact the success of a partnership. Companies that share a common vision and collaborative spirit are more likely to work synergistically, driving a project towards success. This involves assessing the partner's corporate ethos, sustainability commitments, and community engagement practices. A partner that actively prioritizes social responsibility might not only enhance project outcomes but also bolster public perception and support.

Consider scenarios where different approaches might be taken to assess a partner's suitability. Imagine evaluating a company that excels in traditional construction methods versus another that leads in sustainable, cutting-edge technologies. Contemplating these contrasting profiles can refine the decision-making process and highlight the diverse factors at play. Encouraging critical thinking and application of these insights can lead to more informed and strategic partner selection, ultimately maximizing the potential for successful and profitable P3s.

Analyzing Financial Stability and Investment Capacity

In the intricate tapestry of public-private partnerships (P3s), discerning the financial stability and investment capacity of private sector partners becomes paramount. A company's financial health is akin to the bedrock upon which the entire partnership is constructed. It determines not only the feasibility of a project but also its long-term success. To paint a complete picture, one must scrutinize a company's balance sheet, cash flow statements, and profit margins. These documents reveal insights into the company's ability to weather economic fluctuations and sustain long-term commitments. A firm with robust financials is more likely to navigate the uncertainties of large-scale infrastructure projects, ensuring continuity and reliability.

A deeper dive into a partner's investment capacity requires examining their historical investments in similar ventures. This historical lens provides a window into their strategic priorities and their willingness to allocate resources toward infrastructure projects. Companies with a history of substantial investments in similar P3 projects often possess the requisite experience and risk tolerance necessary for future endeavors. Moreover, understanding their funding sources—whether through equity, debt, or a mix—can illuminate their approach to financing and risk management. This knowledge is vital for assessing whether their investment philosophy aligns with the project's goals and timelines.

In the evolving landscape of infrastructure development, emerging trends like green bonds and sustainable financing are reshaping how projects are funded. Evaluating a partner's engagement with these innovative financial instruments can offer additional insights into their forward-looking strategies and adaptability. Companies that actively pursue sustainable financing options are often at the forefront of industry shifts, demonstrating a commitment to future-proofing their investments. This foresight can be a valuable asset in a partnership, aligning with governmental priorities for sustainable development and enhancing the project's appeal to a broader range of stakeholders.

Critical thinking about potential partners' financial stability also involves considering diverse perspectives. Some analysts might argue that traditional financial metrics do not fully capture a company's resilience. For instance, a firm's adaptability to technological advancements or its agility in navigating regulatory changes could be just as indicative of its stability as its financial statements. By incorporating such non-traditional factors, investors can build a more nuanced understanding of a partner's capacity to deliver on a P3 project, beyond the surface-level financials.

In practical terms, investors can employ a checklist approach, evaluating potential partners against a set of criteria that encompasses both financial metrics and strategic considerations. This checklist might include questions like: Does the company have a track record of completing projects on time and within budget? How do they manage financial risks, and what contingency plans are in place for unforeseen challenges? By systematically addressing these questions, investors can make informed decisions, positioning themselves to capitalize on promising P3 opportunities while minimizing exposure to risk.

Assessing Strategic Alignment and Long-Term Goals

Aligning strategic objectives and long-term goals with key private sector partners is an essential skill for anyone seeking to capitalize on public-private partnerships (P3s). Understanding the motivations and aspirations of potential partners requires a deep dive into their corporate mission statements, project histories, and public communications. Strategic alignment ensures that both public and private entities are moving towards a common vision, which can lead to smoother project execution and enhanced profitability. Partners with shared goals are more likely to commit resources and expertise, fostering an environment where innovation and efficiency thrive. This alignment reduces friction, facilitates consensus, and ultimately accelerates project timelines, allowing investors to anticipate and exploit opportunities as they arise.

The pursuit of strategic alignment involves assessing the long-term objectives of potential partners and how these objectives might intersect with public infrastructure goals. For instance, a company with a robust track record in sustainable development may be an ideal candidate for eco-friendly infrastructure projects. Analyzing their past ventures, future plans, and industry positioning provides valuable insight into their strategic direction. This information, combined with an understanding of governmental priorities, can highlight synergies that are ripe for exploitation. By identifying companies whose long-term goals dovetail with public policy trends, such as renewable energy or digital infrastructure, investors position themselves to capitalize on a wave of public interest and funding.

Beyond the examination of stated goals, scrutiny of a partner's adaptability and openness to innovation proves invaluable. The most successful P3s often involve partners who are not just aligned in their goals but are also adaptable, willing to pivot in response to new challenges and changing landscapes. Organizations that embrace cutting-edge technology, prioritize research and development, and demonstrate a willingness to innovate are better equipped to navigate the complexities of modern infrastructure projects. Such partners are likely to drive projects forward with fresh perspectives that can yield unique solutions to seemingly intractable problems, offering investors a competitive edge in anticipating project success.

A nuanced understanding of strategic alignment extends to the cultural and operational philosophies of potential partners. Beyond public statements and financial reports, the culture within a company can reveal much about its likely behavior in a partnership. A culture that values transparency, collaboration, and ethical practices can be an excellent match for public sector projects, which often require a high degree of accountability. Observing how a company engages with stakeholders, manages internal challenges, and responds to external pressures can inform predictions about their potential role in a P3. Savvy investors will look beyond the numbers to assess whether a partner's internal ethos aligns with the collaborative spirit required in complex infrastructure endeavors.

To effectively assess and engage with potential partners, consider posing critical questions that probe deeper into their strategic fabric. What are the potential partners' priorities over the next decade, and how do these align with anticipated public sector initiatives? How does the company respond to regulatory changes, and what measures do they have in place to adapt to technological advancements? These questions encourage a deeper evaluation of a partner's strategic compatibility, enabling investors to craft a nuanced approach to partnership selection. By rigorously analyzing strategic alignment and long-term goals, investors can not only identify promising partners but also anticipate shifts in the market, positioning themselves to profit from emerging infrastructure opportunities.

Analyzing the Structure of P3 Agreements

Visualize a future where infrastructure seamlessly integrates public ambition with private innovation, creating landscapes that are not only functional but visionary. Public-private partnerships, or P3s, stand at the crossroads of this transformational journey, acting as catalysts for major projects that redefine how societies grow and thrive. These partnerships are more than mere collaborations; they are strategic alliances that harness the strengths of both sectors to deliver projects that might otherwise remain unfulfilled. As we embark on this exploration, we uncover the intricate structures of P3 agreements, which serve as blueprints for success and as indicators of significant developments on the horizon. Understanding these frameworks is crucial, as they reveal the foundational elements that drive project viability and profitability.

In this section, the focus shifts to dissecting the anatomy of P3 agreements, unveiling the key components and the roles of stakeholders that shape these complex arrangements. Each agreement is a unique tapestry woven with threads of risk allocation and financial structuring, providing insight into the delicate balance of interests. The legal and regulatory landscapes further contour the success of these partnerships, highlighting the critical pathways that guide projects from concept to completion. As we navigate through these subtopics, the knowledge gained will illuminate how early collaborations can signal lucrative opportunities, setting the stage for informed investment decisions that capitalize on the potential of future infrastructure endeavors.

Key Components and Stakeholder Roles in P3 Agreements

Public-private partnership agreements, or P3s, are intricate constructs that serve as the backbone for transformative infrastructure projects. At their core, these agreements are collaborations where the public and private sectors unite their strengths to deliver large-scale ventures. A critical component of P3 agreements is the delineation of roles among stakeholders, which includes government entities, private investors, and sometimes third-party facilitators. Each party brings unique expertise and resources to the table, and their involvement is often dictated by the specific needs and objectives of the project. Government bodies typically oversee regulatory compliance and public interest, while private partners are tasked with innovation, funding, and efficient execution, creating a synergy that neither could achieve independently.

An essential aspect of understanding P3 agreements lies in recognizing the multifaceted roles stakeholders play. For instance, government agencies not only act as regulators but also as guarantors of public welfare, ensuring that projects align with broader social and economic goals. Private sector partners, on the other hand, are driven by profitability and efficiency. They often introduce cutting-edge technologies and practices that can significantly reduce costs and timelines. This alignment of interests is crucial; when effectively managed, it results in projects that are both beneficial to the public and financially viable for private investors. Advanced insights into these dynamics can reveal potential investment opportunities by highlighting which sectors are ripe for innovation and growth.

The structural complexity of P3 agreements also extends to the nature of the partnerships themselves. These can range from simple contractual arrangements to more intricate joint ventures, each with specific stakeholder responsibilities and expectations. Recent research indicates a shift toward more flexible, adaptive agreements that can better accommodate changing circumstances and emerging technologies. This adaptability is crucial in an era where technological advancements and environmental considerations are rapidly reshaping infrastructure needs. Investors who can anticipate and adapt to these evolving structures are better positioned to capitalize on the opportunities presented by these partnerships.

Recent trends emphasize the importance of stakeholder engagement and transparent communication throughout the life of a P3 project. Successful partnerships necessitate clear communication channels and shared objectives, ensuring that all parties are aligned and committed to the project's success. This approach not only mitigates potential conflicts but also builds trust and accountability among stakeholders. By fostering an environment of collaboration and mutual respect, P3 agreements can achieve outcomes that are both innovative and sustainable. Investors who recognize the value of these principles can better navigate the complexities of P3 agreements and identify potential areas for strategic involvement.

The intricacies of P3 agreements require a keen understanding of the interplay between public policy and private interests. As infrastructure demands evolve, so too do the frameworks that support P3 projects. Forward-thinking investors are encouraged to engage with the latest research and emerging methodologies that influence these agreements. By doing so, they can develop a nuanced perspective on how to best position themselves within this landscape, leveraging their insights to make informed decisions that align with both current trends and future possibilities. This depth of understanding is not only a competitive advantage but a vital tool for navigating the dynamic world of public-private partnerships.

Risk Allocation and Financial Structuring in P3 Projects

Public-Private Partnerships (P3s) represent a sophisticated dance between the public and private sectors, where the allocation of risk and financial structuring are critical to the project's fruition. At the heart of a successful P3 lies a well-negotiated balance of risk allocation, ensuring that the party best equipped to manage a specific risk assumes responsibility for it. This delicate balance is informed by an array of considerations, such as project scale, geographical nuances, and sector-specific challenges, each impacting the risk distribution. For instance, construction risks might be more aptly managed by the private sector, while regulatory risks remain under the public domain. This strategic allocation not only mitigates potential pitfalls but also aligns incentives, fostering a collaborative environment where both parties are invested in the project's success.

Modern P3 agreements often incorporate innovative financial structures that blend public and private funding sources, crafting a robust framework for project financing. The inclusion of mechanisms like availability payments, where the public sector compensates the private partner based on the project's availability and performance, exemplifies a shift from traditional financing methods. Such financial constructs not only provide predictability but also incentivize quality and efficiency. The burgeoning trend of using green bonds and sustainable financing within P3s further underscores the evolving landscape, reflecting an increasing prioritization of environmental and social governance (ESG) criteria. This evolution not only attracts a broader spectrum of investors but also aligns infrastructure development with global sustainability goals, offering a dual benefit of financial return and positive societal impact.

Legal and regulatory frameworks serve as the backbone of P3 success, shaping the risk and financial architecture within these complex agreements. Jurisdictions across the globe have crafted bespoke legal frameworks that facilitate P3s, each with unique nuances reflecting local governance and market dynamics. The sophistication of these frameworks varies, with some regions offering mature, well-tested models while others are in nascent stages of development. Understanding these legal landscapes is paramount for stakeholders aiming to navigate P3 opportunities effectively. For instance, recent legislative trends towards increasing transparency and accountability within P3s have significant implications for risk management and financial structuring, influencing contract negotiations and project outcomes.

Examining the cutting-edge developments in P3 financial structuring reveals a shift towards more collaborative models that integrate community and stakeholder engagement. This participatory approach not only enhances project acceptance but also mitigates social risks that could derail project timelines. Furthermore, the integration of digital tools and data analytics in managing P3 projects heralds a new era of efficiency and transparency. These technologies enable real-time monitoring and predictive analytics, offering stakeholders unprecedented insights into project performance and risk management. Such advancements not only optimize resource allocation but also create a resilient framework capable of adapting to unforeseen challenges, ensuring project longevity and success.

In practice, identifying and capitalizing on the subtle signals within P3 agreements requires a strategic approach. Investors who cultivate a deep understanding of risk allocation and financial structuring within these projects are better positioned to anticipate market movements and seize opportunities. This involves not only analyzing existing agreements but also tracking policy shifts and emerging trends that could redefine risk landscapes and financial models. By maintaining a vigilant eye on these developments, astute investors can craft strategies that align with the evolving P3 environment, securing a competitive edge in the ever-dynamic world of infrastructure investment.

Legal and Regulatory Frameworks Shaping P3 Success

Public-private partnerships (P3s) thrive within a complex legal and regulatory tapestry that critically influences their success. Understanding the framework that governs these partnerships is essential for identifying potential investment opportunities. This framework often consists of multifaceted regulations, which vary significantly across different jurisdictions. For instance, while some regions have comprehensive legislation specifically tailored for P3s, others may operate under more generalized procurement laws. These legal environments can dictate everything from the tendering process to financial closure, impacting the feasibility and profitability of projects. As such, savvy investors must assess how these regulations shape the development landscape. The nuanced legalities not only define the operational boundaries but also create opportunities for those who can navigate them adeptly.

Stakeholders in P3 arrangements include a multitude of entities, each governed by distinct legal mandates. Government bodies, private sector partners, financiers, and sometimes even community groups all play pivotal roles within this framework. Each stakeholder has specific obligations and rights, which are often articulated within the legal agreements binding the partnership. For instance, the risk-sharing arrangements between public and private entities are often enshrined in these legal documents. Investors who can decipher these agreements gain insights into which stakeholder bears the financial risks, be it cost overruns, project delays, or operational inefficiencies. Recognizing these allocations allows investors to anticipate where potential vulnerabilities or strengths may lie within a project.

Financial structuring within P3s is another crucial element molded by legal and regulatory frameworks. Innovative financing models often emerge in response to these frameworks, including mechanisms like availability payments or shadow tolls. Such models can significantly impact the cash flow and financial stability of a project, thereby influencing its attractiveness as an investment opportunity. Investors must be proficient in analyzing these structures, understanding how legal stipulations affect financial performance. The choice of financing model often reflects the risk appetite and strategic objectives of private partners, and being able to interpret these choices can provide a competitive edge in forecasting project viability.

The regulatory landscape surrounding P3s is continually evolving, shaped by both technological advancements and shifting political climates. Recent developments in areas such as environmental regulations or data privacy laws can impose new requirements on P3 projects, altering their trajectory. Staying abreast of these changes is vital for investors aiming to capitalize on upcoming projects. For example, a shift towards more stringent environmental regulations might favor projects with sustainable development goals, opening avenues for investment in green infrastructure. Thus, a dynamic understanding of regulatory trends can illuminate future pathways for investment opportunities, allowing investors to position themselves advantageously.

Legal frameworks not only present challenges but also offer opportunities for innovation and growth. As governments seek to address infrastructure deficits, they often modify regulatory frameworks to encourage private sector involvement. This can result in streamlined approval processes or incentives for certain types of infrastructure projects. Investors who are proactive in identifying these legislative shifts can capitalize on new opportunities before they become widely apparent. By meticulously tracking legal developments and understanding their implications, investors can craft strategies that are both informed and adaptable, ensuring they remain at the forefront of infrastructure investment trends.

Tracking Early Collaborations for Profit

In the intricate web of infrastructure development, early collaborations often serve as the subtle yet powerful threads that foreshadow significant projects. These early-stage partnerships, particularly within the realm of public-private collaborations, can offer astute investors a glimpse into the future of urban landscapes and transport networks before they become headline news. As the initial sparks of these collaborations ignite, they illuminate pathways to potential investment opportunities that, when recognized early, can yield substantial rewards. Understanding the dynamics of these early interactions is akin to reading the first chapters of an unfolding story—where the characters and their intentions lay the groundwork for the plot ahead.

As we navigate this landscape, the ability to dissect Memorandums of Understanding and other preliminary agreements becomes crucial. These documents, often laden with industry-specific jargon and legal nuances, hold the keys to decoding intentions and commitments between key stakeholders. By focusing on the stakeholders involved and the structures of these initial agreements, investors can position themselves strategically, aligning their interests with those driving these ventures. Through careful analysis and strategic foresight, one can transform these early signals into actionable insights, ensuring a competitive edge in the ever-evolving world of infrastructure investment.

Identifying Key Stakeholders in Early-Stage Public-Private Partnerships

Unveiling the intricate web of stakeholders in early-stage public-private partnerships (P3s) offers a unique vantage point for astute investors. These collaborations, often involving a matrix of government agencies, private entities, and sometimes non-profit organizations, serve as a fertile ground for identifying key players who wield influence over project trajectories. An astute observer can discern patterns by examining the roles and reputations of these stakeholders, noting which entities consistently emerge in successful ventures. These insights become invaluable when predicting the viability and potential impact of future projects. Consider, for instance, a private corporation with a history of successful P3 involvement; their participation often signals a robust project outcome, making their moves worth tracking.

Navigating this landscape requires a keen eye for detail and an understanding of the nuanced dynamics at play. Stakeholders in P3s are not always the most visible or vocal, yet their influence is palpable in decision-making processes and resource allocation. By mapping these relationships, one can ascertain not only the power structures but also the priorities and potential pitfalls of a project. Advanced software tools and analytical frameworks can aid in this endeavor, sifting through vast amounts of data to highlight unexpected partnerships and alliances. This detective work, though demanding, provides a strategic edge, offering insights that are both actionable and timely.

Recent studies illuminate the importance of early-stage stakeholder engagement in predicting project success. The presence of seasoned industry players often correlates with innovative project approaches and higher completion rates. Moreover, the involvement of stakeholders with a track record of sustainability and community engagement frequently results in initiatives that are both financially and socially rewarding. By understanding these patterns, investors can position themselves advantageously, aligning their strategies with entities that prioritize long-term value over short-term gains. This approach not only diversifies risk but also ensures alignment with evolving market trends and societal expectations.

The evolving landscape of P3s also reflects broader shifts in economic and political priorities. As governments increasingly seek to mitigate risk and leverage private sector expertise, the selection of stakeholders becomes a reflection of policy priorities and market demands. Savvy investors must remain attuned to these shifts, recognizing that stakeholder involvement can signal emerging trends in technology, infrastructure, and regulatory environments. By anticipating these changes, one can craft investment strategies that are not only responsive but also anticipatory, capitalizing on the opportunities that arise from the confluence of public and private interests.

Engagement in this domain demands a proactive approach. Investors should cultivate networks that include industry insiders, policy analysts, and community leaders. These connections provide firsthand insights into stakeholder motivations and project nuances that are often obscured in official documents. By fostering these relationships, investors can gain a more holistic understanding of P3 dynamics, enabling them to make informed decisions that transcend conventional analysis. This strategic foresight, built on a foundation of in-depth stakeholder knowledge, positions investors to not only participate in but also shape the future of infrastructure development.

Analyzing Memorandums of Understanding for Investment Signals

Memorandums of Understanding (MOUs) serve as early indicators of collaboration, offering a window into potential infrastructure initiatives. These preliminary agreements, though non-binding, outline the intentions and mutually beneficial goals of the involved parties, often signaling the onset of significant projects. By examining MOUs, one can discern the strategic priorities and resource allocations of both public and private entities. This insight allows savvy investors to identify emerging trends and opportunities before they become widely recognized. Understanding the language and implications of MOUs can thus provide a competitive edge, revealing the shared objectives that could shape future developments.

Decoding MOUs requires a keen eye for detail and an understanding of the nuanced language often embedded within these documents. Investors should focus on the specific commitments and timelines mentioned, as well as the scope of the projects outlined. Key phrases often hint at the scale and ambition of the planned undertakings, offering clues about potential market impacts. For example, terms like "pilot program" or "feasibility study" might suggest early-stage exploration, while "implementation phase" indicates a more advanced stage. By dissecting these elements, investors can anticipate the trajectory of projects and position themselves strategically in the marketplace.

Beyond the language of the MOUs, the stakeholders involved can provide further insights into the potential success and scale of a project. Identifying the organizations and individuals named within these agreements helps to map out the network of influence and expertise driving the initiative. Recognizing the presence of prominent industry leaders or innovative firms may suggest a project with considerable momentum and likelihood of success. Additionally, the historical performance and reputation of these stakeholders can serve as a barometer for the project's potential outcome, offering yet another layer of analysis for investors aiming to capitalize on early-stage information.

Critical examination of the timeline and conditions set forth in MOUs can also yield valuable investment signals. Investors should assess the milestones and contingencies outlined to understand the project's dependencies and potential risks. This analysis can reveal potential delays or accelerations in the project's lifecycle, allowing investors to adjust their strategies accordingly. For instance, if an MOU outlines dependencies on regulatory approval, investors may gauge the likelihood of these conditions being met based on current political and regulatory climates. Such insights enable investors to better manage risk and time their market entries or exits with precision.

Engaging with MOUs demands not just reading, but comprehending the broader context in which they operate. Investors should consider the geopolitical and economic environments that influence the agreements, recognizing that external factors can significantly impact the projects' feasibility and attractiveness. Critical thinking about how these variables interact with the information in MOUs can lead to innovative investment strategies. By nurturing a holistic understanding of MOUs, investors can transform these early-stage documents from mere formalities into robust tools for predicting and profiting from future infrastructure developments.

Leveraging Early Contract Announcements for Strategic Positioning

Recognizing the potential embedded within early contract announcements is invaluable for strategically positioning oneself in the realm of public-private partnerships (P3s). These announcements often serve as precursors to significant developments, revealing the initial commitments between governmental bodies and private entities. By scrutinizing these early communications, investors can discern patterns and trends that signal forthcoming infrastructure projects. The ability to interpret these contracts not only offers a glimpse into the project's scope and scale but also provides foresight into the economic ripple effects that may follow. This foresight empowers investors to align their strategies with emerging opportunities, ensuring they are well-positioned to capitalize on market shifts.

An astute investor must delve into the intricacies of early contract announcements to extract actionable insights. This involves understanding the language and terms used to describe the partnerships, which often reveal the project's priorities and potential challenges. By identifying the key performance indicators (KPIs) and deliverables outlined in these contracts, investors can assess the likelihood of a project's success and the speed at which it will progress. Furthermore, the financial commitments and risk-sharing arrangements detailed within these documents can provide clues about the project's viability and the level of confidence that both parties have in its future.

In addition to the contractual details, the timing of these announcements can be equally telling. Early contract announcements often coincide with broader economic or political initiatives, suggesting a favorable environment for infrastructure investment. For instance, a surge in contract activity may align with new policy directions, government funding inflows, or shifts in regulatory landscapes. By tracking these temporal patterns, investors can identify windows of opportunity where the alignment of political will and financial resources creates fertile ground for infrastructure growth. This temporal analysis, when combined with a thorough understanding of the contractual landscape, offers a comprehensive view of the investment horizon.

The geographical context also plays a crucial role in interpreting early contract announcements. Projects announced in regions experiencing rapid urbanization, technological advancement, or demographic changes are likely to gain momentum quickly. By mapping these announcements against demographic and economic data, investors can pinpoint regions where infrastructure demand is set to outpace supply. This geographic insight allows for targeted investment strategies that focus on areas poised for transformational growth, thus maximizing potential returns. Employing Geographic Information Systems (GIS) and other spatial analysis tools can further enhance this geographic strategy, offering a visual representation of where opportunities are most concentrated.

Considerations of diverse viewpoints within the field provide a rich tapestry of insights into strategic positioning. While some experts advocate for aggressive positioning in response to early announcements, others suggest a more measured approach, emphasizing the importance of risk management and due diligence. Evaluating these perspectives alongside one's own risk tolerance and investment objectives can lead to a more nuanced strategy. Engaging with this range of expert advice not only broadens an investor's understanding but also sharpens their ability to adapt strategies in response to evolving market conditions. This nuanced approach ensures that investors are not merely reacting to announcements but are proactively strategizing to harness their full potential.

Public-Private Partnerships (P3s) serve as pivotal indicators for upcoming infrastructure projects, offering a window into future developments through their distinctive blend of public initiative and private sector involvement. Recognizing the significance of P3s allows investors to anticipate substantial projects before they break ground. Within this chapter, we explored the intricacies of identifying key private sector partners and understanding the structure of P3 agreements. These elements are crucial for discerning the potential impact and success of these collaborations. By tracking early-stage partnerships, readers can position themselves advantageously to capitalize on impending opportunities.

This strategic insight reinforces the broader theme of the book: harnessing detailed research and foresight to gain a competitive edge in investment. As we transition to the next chapter, consider how these insights into P3s could shape your approach to identifying and leveraging other governmental and private sector interactions. What patterns might emerge when you connect the dots between policy and profit? This continuous exploration and application of knowledge are essential for mastering the art of predictive investment, encouraging readers to refine their strategies and remain vigilant in their pursuit of financial success.

Chapter Six

Using Geographic Information Systems GIS for Insights

Venturing into the realm of Geographic Information Systems (GIS) is akin to wielding a powerful lens, one that unveils layers of hidden potential in the world around us. Imagine standing atop a hill, surveying a vast landscape. At first glance, it might seem like an ordinary stretch of land, but with a keen eye and the right tool, you begin to discern the intricate patterns and possibilities beneath the surface. This chapter invites you to explore how GIS can transform the way you perceive infrastructure investments, turning seemingly mundane data into a treasure map of opportunity. As technology continues to redefine the boundaries of what we see and understand, GIS stands out as a pivotal resource in predicting and capitalizing on future developments.

Throughout our journey, we'll uncover how GIS layers can reveal trends and shifts that often elude the untrained eye. Just as a cartographer charts unknown territories, you'll learn to map infrastructure investments with precision, identifying areas ripe for development and growth. GIS allows us to visualize data in a way that is both intuitive and impactful, offering insights into where governments might be directing their resources. By mastering these skills, you can position yourself ahead of the curve, recognizing opportunity zones long before they become common knowledge. This is not just about reading maps; it's about interpreting the story they tell and using that narrative to guide smart investment decisions.

As we delve deeper, you'll encounter compelling stories and case studies that illustrate the power of GIS-driven strategies. These examples serve as a testament to the transformative impact this technology can have on your investment approach. Armed with GIS insights, you'll be equipped to make informed decisions that align with your financial goals, maximizing returns by capitalizing on infrastructure trends before they reach the mainstream. This chapter aims to demystify GIS, making it an accessible and invaluable tool in your investment arsenal, empowering you to see beyond the horizon and seize opportunities that others might overlook.

How GIS Layers Reveal Infrastructure Trends

Let's start by examining how Geographic Information Systems (GIS) serve as a powerful lens through which infrastructure trends come into focus. At the crossroads of technology and urban planning, GIS offers a vibrant palette of spatial data that paints a detailed picture of our evolving environments. This technology is not just a tool but a revelation, transforming raw data into a narrative of growth, opportunity, and foresight. As governments and businesses increasingly rely on geospatial intelligence, the ability to decode these layers becomes indispensable for investors seeking to capitalize on upcoming projects. By visualizing the trajectory of infrastructure development, GIS unveils hidden patterns that can be the difference between merely observing progress and actively participating in its economic benefits.

As we navigate through the intricacies of GIS, the subsequent sections will illuminate how spatial data analysis can spotlight infrastructure growth in its nascent stages. From identifying urban development anomalies that signal change to integrating diverse datasets for a refined predictive model, this exploration of GIS will equip you with a nuanced understanding of its capabilities. By the time we delve into the case studies, these concepts will have coalesced into a robust framework for recognizing and acting upon geospatial signals. Through this journey, the symbiosis between data and decision-making will become ever clearer, setting the stage for strategic investments grounded in the foresight that GIS uniquely provides.

Visualizing Infrastructure Growth Through Spatial Data Analysis

Harnessing the power of Geographic Information Systems (GIS) to visualize infrastructure growth offers a profound understanding of spatial data analysis that transcends traditional methods. GIS provides a dynamic lens through which infrastructure trends can be anticipated, allowing investors and planners to pinpoint areas ripe for development. By layering various datasets, such as demographic shifts, traffic patterns, and land use changes, GIS enables the creation of intricate maps that reveal the underlying currents of urban expansion. These maps serve as predictive tools, guiding strategic decisions by highlighting where new roads, utilities, or public services are likely to emerge. This capability to visualize potential growth areas equips investors with a foresight that can significantly inform investment strategies.

The capacity of GIS to identify patterns and anomalies in urban development is instrumental in recognizing opportunities that might otherwise remain hidden. While traditional analysis might overlook subtle shifts in land use or traffic density, GIS excels in uncovering these nuances. For instance, a sudden increase in building permits within a specific region, when visualized on a GIS map, might indicate an impending urban sprawl. Conversely, areas with stagnant development amidst booming surroundings might signal untapped potential or underlying issues. Recognizing these patterns allows stakeholders to make informed predictions about future infrastructure needs and align their investments accordingly, ensuring they are poised to capitalize on emerging trends.

Integrating multi-layered data for predictive modeling is where GIS truly shines, transforming raw information into actionable insights. By combining layers such as environmental constraints, economic indicators, and existing infrastructure, GIS models can simulate various scenarios of urban growth and development. This predictive power is invaluable for investors aiming to stay ahead of the curve. For example, a GIS model might reveal how an upcoming transportation project could boost property values in its vicinity, presenting a lucrative investment opportunity. The ability to conduct such detailed simulations enhances the decision-making process, enabling stakeholders to devise strategies that align with projected infrastructure trajectories.

The adaptability of GIS in visualizing infrastructure growth is further exemplified through its application in real-world case studies. Consider a city planning initiative that utilized GIS to optimize the placement of new public transit lines. By analyzing commuter data and population density, the project not only improved accessibility but also sparked a wave of residential and commercial investments along the new routes. Such examples underscore the transformative potential of GIS in reshaping urban landscapes and highlight its critical role in driving economic growth. These case studies provide a wealth of lessons and strategies that can be adapted and applied to diverse contexts, offering readers a tangible blueprint for navigating the complex terrain of infrastructure investments.

To maximize the benefits of GIS in infrastructure forecasting, practitioners should adopt a proactive approach, continuously refining their analytical skills and staying abreast of technological advancements. Engaging with the latest GIS software and tools, participating in industry forums, and collaborating with experts can deepen one's understanding and application of GIS insights. Encouraging critical thinking by posing questions such as, "How might changing zoning laws impact infrastructure development?" or "What unforeseen variables could alter predicted growth patterns?" fosters a mindset geared towards innovation and adaptability. By embracing these strategies, readers not only enhance their predictive acumen but also position themselves at the forefront of infrastructure investment opportunities, ready to transform insights into successful ventures.

Identifying Patterns and Anomalies in Urban Development

Geographic Information Systems (GIS) offer a powerful lens through which urban development patterns and anomalies can be discerned, providing invaluable foresight into infrastructure trends. By meticulously layering spatial data, GIS enables a detailed examination of urban growth, revealing patterns that might otherwise remain obscured. Imagine a sprawling cityscape, where new developments sprout like mushrooms after a rainstorm. Through GIS, it becomes possible to map these growth spurts in real-time, offering investors a dynamic view of where infrastructure investments might yield the greatest returns. The technology captures micro-level changes and broad-scale trends, illustrating how urban spaces evolve over time and highlighting potential anomalies that could signal unique investment opportunities.

Within this framework, identifying patterns in urban development becomes a strategic endeavor. GIS can illuminate areas of consistent growth, such as clusters of new residential projects or emerging commercial hubs. These patterns often correlate with governmental investments in infrastructure, such as new transport links or utility upgrades. By tracking such developments, one can construct a narrative of urban expansion that informs future investment decisions. For instance, a sudden spike in building permits within a particular district could indicate an impending infrastructure boom. GIS tools make it possible to visualize these changes spatially, aligning growth patterns with planned infrastructures like highways or new transit lines, hence enabling predictive insights about where to allocate investment resources.

Anomalies, on the other hand, present rich opportunities for those equipped to recognize them. These deviations from expected patterns may arise from unforeseen government projects, shifts in regulatory policies, or changes in market dynamics. GIS, with its capacity to integrate diverse data layers, helps in spotting these irregularities. For example, unexpected infrastructure developments might appear when GIS analysis reveals a surge in land acquisition by public agencies in areas previously marked as low-priority. Such anomalies can provide early warnings of potential investments that are not yet common knowledge, allowing investors to position themselves advantageously before the market catches on.

Incorporating multi-layered data into GIS analyses enhances the ability to predict infrastructure changes with greater precision. By combining datasets such as zoning laws, demographic shifts, and historical land use patterns, GIS offers a composite view of the forces shaping urban development. This enriched perspective aids in distinguishing fleeting trends from long-term growth trajectories. Consider the impact of an upcoming metro line extension—GIS can project its influence on surrounding areas, forecasting increased property values or commercial opportunities. By synthesizing these data layers, investors can craft predictive models that inform strategic decision-making, reducing uncertainties and maximizing potential gains.

Thought-provoking questions arise when considering how GIS might revolutionize investment strategies. How might shifts in population density affect urban infrastructure demands? In what ways could emerging technologies like AI further enhance GIS capabilities, providing even more nuanced insights into urban planning? Encouraging readers to contemplate these questions fosters a proactive mindset, prompting them to continuously refine their analytical approaches. By applying GIS insights, investors can not only identify lucrative opportunities but also contribute to sustainable urban development, aligning profit motives with broader societal benefits. The ability to anticipate and act upon these insights distinguishes informed investors from the crowd, empowering them to capitalize on the hidden narratives of urban growth before they unfold in the public domain.

Integrating Multi-Layered Data for Predictive Infrastructure Modeling

Integrating multi-layered data for predictive infrastructure modeling enables a nuanced understanding of how various factors intersect and influence future developments. Geographic Information Systems (GIS) offer a sophisticated platform for such integration, allowing users to overlay diverse datasets. By harmonizing information like demographic trends, transportation networks, zoning laws, and environmental constraints, GIS facilitates a holistic view of potential infrastructure growth. This intersectionality presents an opportunity to anticipate shifts before they become apparent, offering a competitive edge to those adept at reading these signals. The process of layering data can unveil hidden connections, such as how certain zoning changes might align with planned public transit expansions, potentially signaling imminent urban transformation.

The synergy between GIS layers and predictive modeling showcases a profound shift from traditional methods of analysis. By adopting a multi-faceted approach, users can discern patterns that single-layer assessments might overlook. For example, a rise in permit applications in a specific area, when viewed alongside projected population growth, could suggest an upcoming infrastructure project aimed at accommodating increased residential demand. This kind of integrated analysis not only aids in pinpointing valuable investment opportunities but also provides context, helping to discern whether observed trends are part of a broader strategic initiative or isolated incidents.

In recent years, advancements in machine learning and AI have further enhanced the capability of GIS for predictive modeling. Algorithms can now process vast amounts of layered data with remarkable speed and precision, uncovering trends and anomalies that might elude human analysts. These technologies empower investors to simulate various scenarios, evaluating the potential impact of different infrastructure projects on local economies and property markets. By integrating predictive analytics with GIS, stakeholders can test hypotheses and refine their strategies, aligning investment decisions with the most likely outcomes based on comprehensive data analysis.

The practical application of these insights requires a keen understanding of both the technical tools and the broader economic and social context. For instance, utilizing GIS to identify opportunity zones involves not only recognizing areas with favorable conditions for growth but also understanding the socio-political dynamics that might affect development. This means considering factors such as community engagement, potential regulatory changes, and public sentiment, all of which can influence the trajectory of infrastructure projects. By maintaining a balanced view that incorporates both quantitative data and qualitative assessments, investors can position themselves to make informed, strategic decisions.

Imagining scenarios where GIS-driven insights lead to tangible benefits, consider an investor who identifies a region with overlapping indicators of growth, such as new road construction plans, an influx of young professionals, and favorable government incentives. By acting on these insights, they might acquire properties before prices surge, ensuring a profitable return on investment. This scenario highlights the importance of not only understanding how to integrate multi-layered data but also how to translate that understanding into concrete, actionable steps. This approach underscores the transformative potential of GIS in the realm of infrastructure investment, offering a pathway to foresight-driven success.

Mapping Infrastructure Investments

Imagine waking up one morning to find a bustling new transit line weaving through your neighborhood, or a sleek bridge connecting two once-separated parts of your city. While such transformations appear sudden, they are the fruits of meticulously planned infrastructure investments—projects often visible long before their physical manifestations through the lens of Geographic Information Systems (GIS). In the world of investment, the ability to map these infrastructure developments offers a unique vantage point, one where the seemingly mundane layers of roads, utilities, and land use tell a story of future economic shifts. GIS technology has evolved into an indispensable tool for those seeking to anticipate these changes, offering a dynamic canvas where real-time data and projections converge. By understanding how to navigate this digital landscape, investors can uncover the subtle signs of growth and opportunity that might otherwise go unnoticed.

Mapping infrastructure investments with GIS involves more than just pinpointing locations; it transforms data into a powerful narrative of possibilities. As you explore the symbiotic relationship between socioeconomic factors and infrastructure patterns, you'll discover a realm where traditional investment strategies meet cutting-edge technology. The integration of diverse datasets not only enriches the analysis but also enhances the predictive accuracy of potential investment hotspots. This chapter embarks on a journey through advanced predictive modeling techniques, showing how GIS can forecast not just where growth will occur, but also when and how it might unfold. By harnessing GIS as a tool for investment forecasting, you'll gain the insight needed to navigate the evolving landscape of infrastructure, turning potential into profit with precision and foresight.

Leveraging GIS for Real-Time Infrastructure Monitoring

Harnessing the power of Geographic Information Systems (GIS) for real-time infrastructure monitoring offers a dynamic toolset for investors eager to uncover hidden opportunities in the infrastructure landscape. GIS technology provides a layered, multidimensional view of the world, permitting users to examine the intricate tapestry of infrastructure networks as they evolve. By visualizing data in real-time, stakeholders can detect emerging trends and patterns that might otherwise go unnoticed. This capability is invaluable for recognizing shifts in infrastructure projects, from transportation networks to utility expansions, allowing investors to anticipate areas of growth and pivot their strategies accordingly.

Investors can capitalize on the sophistication of GIS by integrating this data with live feeds from public agencies and private sector sources. This continuous stream of information furnishes a comprehensive picture of infrastructure dynamics, revealing not only what is being built but also how it interconnects with existing frameworks. For instance, the expansion of a highway or the development of a new rail line can be monitored alongside demographic shifts and economic data, offering a holistic view of potential impacts on surrounding real estate markets. By aligning this data with their investment objectives, savvy investors can position themselves advantageously, targeting regions poised for significant appreciation.

The incorporation of real-time GIS data into investment strategies also enables a nuanced understanding of risk factors. By analyzing historical data alongside current developments, users can identify areas prone to volatility or disruption. This foresight empowers investors to mitigate risks, ensuring that their portfolios remain robust in the face of unforeseen challenges. Additionally, GIS can highlight regions where infrastructure improvements are likely to spur economic growth, providing a clear roadmap for strategic investments. This risk-awareness, combined with a forward-looking approach, ensures a balanced investment strategy that capitalizes on opportunities while safeguarding against potential pitfalls.

Beyond its immediate applications, GIS serves as a catalyst for innovation in infrastructure investment. Recent advancements in machine learning and artificial intelligence are enhancing the predictive capabilities of GIS, enabling more precise forecasting of infrastructure trends. Investors can leverage these technological breakthroughs to refine their models, harnessing the power of predictive analytics to anticipate future developments with greater accuracy. This edge is crucial in a competitive market, where the ability to foresee and act on emerging opportunities can make a significant difference in investment outcomes.

Proactive investors are encouraged to explore how real-time GIS monitoring can be woven into their broader investment framework. By embracing this technology, they can not only gain a deeper understanding of the infrastructure landscape but also cultivate the agility needed to respond swiftly to changes. Thought-provoking scenarios, such as the impact of a new tech hub on local infrastructure or the effects of climate change on transportation networks, underscore the importance of GIS in strategic planning. As investors refine their approaches, the integration of GIS offers a pathway to informed decision-making, unlocking hidden value in the ever-evolving infrastructure sector.

Integrating Socioeconomic Data for Enhanced Investment Analysis

Geographic Information Systems (GIS) offer an exceptional opportunity to integrate socioeconomic data into infrastructure investment analysis, transforming a mass of disparate information into a cohesive, actionable narrative. By fusing layers of demographic, economic, and social statistics with spatial data, investors can uncover nuanced insights that go far beyond traditional financial analysis. This approach enables a deeper understanding of how infrastructure projects interact with local communities, influencing factors such as property values, business growth, and even social equity. For instance, analyzing patterns of income distribution or educational attainment in conjunction with proposed transport networks can reveal untapped areas poised for growth. This multidimensional perspective not only highlights potential investment hotspots but also guides strategic decision-making that aligns with broader societal trends.

Harnessing GIS for socioeconomic integration involves employing sophisticated data visualization techniques that can transform static numbers into dynamic maps, revealing patterns that might otherwise remain obscured. Tools like heat maps, choropleth maps, and spatial analytics allow investors to visualize data such as population density, median income, or employment rates in relation to proposed infrastructure developments. This spatial context provides a clearer picture of how infrastructure investments might affect or be affected by local conditions. For example, a new subway line planned through an economically burgeoning area can be mapped alongside median income growth, offering a predictive glimpse into future real estate appreciation. Such insights enable proactive investment strategies, positioning stakeholders to capitalize on emerging opportunities before they become evident to the wider market.

Incorporating advanced predictive analytics into GIS models further enhances the potential for insightful investment forecasts. Machine learning algorithms can analyze historical data alongside current socioeconomic indicators to predict future trends, offering a forward-looking lens through which investors can evaluate infrastructure projects. For example, by inputting variables such as current traffic patterns, housing development rates, and economic growth indicators into predictive models, GIS can forecast the potential impact of new highway construction on surrounding areas. This predictive capacity not only aids in identifying lucrative opportunities but also assists in risk management by highlighting potential adverse effects on local communities, allowing investors to devise more robust, ethically sound strategies.

Scenarios where GIS-driven socioeconomic analysis led to significant investment returns are increasingly common, underscoring the method's practical efficacy. In one notable case, an investment firm used GIS to analyze demographic shifts and infrastructure plans in a mid-sized city, identifying neighborhoods where residential and commercial property values were poised to surge. By integrating socioeconomic data, such as rising education levels and a burgeoning tech industry, the firm was able to pinpoint areas with high growth potential well ahead of mainstream recognition. This foresight facilitated timely investments that yielded substantial returns, demonstrating the power of GIS as both a predictive and strategic tool.

To implement this innovative approach, investors should prioritize data acquisition and develop robust analytical skills. Collaborating with GIS specialists or investing in cutting-edge software can provide the necessary expertise and tools. Engaging with local governments and agencies to access socioeconomic data and infrastructure plans is also crucial, as is staying abreast of technological advancements in GIS and related fields. By adopting these proactive measures, investors can transform complex data into clear, actionable insights, enabling them to make informed decisions that harness the full potential of integrated socioeconomic analysis in infrastructure investments.

Advanced Predictive Modeling Techniques in GIS for Investment Forecasting

Geographic Information Systems (GIS) have revolutionized the landscape of investment forecasting by providing a sophisticated toolkit for advanced predictive modeling. At the heart of this transformation lies the ability of GIS to integrate and analyze spatial and non-spatial data, revealing intricate patterns and correlations that are often invisible to the naked eye. These systems enable investors to construct detailed models that factor in a multitude of variables, from transportation networks to environmental impacts, thus painting a comprehensive picture of future infrastructure trends. By overlaying historical data with predictive algorithms, GIS can forecast potential shifts in development zones, offering investors a strategic advantage in anticipating where infrastructure growth is likely to occur.

One of the most powerful aspects of GIS is its ability to synthesize socio-economic datasets with physical infrastructure maps, thereby enhancing investment analysis. This fusion of data allows investors to assess the viability of a project not just based on its physical location, but also through the lens of demographic and economic trends. By employing advanced techniques such as machine learning within GIS, investors can identify correlations between infrastructure projects and socio-economic indicators, like income levels and population growth. This layered approach facilitates a more nuanced understanding of how infrastructure initiatives can influence, and be influenced by, surrounding communities, thus enabling more informed investment decisions.

Forecasting infrastructure developments using GIS is not solely about prediction; it is also about simulation. Advanced modeling techniques allow for the creation of various scenarios, examining how different factors might influence the trajectory of infrastructure projects. For instance, GIS can simulate the impact of policy changes or environmental regulations on future development, providing investors with a spectrum of possible outcomes. This capability not only helps in mitigating risks but also in identifying untapped opportunities that may arise under different conditions. By considering these diverse scenarios, investors can tailor their strategies to capitalize on the most likely outcomes, thus optimizing their investment portfolios.

The application of GIS in investment forecasting is further enriched by recent innovations in data visualization and mapping technologies. Interactive maps and dynamic dashboards make complex data more accessible and actionable, allowing investors to interact with the data in intuitive ways. Such tools enable the exploration of infrastructure trends over time, providing a visual narrative that can aid in identifying patterns and anomalies. By transforming raw data into vivid, interactive visualizations, GIS empowers investors to communicate insights more effectively, fostering better decision-making processes.

To truly capitalize on the predictive power of GIS, investors must adopt a proactive mindset, continuously seeking out the latest advancements and methodologies. Engaging in ongoing education and staying informed about cutting-edge research in the field can significantly enhance one's ability to leverage GIS for investment forecasting. By fostering a culture of innovation and adaptability, investors can refine their predictive frameworks, ensuring they remain at the forefront of infrastructure investment strategies. This dynamic, informed approach not only maximizes the potential for financial gain but also positions investors to contribute positively to the communities impacted by these infrastructure projects.

Identifying Opportunity Zones with GIS

Unveiling the potential of opportunity zones through Geographic Information Systems (GIS) offers a powerful lens for discerning the intricate tapestry of future infrastructure investments. These zones, often teeming with untapped potential, hold the promise of significant financial rewards for those with the foresight to recognize them. By harnessing the capabilities of GIS, investors can transform abstract spatial data into a vivid map of profitable prospects. The digital layers provided by GIS technology illuminate patterns and trajectories that were once obscured, allowing for a nuanced understanding of how various elements converge to create fertile ground for investment. This approach not only identifies where development is likely to occur but also reveals the underlying factors driving these changes, setting the stage for informed decision-making.

As we journey deeper into this realm, the interplay between spatial data and demographic layers becomes a crucial focal point. This synergy sheds light on population dynamics and economic shifts, painting a comprehensive picture of targeted investment opportunities. By weaving zoning regulations into this analytical framework, one can predict development hotspots with remarkable accuracy. This integration of diverse datasets empowers investors to anticipate where infrastructure investments will flourish, enabling strategic positioning long before market trends become obvious. Each subtopic in this section will unravel the layers of GIS, offering tools and insights to navigate these promising landscapes with precision and foresight.

Leveraging Spatial Data to Pinpoint Emerging Market Trends

Geographic Information Systems (GIS) offer a sophisticated lens through which investors can identify burgeoning market trends by analyzing spatial data. This analytical prowess is not merely about mapping locations but about discerning patterns that reveal the underlying dynamics of infrastructure development. By overlaying multiple data layers, such as transportation networks, utility services, and environmental factors, investors can visualize the interplay of these elements and predict where growth is likely to occur. This spatial intelligence transforms raw data into actionable insights, enabling investors to anticipate shifts in the market before they become apparent to the general public.

The integration of spatial data with economic indicators allows for a more nuanced understanding of market movements. Recent advancements in GIS technology have made it possible to incorporate real-time data streams, such as traffic patterns and social media activity, into investment analyses. These innovative approaches expand the traditional boundaries of analysis, facilitating the identification of nascent opportunities. For instance, when a new transit line is proposed, GIS can help investors evaluate the potential impact on nearby property values by correlating transit accessibility with historical appreciation trends. This ability to forecast changes with precision can be a game-changer for those looking to capitalize on early-stage infrastructure projects.

Moreover, leveraging GIS for market trend identification involves a deep dive into demographic shifts. Beyond simple population growth, spatial data can uncover evolving consumer preferences and economic conditions within specific locales. Advanced GIS platforms now include demographic layers that track variables such as income distribution, age brackets, and education levels. By examining these layers in conjunction with infrastructure data, investors can pinpoint areas where demand is likely to surge. For example, a neighborhood with a rising young professional population might signal a growing need for urban amenities, presenting lucrative investment prospects in residential or commercial real estate.

To harness the full potential of GIS, investors must also consider zoning regulations and land use policies. These often-overlooked elements can significantly influence the trajectory of development in a given area. By integrating zoning data with spatial analyses, it becomes possible to forecast where regulatory changes might unlock new opportunities for growth. For instance, a city council's decision to rezone industrial land for mixed-use development can be a catalyst for revitalization, and GIS can help investors identify the properties poised to benefit most from such shifts. This foresight enables strategic positioning well in advance of the market.

The ability to synthesize diverse data sets into a coherent investment strategy is the hallmark of sophisticated GIS use. As investors hone their skills in interpreting spatial data, they cultivate an edge in the competitive landscape of infrastructure investing. By continuously refining their analytical frameworks and embracing cutting-edge technologies, they can stay ahead of the curve and identify trends that others overlook. This proactive approach not only enhances profitability but also reinforces the investor's role as a forward-thinking participant in the ever-evolving world of infrastructure development. Through the strategic application of GIS, investors can transform spatial data into a powerful tool for unlocking untapped potential.

Utilizing Demographic Layers for Targeted Investment Analysis

Harnessing demographic layers within Geographic Information Systems (GIS) unveils a sophisticated approach for discerning market dynamics in infrastructure investment. By examining spatial data intertwined with demographic information, investors can identify shifts in population density, age distribution, income levels, and other vital statistics that signal potential economic growth. For instance, areas with a burgeoning young adult population might indicate a rising demand for residential housing and amenities, while regions with increasing income levels could suggest opportunities for high-end commercial development. This analytical method transcends mere observation, allowing for a strategic forecast of where and how infrastructure ventures might flourish in the near future.

Consider the transformative potential of using demographic layers to evaluate areas of untapped potential. A region that displays a rapid increase in median income and educational attainment could become fertile ground for technological or business hubs. By overlaying this demographic data with existing infrastructure maps, investors can pinpoint locations likely to experience significant development, providing a competitive edge in securing profitable ventures before they gain widespread attention. This data-driven strategy not only highlights current opportunities but also anticipates future demand, laying the groundwork for informed decision-making.

Exploring the intersection of zoning regulations and demographic trends can further refine investment analysis. Understanding how zoning laws interact with demographic shifts allows for the identification of potential development hotspots. For example, if zoning changes are proposed in an area with a growing population and rising property values, investors can anticipate increased construction and infrastructure needs. This insight enables proactive engagement with local authorities and developers, positioning stakeholders to capitalize on impending changes. By strategically aligning zoning knowledge with demographic analysis, investors can better gauge the feasibility and timing of potential projects.

Recent advancements in GIS technology have enhanced the accessibility and accuracy of demographic data, empowering investors with sophisticated tools for analysis. Machine learning algorithms applied to GIS data can reveal patterns and correlations that might otherwise remain hidden. These cutting-edge techniques offer a nuanced understanding of demographic shifts, allowing investors to differentiate between transient trends and sustainable growth. By embracing these innovations, stakeholders can enrich their predictive models, fostering a deeper understanding of the intricate interplay between demographics and infrastructure potential.

Thought-provoking scenarios underscore the need for critical analysis and application of these insights. Consider a hypothetical region where demographic data suggests a decline in population but an increase in average income. This paradox may indicate a shifting market focus towards luxury or niche developments, such as retirement communities or high-end real estate. By questioning assumptions and exploring such nuanced insights, investors can cultivate a more robust strategy that transcends conventional wisdom. Armed with these actionable insights, readers are equipped to apply GIS demographic analysis in real-world scenarios, ultimately transforming abstract data into tangible investment opportunities.

Integrating Zoning Regulations to Forecast Development Hotspots

Understanding the interplay between zoning regulations and infrastructure development is pivotal for identifying potential hotspots for growth. Using GIS technology, investors can scrutinize zoning maps to anticipate where transformative changes might occur. These maps, embedded with layers of data, offer insights into the permissible uses of land across different regions. By examining shifts in zoning designations, such as from industrial to mixed-use or residential, savvy investors can pinpoint areas poised for significant transformation. Such changes often herald increased development activity, suggesting new opportunities for investment. For instance, a city rezoning a large plot near a planned transit hub from low-density residential to mixed-use can signal an impending surge in demand for commercial and residential spaces.

The integration of zoning data with GIS allows for a sophisticated analysis of the spatial and regulatory landscape. Investors can employ advanced spatial analytics to overlay zoning information with other critical data layers, such as proximity to transportation infrastructure or demographic trends. This method uncovers nuanced patterns that might otherwise remain hidden in traditional analyses. A case in point is the use of GIS to identify intersections of zoning flexibility and high population growth, areas often ripe for lucrative investments. This approach transcends conventional wisdom, offering a more dynamic and detailed picture of potential development zones that might not be immediately apparent without the confluence of these data sets.

Incorporating cutting-edge research into zoning trends further enriches the investor's toolkit. Recent studies highlight how cities increasingly adapt zoning regulations to promote sustainable development and accommodate evolving urban needs. For example, the rise of "smart zoning" initiatives aims to balance economic growth with environmental considerations, often prioritizing developments near green transit options. By aligning investment strategies with these forward-thinking policies, investors can position themselves at the forefront of emergent market trends, capitalizing on shifts that align with broader societal and regulatory changes. This alignment not only enhances profit potential but also supports sustainable urban growth.

An innovative perspective involves viewing zoning regulations not as static constraints but as dynamic opportunities. GIS technology enables investors to simulate various zoning scenarios, assessing how potential regulatory changes could impact development possibilities. By hypothesizing different outcomes, such as the relaxation of height restrictions in key areas, investors can craft strategies that anticipate regulatory shifts before they occur. This proactive approach turns zoning regulations into a strategic asset, allowing investors to navigate and even influence the trajectory of urban growth. Such foresight can be invaluable in making informed decisions that align with long-term urban planning goals.

These advanced insights into zoning regulations and GIS provide a robust framework for identifying development hotspots. By meticulously analyzing zoning data alongside demographic and infrastructure trends, investors can uncover hidden opportunities that others might overlook. This strategic foresight enables them to make informed, timely decisions that capitalize on forthcoming urban transformations. Encouraging a mindset of constant inquiry and exploration, readers are empowered to continually refine their understanding of zoning dynamics, ensuring they remain agile and well-prepared to seize emerging opportunities in the infrastructure investment landscape.

Case Studies in GIS-Driven Profits

Starting with an overview of how Geographic Information Systems (GIS) have transformed the landscape of investment forecasting, this topic dives into real-world applications that highlight the power of spatial data. GIS technology is not just a tool; it's a lens through which investors can glimpse the future of infrastructure development. As governments around the world allocate billions to projects that shape cities and landscapes, the ability to visualize these changes before they happen offers a competitive edge. By analyzing multiple layers of data—from zoning maps to transportation networks—GIS can unearth patterns and trends that might otherwise remain hidden in plain sight. This ability to see beyond the obvious can be the difference between seizing an opportunity and watching it slip away.

For investors aiming to harness these insights, understanding the application of GIS is crucial. The upcoming subtopics explore how GIS can illuminate early signals of infrastructure expansion, forecast surges in real estate values, and even merge with economic indicators to refine investment strategies. Each case study presented will illustrate the potential of GIS to turn abstract data into actionable intelligence. As we journey through these examples, the practical integration of GIS into an investment strategy becomes clear, offering not just a glimpse into what's possible, but a guide to making it profitable.

Leveraging GIS for Early Detection of Infrastructure Expansion Zones

Harnessing the power of Geographic Information Systems (GIS) for the early detection of infrastructure expansion zones offers a strategic advantage in the competitive world of investment. By layering spatial data with infrastructure planning information, GIS enables the identification of zones poised for growth, thereby allowing investors to anticipate where government and private sector resources may be directed. This proactive approach hinges on understanding how infrastructure projects affect land use, transportation networks, and economic development patterns. By analyzing these GIS layers, investors can discern subtle shifts that signal major infrastructure undertakings, turning reams of data into actionable insights.

Consider, for instance, the use of GIS analysis in identifying transportation corridors likely to be expanded or developed. Such infrastructure projects often lead to increased accessibility and subsequently higher demand for adjacent real estate. GIS can map these corridors against other data sets, such as population growth statistics and current land use patterns, to pinpoint areas where new developments could spark a surge in property values. By visualizing these intersections, investors gain foresight into the cascading effects of infrastructure projects and can strategically position themselves to capitalize on these impending changes.

GIS also plays a pivotal role in elucidating opportunity zones, areas designated for economic revitalization through tax incentives and other benefits. By integrating GIS data with economic indicators, investors can spot which opportunity zones are most likely to benefit from upcoming infrastructure projects. This fusion of spatial and economic data provides a comprehensive view, enabling investors to make informed decisions about where to allocate resources. Such strategic investments not only promise financial returns but also contribute to the broader economic uplift of the targeted areas, aligning profit with positive community impact.

Advanced GIS tools now offer predictive modeling capabilities, which can simulate the potential impact of proposed infrastructure projects before they even begin. By employing these models, investors can assess various scenarios and forecast the ripple effects of infrastructure development on local economies. These insights allow for a nuanced understanding of both immediate and long-term investment opportunities, providing a competitive edge in timing market entry and exit strategies. Such foresight is invaluable in a landscape where timing can significantly influence the magnitude of returns.

The application of GIS for early detection of infrastructure expansion zones is a testament to the power of technology in transforming raw data into strategic vision. By leveraging these systems, investors are equipped not just to follow trends but to anticipate them. This forward-thinking approach encourages a mindset of continuous learning and adaptation, as new data and methods refine the accuracy and scope of predictions. As investors become more adept at interpreting these complex spatial signals, they position themselves at the forefront of an evolving market, ready to seize opportunities as they arise.

Analyzing Spatial Data to Forecast Real Estate Value Surges

Geographic Information Systems (GIS) offer a robust framework for analyzing spatial data, providing unique insights into potential real estate value surges. By overlaying multiple layers of spatial information, GIS allows investors to visualize hidden patterns and trends that might otherwise go unnoticed. For instance, the proximity of a property to planned infrastructure projects—such as new transit lines or highways—can be a significant indicator of future appreciation. These layers can reveal not only current infrastructure but also planned developments, enabling investors to make informed decisions long before these projects are publicized. The strategic advantage lies in the ability to anticipate growth areas by identifying regions where infrastructure enhancements align with socio-economic trends.

Understanding the relationship between spatial data and real estate values requires a nuanced approach that balances both quantitative and qualitative data. Quantitative metrics, such as distance to amenities or accessibility to major transport routes, are essential. However, qualitative factors like neighborhood characteristics and demographic shifts provide context that numbers alone cannot. By integrating these data points, GIS becomes an indispensable tool for predicting areas where real estate values are likely to experience significant growth. As neighborhoods evolve, GIS analytics offer a comprehensive view of how these changes impact property values, presenting opportunities for astute investors to capitalize on emerging markets.

Significant changes in real estate often follow infrastructure developments, but the key is to recognize these shifts before they occur. GIS enables investors to model potential scenarios, exploring how different infrastructure projects might influence property values across various neighborhoods. Consider a city planning to expand its subway system. By using GIS to map current property values and overlaying the proposed subway routes, investors can identify zones where real estate prices might increase. This spatial foresight allows investors to strategically position themselves in markets poised for growth, maximizing potential returns while minimizing risk.

Innovative GIS applications also incorporate real-time data and predictive analytics to refine investment strategies further. As technology advances, GIS platforms are increasingly capable of processing large datasets from diverse sources, including social media, traffic patterns, and economic indicators. This integration offers a dynamic perspective on real estate trends, allowing investors to respond rapidly to market shifts. By harnessing real-time data alongside traditional GIS layers, investors gain a competitive edge, making more agile and informed decisions. This adaptability not only enhances investment outcomes but also fosters a proactive approach to market changes.

What if investors could predict the next real estate hotspot before it becomes common knowledge? GIS provides the tools to explore such possibilities, encouraging a forward-thinking mindset. By continually refining GIS methodologies and incorporating diverse data sources, investors can stay ahead of the curve, identifying undervalued properties with high growth potential. This proactive strategy not only enhances profitability but also contributes to a more dynamic and resilient investment portfolio. As GIS technology evolves, so too does the potential for innovative and strategic real estate investment, challenging traditional paradigms and opening new avenues for financial success.

Integrating GIS with Economic Indicators for Strategic Investment Decisions

A sophisticated fusion of Geographic Information Systems (GIS) with economic indicators can unlock a treasure trove of strategic investment avenues. This convergence allows investors to pinpoint locations where infrastructure growth and economic trends align, creating fertile ground for lucrative opportunities. GIS technology, with its ability to layer complex spatial data, serves as a powerful lens through which the intricate tapestry of infrastructure can be examined. By integrating economic indicators into this framework, such as employment rates, income levels, and industry growth forecasts, investors can gain a multi-dimensional perspective that transcends traditional analysis.

A practical illustration of this integration can be seen in the predictive modeling of urban growth corridors. These corridors often emerge where economic activity is burgeoning and infrastructure development is imminent. By overlaying GIS maps that showcase existing and planned infrastructure with economic data highlighting areas of robust commercial activity, investors can identify zones poised for exponential real estate appreciation. This approach not only anticipates where the next wave of development will crest but also highlights sectors likely to attract business investments, thus offering dual avenues for financial gain.

Incorporating GIS with economic indicators also empowers investors to assess risk with greater precision. For example, an area might show promising infrastructure developments, yet economic indicators could reveal vulnerabilities, such as declining industries or adverse demographic shifts. By synthesizing these data points, investors can make informed decisions, balancing potential rewards against possible risks. This holistic analysis ensures that investment choices are not based solely on infrastructure potential but are also tempered by economic realities, providing a more resilient strategy.

Cutting-edge research in spatial economics further enriches this approach, offering insights into how infrastructure investments can catalyze regional economic dynamics. Studies have demonstrated that infrastructure projects often lead to increased economic activity, which in turn attracts further investment, creating a virtuous cycle of growth. By using GIS to visualize these spatial relationships, investors can identify patterns that may not be immediately apparent through conventional analysis, granting them a strategic advantage in anticipating future developments.

Engagement with this sophisticated method encourages investors to challenge conventional wisdom and explore diverse perspectives. Consider a scenario where a city plans to expand its public transit network. By analyzing GIS data alongside economic indicators, an investor might discover that the most promising opportunities are not in the immediate vicinity of planned stations, as commonly believed, but rather in underdeveloped areas that will gain connectivity and economic uplift. This insight underscores the importance of moving beyond surface-level assumptions and cultivating a nuanced understanding of spatial economic interactions, ultimately empowering investors to make astute, future-oriented decisions.

GIS technology emerges as a powerful tool in deciphering infrastructure trends, offering investors a distinct edge in identifying and capitalizing on emerging opportunities. By leveraging GIS layers, it's possible to visualize patterns and pinpoint where future infrastructure investments are likely to occur. Mapping these investments provides a strategic lens through which potential growth zones can be identified, revealing opportunity zones ripe for exploration. Through illustrative case studies, the transformative power of GIS in driving profits becomes evident, underscoring its role as an indispensable asset in the investor's toolkit. This chapter not only demystifies the complexities of geographic analysis but also integrates it into a broader investment strategy, reinforcing the book's central theme of transforming information into actionable insights. As the journey progresses, readers are encouraged to apply these GIS techniques, deepening their understanding and enhancing their predictive capabilities. The next chapter will expand on these insights, further equipping readers with the knowledge to turn anticipation into tangible success.

Chapter Seven

Tracking Infrastructure Related Legislation

Step onto the threshold of a bustling construction site, alive with energy and transformation, where the hum of machinery and the towering cranes symbolize not just progress, but opportunity. Beneath the layers of concrete and steel lies a complex web of legislative actions that have set these projects in motion. For many, these legal machinations are a maze of jargon and red tape, but for those with the right tools, they are a treasure map leading to potential prosperity. In this chapter, we embark on a journey to uncover how the seemingly dry world of legislation can become a vibrant source of investment insight. By understanding the laws and regulations that govern infrastructure development, you can transform bureaucratic complexity into a clear path toward financial success.

The pages that follow will guide you in mastering the art of legislative tracking, a crucial skill in predicting the trajectory of future infrastructure projects. We'll explore the intricate dance between legislative agendas and economic impact, revealing how each bill, amendment, and policy can influence the landscape of investment opportunities. By scrutinizing local, state, and federal bills, you'll learn how to anticipate shifts in the infrastructure sector long before they hit the headlines. It's here, in the corridors of power, that the seeds of tomorrow's developments are sown, and understanding this process allows you to plant your own stakes early on.

As we delve deeper, you'll discover how to navigate the policy pipeline, recognizing key deadlines that serve as pivotal action points. These moments, often overlooked by casual observers, are critical junctures where informed decisions can lead to substantial gains. With strategic timing and a keen eye for legislative changes, you'll be poised to capitalize on the next wave of infrastructure growth. By the end of this chapter, you'll not only appreciate the significance of legislative tracking but also be equipped to leverage it as a cornerstone of your investment strategy. Prepare to see beyond the construction sites and into the legislative engines that power them, ready to seize the opportunities they present.

Legislative Agendas and Their Economic Impact

Experts have long debated the intricacies of legislative agendas and their profound economic implications. At the heart of these discussions lies the understanding that legislative proposals, while often complex and multifaceted, contain a wealth of economic signals waiting to be deciphered. These signals can offer foresight into potential shifts in the economic landscape, providing informed investors with the opportunity to align their strategies with upcoming changes. Legislation can act as a powerful catalyst, setting in motion financial ripple effects that touch markets, industries, and individual investments. Grasping the nuances of these proposals not only provides a glimpse into the future but also equips astute investors with a strategic edge.

Navigating the world of legislative tracking involves more than just monitoring bills; it demands a keen eye for detail and an understanding of the policy pipeline. As bills move from proposals to enacted policies, they often follow a timeline that can serve as a roadmap for strategic investment decisions. Legislative deadlines, often viewed as mere bureaucratic checkpoints, transform into action points for those who are adept at reading between the lines. By aligning investment strategies with these timelines, investors can position themselves advantageously, poised to capitalize on the economic shifts that follow legislative changes. The ensuing subtopics will unravel the techniques to decode these legislative cues, offering a pathway to strategically timed investments.

Analyzing Legislative Proposals for Economic Signals

Government legislative proposals often serve as precursors to economic shifts, offering astute investors a glimpse into future market conditions. By scrutinizing these proposals, one can detect subtle indicators of impending infrastructural developments that might not be immediately apparent. For instance, a bill proposing increased funding for renewable energy infrastructure could signal forthcoming construction projects, potentially benefiting companies involved in solar panel manufacturing or grid modernization. Analyzing such proposals requires a keen eye for detail and an understanding of how legislative language can translate into economic action. This approach allows investors to anticipate market changes and align their strategies accordingly.

The economic signals embedded in legislative proposals often extend beyond direct monetary allocations. Consider the broader implications of policy changes that might affect labor markets, supply chains, or regional development. A proposal aimed at improving public transportation might suggest an uptick in urban development, resulting in increased demand for residential and commercial real estate in affected areas. Investors who understand these connections can position themselves advantageously, capitalizing on the ripple effects that follow legislative enactments. By doing so, they not only gain a financial edge but also contribute to informed decision-making that reflects a comprehensive understanding of policy-driven economic dynamics.

To effectively analyze legislative proposals for economic signals, one must adopt a multifaceted approach that combines both quantitative and qualitative assessments. Quantitative analysis involves examining projected budgets, funding allocations, and economic forecasts linked to proposed legislation. On the qualitative side, understanding the political context and stakeholder interests can provide deeper insights into the viability and potential impact of a proposal. This dual approach ensures a robust evaluation, allowing investors to distinguish between proposals likely to succeed and those that may encounter obstacles. By integrating these methods, one can develop a nuanced perspective that informs strategic investments tailored to legislative timelines.

Innovative tools and resources have emerged to assist investors in deciphering the complexities of legislative proposals. Platforms that aggregate and analyze legislative data offer invaluable insights, highlighting key trends and potential economic impacts. These tools often employ sophisticated algorithms to forecast the likelihood of a proposal's passage, offering users a probabilistic view of future developments. Embracing such technology can enhance an investor's ability to anticipate changes, providing a competitive edge in a rapidly evolving market landscape. Engaging with these resources not only streamlines the analysis process but also empowers investors to make data-driven decisions that align with emerging policy trends.

In exploring legislative proposals, it is crucial to remain adaptable and open to diverse perspectives, recognizing that economic signals can manifest in myriad ways. What might initially appear as a niche proposal could have far-reaching implications, influencing sectors beyond its immediate scope. Encouraging critical thinking and scenario analysis can help investors identify less obvious opportunities that others might overlook. Consider, for instance, the indirect benefits of a proposal aimed at enhancing broadband infrastructure in rural areas, which could spur technological innovation and business growth. By fostering a mindset that embraces complexity and seeks out unconventional insights, investors not only enrich their strategic framework but also position themselves to capitalize on legislative developments with precision and foresight.

Evaluating the Financial Ripple Effects of Policy Changes

Evaluating the financial ripple effects of policy changes requires an astute understanding of the intricate interplay between legislation and market dynamics.

Legislative proposals, especially those pertaining to infrastructure, can profoundly shape economic landscapes by altering cost structures, creating new market opportunities, or shifting regulatory environments. For instance, a policy aimed at bolstering renewable energy infrastructure could ignite demand for solar panels and related technologies, thereby impacting sectors ranging from manufacturing to real estate. Such policies don't operate in isolation; they reverberate through supply chains, affecting everything from raw material procurement to the end-user. By comprehensively analyzing these chain reactions, investors can anticipate shifts in market sentiment and position themselves strategically.

A nuanced approach to assessing these ripple effects involves dissecting the language of legislative texts and understanding their potential economic implications. Legislative language often holds subtle clues about the scope and scale of intended infrastructure projects. By parsing these documents, investors can uncover early indicators of industry trends, such as increased funding allocations for smart city projects or transportation upgrades, which may suggest burgeoning opportunities in related sectors like technology or construction. Furthermore, understanding the legislative intent—whether it's fostering innovation, addressing climate change, or improving public health—can provide context for anticipating which industries might experience growth or contraction.

Recent studies underscore the importance of timing when capitalizing on legislative changes. Research indicates that early movers often enjoy a competitive edge, as they can capitalize on market inefficiencies before these opportunities become widely recognized. Investors who understand the legislative timeline can anticipate when funds will be released and projects initiated, allowing them to position their portfolios to benefit from these developments. By aligning investment decisions with legislative milestones, such as budget approvals or project announcements, astute investors can effectively manage risks and maximize returns.

Diverse perspectives reveal that while some view policy changes as a source of uncertainty, others see them as catalysts for innovation and economic growth.

For example, the introduction of stringent environmental regulations might initially be perceived as a burden, yet it can spur advancements in green technology and sustainable practices. By recognizing the transformative potential of such policies, investors can adopt a forward-thinking approach, identifying sectors poised for growth due to regulatory shifts and investing in companies that are agile enough to adapt and thrive in changing environments.

Thought-provoking scenarios encourage readers to consider what might happen if a particular policy doesn't pass or if its implementation faces delays. How would that affect the anticipated economic ripple effects? This kind of critical thinking enables investors to develop contingency plans, ensuring they remain adaptable in the face of legislative uncertainty. By continuously refining their predictive frameworks and seeking out diverse perspectives, readers can transform complex legislative signals into actionable investment strategies, ultimately gaining a competitive advantage in an ever-evolving economic landscape.

Strategic Investments Aligned with Legislative Timelines

Aligning investments with legislative timelines requires a sophisticated understanding of how policy shifts can reshape economic landscapes. Savvy investors recognize that proposed bills and legislative agendas, from local councils to federal chambers, often serve as harbingers of change, signaling where public funds might flow. By interpreting these signals, investors can position themselves strategically, capitalizing on upcoming infrastructure ventures. For instance, a proposed transportation bill might hint at future road expansions or public transit enhancements, offering opportunities in related sectors like construction, materials, or urban development. The art lies in discerning which legislative items will garner the necessary support to transition from proposal to enacted law, translating legislative intent into tangible projects.

Timing is a critical component in this strategic dance. Understanding the legislative calendar, including key sessions, committee reviews, and voting schedules, provides crucial insights into when investments should be made. Legislative processes often follow a rhythmic pattern, with certain times of the year more likely to yield decisive actions. Recognizing these patterns allows investors to act with precision, entering markets ahead of competitors. This predictive prowess is bolstered by real-time legislative tracking tools, which provide updates on the status of bills and amendments, ensuring investors remain informed and agile. The ability to anticipate and respond swiftly to legislative changes can transform potential risks into lucrative opportunities.

Incorporating legislative analysis into investment strategy also involves evaluating the broader economic implications of policy decisions. This requires a nuanced approach that considers not only direct effects but also secondary and tertiary impacts across various industries. For example, legislation aimed at renewable energy development might initially benefit solar panel manufacturers, but its ripple effects could extend to industries such as battery storage, grid infrastructure, and even real estate in areas poised to become green energy hubs. By mapping these potential outcomes, investors can diversify their portfolios, minimizing risk while maximizing potential returns.

Advanced investors often employ scenario analysis as a tool to forecast the outcomes of legislative decisions. By constructing different scenarios based on potential legislative paths, investors can prepare for a range of outcomes, ensuring readiness regardless of which direction policy takes. This approach not only enhances strategic foresight but also aids in developing robust investment portfolios that account for various contingencies. Engaging with legislative analysts or policy experts can further enrich this process, providing insights that transcend conventional market speculation and offering a competitive edge in anticipating legislative-driven market shifts.

Ultimately, the key to leveraging legislative timelines for investment success lies in a proactive mindset. Rather than reacting to changes as they occur, astute investors cultivate a habit of anticipation, constantly scanning the horizon for legislative developments that could signal new opportunities. By fostering a culture of continuous learning and adaptation, investors can refine their strategies, ensuring they not only keep pace with legislative changes but also harness these shifts to drive long-term financial success. This dynamic approach transforms the often opaque world of legislation into a transparent roadmap for strategic investment, aligning financial goals with the ebb and flow of policy evolution.

How to Monitor Local, State, and Federal Bills

What sets this apart is the intricate dance of timing, precision, and insight required to navigate the legislative landscape effectively. Understanding how to monitor local, state, and federal bills is perhaps one of the most vital skills for anyone seeking to capitalize on the vast sea of opportunity hidden within government infrastructure projects. The legislative process, often perceived as labyrinthine and inaccessible, is a treasure trove of information for those who know where to look. Each bill, motion, and amendment carries the potential to reshape the economic landscape, making it imperative for savvy investors to stay ahead of the curve. This isn't just about knowing what's on the docket; it's about anticipating the ripple effects of legislation that can lay the groundwork for transformative infrastructure endeavors. By mastering this skill, investors can position themselves at the forefront of emerging trends and potential windfalls.

To navigate this arena, one must be armed with the right tools and strategies. As we move forward, the focus shifts to practical methodologies that transform legislative tracking from an overwhelming task into a streamlined and insightful practice. Utilizing online legislative tracking tools for real-time updates allows investors to maintain a pulse on the ever-shifting political landscape. Understanding the role of legislative committees and their influence on bill progression sheds light on the power dynamics that can accelerate or stall crucial developments. Finally, interpreting amendments and riders unveils hidden infrastructure opportunities that might otherwise go unnoticed. Together, these subtopics form a cohesive framework, empowering readers to not just follow but anticipate legislative movements that could herald profitable infrastructure projects.

Utilizing Online Legislative Tracking Tools for Real-Time Updates

Modern technology has revolutionized the way we track legislative developments, offering an array of sophisticated online tools that provide real-time updates on bills at local, state, and federal levels. Platforms such as GovTrack, LegiScan, and Congress.gov enable investors to stay informed about the legislative pulse, offering comprehensive information on bill status, sponsors, and upcoming votes. These tools utilize APIs and data feeds to deliver instantaneous updates, ensuring that users are always at the forefront of legislative changes. By leveraging these digital resources, investors can identify which bills have the potential to impact infrastructure projects, allowing them to make informed decisions promptly. This instant access to legislative proceedings eliminates the lag time traditionally associated with monitoring government activities, providing a strategic advantage in a competitive market.

An in-depth understanding of the structure and function of legislative committees is crucial for anyone looking to capitalize on infrastructure-related opportunities. Committees play a pivotal role in shaping the trajectory of bills, often determining their success or failure. By analyzing committee compositions and their historical voting patterns, investors can anticipate how a particular bill might progress. For instance, a committee with a majority of members who have previously supported infrastructure development is more likely to advance related bills. Furthermore, understanding the influence of key committee members, such as chairs and ranking members, can offer nuanced insights into the legislative process. By identifying these influential figures and monitoring their public statements and affiliations, investors can gain a clearer picture of the legislative landscape and its implications for future infrastructure projects.

The subtleties of legislative amendments and riders often hold the key to uncovering hidden opportunities within infrastructure bills. While the primary text of a bill might appear straightforward, it is in the amendments and riders where significant changes can occur, sometimes redirecting funds or altering project scopes. Investors who can interpret these modifications stand to gain a strategic edge, as these changes may not be immediately apparent to the casual observer. For instance, a seemingly minor amendment could introduce new funding for a specific type of infrastructure, signaling potential investment opportunities. By developing the ability to discern these nuanced shifts, readers can position themselves ahead of the curve, capitalizing on developments that might otherwise go unnoticed.

The dynamic nature of legislative deadlines presents both challenges and opportunities for astute investors. Each stage of the legislative process is governed by specific timelines, from the introduction of a bill to its potential enactment. Understanding these deadlines enables investors to anticipate critical junctures that could influence infrastructure projects. For example, an impending deadline for a committee vote might indicate a surge in lobbying efforts or public interest, which in turn could impact the bill's likelihood of passing. By aligning investment strategies with these legislative timelines, investors can better manage risk and optimize their decision-making process. This temporal awareness ensures that they are not only reacting to changes but strategically positioning themselves to benefit from them.

Engaging with the legislative process on this level invites investors to adopt a proactive mindset, transforming passive observation into active participation. By leveraging online legislative tracking tools, analyzing committee dynamics, interpreting amendments, and understanding deadlines, investors are equipped to navigate the complex web of government proceedings with confidence. This approach encourages critical thinking and fosters a deeper understanding of the intricate interplay between legislation and infrastructure development. As readers embrace these methodologies, they not only enhance their investment acumen but also contribute to a more informed and dynamic market landscape. Through continuous refinement of these skills, investors can transform potential challenges into unparalleled opportunities, setting the stage for sustained financial success in the ever-evolving world of infrastructure projects.

Analyzing Legislative Committees and Their Influence on Bill Progress

Legislative committees serve as pivotal gatekeepers in the progression of bills, wielding considerable influence over the fate of proposed infrastructure projects. Each committee, typically composed of a group of lawmakers with specific expertise, evaluates bills pertinent to their domain, shaping their content, and determining their viability. Understanding the composition and interests of these committees is crucial for investors seeking to anticipate legislative outcomes that may impact infrastructure investments. For instance, a committee focused on transportation might prioritize bills that address public transit funding or road maintenance, offering early indicators of where government resources will be allocated. By examining the backgrounds and priorities of committee members, investors can glean insights into potential project approvals or rejections that could influence market dynamics.

The intricate process within these committees often involves negotiations, hearings, and deliberations, where bills can be amended, combined, or stalled. These stages are critical junctures for investors to monitor, as they can significantly alter the trajectory of a bill. Real-time updates from committee meetings can reveal shifts in legislative focus or emerging trends, such as a sudden emphasis on sustainable infrastructure or renewable energy projects. Advanced tracking tools and legislative platforms provide access to detailed committee reports and hearing transcripts, enabling investors to stay informed about the latest developments and adjust their strategies accordingly. This proactive approach allows investors to anticipate changes in infrastructure policy that might affect market opportunities.

Committees also play a strategic role by deciding which bills advance to the legislative floor for a vote, often serving as the first line of defense against poorly conceived proposals. Bills that pass through rigorous committee scrutiny are more likely to reach implementation, making these deliberations essential focal points for investors. Observing committee endorsements or opposition can offer predictive insights into the bill's success, impacting sectors like construction, transportation, and utilities. Investors who understand these dynamics can position themselves advantageously by aligning their portfolios with projects that have a higher likelihood of gaining legislative approval.

In addition to public meetings, committees often engage in private discussions and negotiations, where informal alliances and compromises can shape legislative priorities. Networks and relationships within these committees can influence which projects receive attention and funding, providing a nuanced layer of analysis for investors. Understanding these dynamics requires a deep dive into the political landscape and an awareness of the underlying motivations driving committee members. By cultivating a network of contacts within government and industry circles, investors can gain access to valuable intelligence that may not be readily available through public channels.

Encouraging a more proactive stance, consider the implications of a bill that successfully navigates the committee stage and becomes law. This transition can set off a chain reaction, triggering public-private partnerships, influencing regional economic development, and offering a multitude of investment opportunities. Investors should remain vigilant, using insights gained from committee dynamics to guide their decision-making process. As legislative landscapes evolve, staying ahead of the curve requires not only a keen understanding of committee operations but also a readiness to adapt strategies in response to legislative shifts. By mastering the intricacies of committee influence, investors can effectively capitalize on the legislative process to maximize their returns.

Interpreting Amendments and Riders for Hidden Infrastructure Opportunities

Amendments and riders within legislative documents often serve as hidden passageways to lucrative infrastructure opportunities. These modifications can quietly introduce provisions for infrastructure projects, sometimes embedded within broader legislative packages that are seemingly unrelated. For instance, a rider attached to a transportation bill might allocate funds for the development of digital infrastructure in rural areas, a detail easy to overlook amidst the primary focus on road and bridge repairs. It is crucial to approach these documents with a discerning eye, recognizing that the true value lies not just in the headline legislation but in the fine print that accompanies it. By systematically analyzing amendments and riders, savvy investors can uncover these concealed opportunities long before they are widely recognized.

Tools like keyword alerts and legislative tracking software can provide real-time updates on amendments and riders, offering a competitive edge. Such tools allow users to specify terms related to infrastructure, ensuring that any relevant legislative changes are flagged immediately. However, the real skill comes in interpreting these changes, distinguishing between minor procedural adjustments and significant shifts in policy direction. For instance, a simple amendment might redirect funds from an existing project to a new, high-priority initiative, signaling a shift in governmental focus and potential new investment opportunities. By closely monitoring these developments, investors can position themselves to benefit from the ripple effects of legislative changes.

Understanding the context and intent behind amendments and riders is also essential. Legislative language can be complex and nuanced, often requiring a grasp of political dynamics and stakeholder interests. Engaging with policymakers, attending committee meetings, or even consulting with legal experts can provide deeper insights into the motivations driving these changes. This knowledge can illuminate potential infrastructure projects that align with broader policy goals, such as sustainability or technology advancement. For example, a rider promoting green energy projects might align with broader governmental goals for reducing carbon emissions, indicating a likely increase in funding and support for related infrastructure initiatives.

A sophisticated approach to analyzing amendments and riders involves considering the broader legislative ecosystem. This includes understanding how amendments interact with existing laws and the potential for future legislative developments. For instance, an amendment that introduces a pilot program for smart city technologies might signal a future wave of related initiatives, offering a strategic entry point for investments in emerging tech infrastructure. By mapping these interconnections, investors can develop a predictive framework that anticipates where and how government priorities will manifest in infrastructure projects.

To maximize the potential of these hidden opportunities, investors should cultivate a proactive strategy. This involves not only tracking legislative changes but also acting swiftly on insights gained. Establishing relationships with key stakeholders, such as local government officials and industry leaders, can provide additional intelligence and facilitate timely decision-making. By integrating legislative analysis into a broader investment strategy, investors can enhance their ability to capitalize on infrastructure opportunities that others might overlook, ultimately turning legislative nuances into profitable ventures.

Understanding the Policy Pipeline

Imagine waking up one morning to find that a seemingly obscure piece of legislation has suddenly opened the floodgates to a new wave of infrastructure projects, sending ripple effects through the economy. This scenario may feel like a stroke of luck, but for those versed in the art of understanding the policy pipeline, it's a predictable outcome rather than a surprise. In this dynamic world of infrastructure investment, the legislative process acts as both a catalyst and a compass, guiding investors toward opportunities that others might overlook. The policy pipeline is not merely a sequence of bureaucratic steps; it is a living, breathing entity that embodies the intentions, priorities, and ambitions of those in power. By learning to decode this complex system, investors can position themselves to anticipate changes before they happen, gaining a significant competitive edge.

As we navigate this intricate landscape, the ability to discern legislative intent and priorities becomes paramount. Understanding the political and bureaucratic influences at play provides a clearer picture of how policies are shaped and steered. This insight is crucial for forecasting policy outcomes and discerning their potential impact on investment landscapes. Armed with this knowledge, investors can not only predict which projects might emerge but also understand the broader economic implications. This foresight transforms legislative timelines into strategic action points, allowing for well-timed investments that align with policy shifts. Each subtopic in this chapter will unravel these layers, offering practical insights and techniques to master the art of tracking and interpreting infrastructure-related legislation.

Analyzing Legislative Intent and Priorities

Understanding the intent behind legislative agendas is akin to reading between the lines of a complex narrative. Lawmakers craft these agendas with underlying priorities that often cater to long-term strategic goals, regional needs, or political promises. To uncover the true implications for infrastructure projects, one must scrutinize not just the language of the bill, but also the motivation driving its creation. For instance, a bill proposing enhancements to public transit systems may be rooted in a city's overarching goal to reduce traffic congestion and emissions, signaling potential opportunities in sectors aligned with sustainable transportation. This nuanced understanding allows investors to anticipate shifts in focus and allocate resources accordingly, tapping into projects poised for legislative support.

Political dynamics and bureaucratic forces play decisive roles in shaping the legislative landscape. These influences can significantly alter the trajectory of a bill, making it vital for investors to navigate these waters with discernment. A policy might initially appear promising, only to be stalled or transformed by political bargaining or bureaucratic inertia. Recognizing key stakeholders and understanding their agendas can provide foresight into how these forces may impact a bill's progression. For example, a proposal for new energy infrastructure might gain momentum with the backing of influential committees or be delayed due to opposition from entrenched interests. By mapping these connections, investors can better forecast the likelihood of a bill's advancement and prepare strategic responses.

Predicting policy outcomes and their investment implications requires a blend of analytical rigor and market intuition. Legislative developments can catalyze significant economic shifts, with direct and indirect effects on various sectors. Investors need to anticipate how new laws will manifest in real-world scenarios, affecting everything from construction timelines to regulatory landscapes. Consider a government initiative to bolster broadband infrastructure in rural areas; such a policy could spur growth in telecommunications, real estate, and local economies. By crafting scenarios and examining potential ripple effects, investors can position themselves to capitalize on these changes, transforming legislative foresight into tangible financial returns.

Innovative approaches are emerging to enhance the precision of legislative analysis. Advanced data analytics and machine learning models are being employed to predict legislative outcomes with increasing accuracy. These technologies can sift through vast datasets to identify patterns and predict shifts in policy priorities, offering insights previously beyond reach. By integrating these tools into their analysis, investors can refine their predictive models, gaining a competitive edge in identifying forthcoming opportunities. However, while technology provides powerful enhancements, the value of human judgment and expertise remains indispensable, ensuring that predictions are grounded in practical realities and contextual understanding.

Applying this knowledge in real-world scenarios involves strategic patience and decisive action. Legislative processes are often protracted, requiring investors to maintain vigilance and adaptability as bills evolve. Critical deadlines, such as committee reviews or voting sessions, serve as pivotal points for reassessment and strategy refinement. By aligning investment decisions with these legislative milestones, investors can optimize timing and minimize risks. This approach not only enhances the potential for profit but also cultivates a deeper understanding of the intricate dance between policy and market forces. Through continuous learning and adaptation, investors can transform legislative insights into a robust framework for infrastructure investment success.

Navigating Political and Bureaucratic Influences

Deciphering the intricate web of political and bureaucratic influences within the infrastructure landscape demands a keen understanding of both overt and subtle dynamics. The political arena, rife with competing interests and shifting alliances, often dictates the trajectory of governmental priorities. Political leaders may champion particular infrastructure projects to gain favor with constituents or align with broader party agendas. Recognizing these motivations allows investors to anticipate policy shifts and their potential impact on infrastructure initiatives. For instance, a mayor advocating for sustainable transport might signal forthcoming investment in green infrastructure, an opportunity for astute investors to explore related markets.

Amidst political maneuvering, bureaucratic forces play a pivotal role in shaping infrastructure policies. The bureaucratic machinery, often perceived as slow and cumbersome, actually wields significant influence through regulatory frameworks, permitting processes, and funding allocations. Understanding the inner workings of relevant agencies and their historical precedents can yield valuable insights. An agency's past decisions, for example, may highlight its propensity to favor certain types of projects or its response to public pressure. Investors who can map these patterns are better positioned to predict which projects will advance smoothly and which might encounter obstacles.

The interplay between political and bureaucratic elements is further complicated by external pressures, such as lobbying efforts and public opinion. Lobbyists, representing myriad interests from construction firms to environmental groups, exert considerable influence over legislative and bureaucratic decision-making. By analyzing lobbying activities, investors can gain foresight into which sectors might see increased investment or regulation. Simultaneously, public sentiment can sway political priorities, as elected officials seek to align with voter concerns. Staying attuned to public discourse can therefore provide early warnings of shifts that could affect infrastructure planning.

Navigating these complexities requires not only awareness but also strategic foresight. Investors must develop an agile mindset, constantly scanning the horizon for emerging political and bureaucratic trends. This involves cultivating a network of reliable sources, including industry insiders and policy analysts, who can offer real-time insights. Engaging with think tanks and academic institutions can also provide advanced perspectives on potential policy developments, enabling investors to refine their predictive models. By integrating these diverse viewpoints, investors can construct a more nuanced understanding of the policy landscape.

To translate these insights into actionable strategies, investors should adopt a proactive approach, identifying key legislative windows and aligning their investments accordingly. For instance, tracking legislative calendars and committee meetings can reveal critical deadlines and decision points. By aligning investment timing with these moments, investors can maximize their advantage, positioning themselves ahead of market reactions. This strategic alignment not only enhances potential returns but also mitigates risks associated with sudden policy shifts. By mastering the art of navigating political and bureaucratic influences, investors can secure a competitive edge in the ever-evolving infrastructure domain.

Forecasting Policy Outcomes and Investment Implications

Forecasting policy outcomes and their investment implications requires a nuanced understanding of legislative processes and their potential to drive economic change. By examining the legislative framework, investors can anticipate shifts in infrastructure priorities and align their strategies accordingly. For instance, when a bill is introduced proposing significant funding for renewable energy projects, astute investors recognize the potential ripple effects across various industries such as construction, technology, and manufacturing. Identifying these connections requires a keen eye for detail and an understanding of how legislative initiatives can reshape market dynamics. This foresight can guide investment decisions, allowing investors to position themselves advantageously long before the broader market responds.

The ability to predict policy outcomes also hinges on understanding the interplay between political motivations and bureaucratic procedures. Legislation often reflects a complex web of interests, from economic agendas to social imperatives, and recognizing these underlying drivers is crucial. For example, infrastructure bills tied to job creation in economically distressed regions may signal an influx of development opportunities. Savvy investors who grasp these subtleties can anticipate where and when capital flows will materialize, enabling them to make informed choices about property acquisitions or partnerships. This strategic anticipation transforms seemingly abstract policy developments into concrete investment pathways.

Navigating the intricacies of the policy pipeline also involves staying abreast of legislative trends at multiple levels of government. Local, state, and federal policies can converge, diverge, or even collide, each influencing infrastructure projects in distinct ways. For example, a federal push for electric vehicle infrastructure might be bolstered or impeded by state-level regulations. A comprehensive understanding of these multilevel interactions equips investors with a holistic view, allowing them to adapt their strategies to both opportunities and obstacles. This multifaceted approach requires continuous monitoring and analysis, ensuring that decisions are grounded in the most current legislative landscape.

An astute investor also recognizes the potential for policy outcomes to deviate from their original intent. Bureaucratic delays, political opposition, or shifts in public opinion can alter the trajectory of legislation. By analyzing these potential disruptions, investors can better assess the risks associated with their predictions. For instance, if a proposed infrastructure project faces significant public backlash, it may be delayed or modified, impacting its investment viability. Simultaneously, this unpredictability can present opportunities for those prepared to pivot their strategies. By incorporating scenario planning into their analysis, investors can maintain flexibility and resilience in their approach.

Ultimately, the ability to forecast policy outcomes and derive investment implications is a skill that combines research, intuition, and experience. It involves connecting the dots between seemingly disparate pieces of information and constructing a coherent narrative that guides investment decisions. This process is not static but dynamic, requiring constant refinement and adaptation. By cultivating this skill, investors can transform legislative insights into actionable strategies, positioning themselves to capitalize on infrastructure developments long before they become mainstream knowledge. This proactive approach not only enhances investment potential but also contributes to a deeper understanding of the ever-evolving intersection of policy and economics.

Legislative Deadlines as Action Points

Imagine waking up one morning to find that a single legislative deadline has sent ripples through the financial markets, altering investment landscapes almost overnight. Such is the power of understanding legislative timelines in the realm of infrastructure projects. These seemingly mundane dates are, in fact, the hidden gears of a complex machinery that can dictate the flow of billions of dollars. For the astute investor, these deadlines represent more than just bureaucratic checkpoints; they are pivotal moments that can be harnessed for strategic advantage. As legislative agendas evolve, each milestone on their timeline can signal a shift in market dynamics, offering early indicators of where opportunities might crystallize next. Recognizing these critical junctures enables the investor to not only anticipate changes but to capitalize on them, transforming legislative awareness into actionable investment strategies.

Transitioning from the abstract to the concrete, the task then becomes identifying which legislative milestones hold the most potential for infrastructure projects and how they might translate into economic impacts. By mapping out these timelines, investors can pinpoint when to act, navigating the policy pipeline with precision. This approach requires an advanced understanding of how legislative processes unfold and their subsequent influence on market behavior. With the right techniques, these deadlines become more than mere dates on a calendar; they become action points, each one a beacon guiding investment decisions. In this context, the ability to foresee and respond to legislative developments distinguishes the successful from the merely informed, offering a robust framework for turning foresight into financial gain.

Identifying Critical Legislative Milestones for Infrastructure Projects

Infrastructure projects often hinge on specific legislative milestones that drive their progression from concept to reality. These milestones can be thought of as pivotal junctures where the trajectory of a project is determined, and understanding them is essential for making astute investments. For instance, the approval of a major infrastructure bill or the passing of budget allocations can signal the green light for significant development activities. Identifying these critical points requires an acute awareness of the legislative process, including knowing when and where to access the information that indicates when a project moves from planning to execution. This knowledge enables investors to anticipate shifts in market conditions and align their strategies with upcoming changes.

One effective method for pinpointing these milestones involves monitoring legislative calendars and agendas, which outline key dates and deadlines for bills that impact infrastructure initiatives. These calendars are often public and provide a roadmap of upcoming legislative activities. By analyzing these documents, investors can recognize patterns in legislative behavior that highlight when critical decisions are likely to occur. For example, understanding the budget cycle and the timing of appropriations can reveal when funds are likely to be released for new infrastructure work, allowing investors to position themselves advantageously before market reactions occur.

Advanced techniques in legislative tracking, such as utilizing data analytics and machine learning algorithms, can further enhance the ability to identify significant legislative milestones. These technologies can sift through vast amounts of legislative data to detect trends and predict future developments. By employing such cutting-edge tools, investors can gain a competitive edge, as they are not only able to react swiftly to legislative changes but also predict them with a higher degree of accuracy. This proactive approach can lead to more strategic investment decisions, minimizing risk and maximizing potential returns.

Engaging with multiple sources of information, including non-traditional and independent perspectives, can also provide valuable insights into legislative developments. By considering diverse viewpoints, investors can uncover hidden opportunities that may not be immediately apparent through mainstream channels. This approach encourages critical thinking and provides a fuller understanding of the legislative landscape. By challenging conventional narratives and exploring alternative analyses, investors can develop a more nuanced perspective that informs their investment strategies.

Thoughtful application of this information involves not only recognizing legislative milestones but also acting upon them with precision. For investors, this means developing a clear plan of action that aligns with legislative timelines, identifying specific investment targets, and executing decisions in a timely manner. By applying these insights, investors can effectively harness the power of legislative milestones, turning them into actionable opportunities that drive financial success. This strategic foresight transforms complex legislative processes into a clear path for capitalizing on infrastructure investments.

Leveraging Legislative Timelines for Strategic Investment Decisions

In the intricate dance of infrastructure investment, understanding legislative timelines becomes a powerful compass for navigating potential opportunities. Recognizing the rhythm of these timelines allows investors to anticipate when legislative actions may trigger market movements or unveil new avenues for profit. Legislative calendars, often dense and convoluted, can be decoded to reveal critical intervention points where the approval or rejection of a bill may directly influence infrastructure projects. By tracking these legislative milestones, investors can position themselves to capitalize on projects that are primed for advancement, turning bureaucratic processes into strategic assets.

The art of timing investments around legislative actions requires a keen understanding of the policy life cycle. Each phase of a bill—from introduction to committee discussions and eventual voting—holds the potential to impact market dynamics. Investors must develop a nuanced appreciation for how different stages of legislation can affect infrastructure initiatives. For instance, the approval of a transportation bill might signal impending developments in public transit projects, offering a window of opportunity for strategic investment. This proactive approach demands not only vigilance but also the ability to interpret legislative nuances that may not be immediately evident.

In harnessing legislative timelines, investors should employ sophisticated analytical tools and methodologies to forecast potential outcomes. Advanced data analytics and machine learning can be utilized to track historical legislative patterns and predict future trajectories. By integrating these technologies, investors gain a competitive edge, transforming legislative data into actionable insights. This approach underscores the importance of marrying traditional investment strategies with cutting-edge technology, ensuring that decisions are informed by the most comprehensive datasets available.

Developing a keen sense for legislative impacts also involves considering the broader socio-economic context in which these decisions are made. Policy changes are often reflective of societal needs and political priorities, and understanding these underlying currents can provide additional layers of insight. For instance, a government's focus on sustainable energy or urban development can influence the type of infrastructure projects prioritized within legislative agendas. By aligning investment strategies with these broader trends, investors can better anticipate shifts in the market landscape and align their portfolios accordingly.

Navigating the complexities of legislative timelines entails more than just tracking bills; it involves a strategic mindset that anticipates change and adapts swiftly. Investors must cultivate an agile approach, ready to pivot as legislative scenarios evolve. This adaptability, combined with a robust understanding of legislative processes, positions investors to not only react to changes but to foresee them, transforming potential obstacles into opportunities. Such foresight, when coupled with a disciplined investment strategy, empowers investors to make informed decisions that are both timely and impactful.

Advanced Techniques for Anticipating Legislative Impacts on Market Dynamics

Understanding the intricacies of legislative impacts on market dynamics requires a nuanced approach that goes beyond surface-level analysis. One of the key methods is to examine the historical precedents of similar bills and their outcomes on market behavior. This involves dissecting past legislative cycles, identifying patterns, and correlating them with market shifts. For instance, if a previous transportation bill led to a surge in infrastructure stocks, similar proposals in the current legislative session might suggest analogous opportunities. By employing statistical tools and data analytics, investors can quantify these correlations, offering a data-driven edge in predicting future market movements.

Harnessing predictive analytics in understanding legislative effects is an innovative technique that transforms seemingly abstract timelines into actionable insights. Machine learning algorithms can process vast datasets, identifying subtle trends and anomalies that human analysis might overlook. By feeding these models with information such as bill sponsorship, frequency of amendments, and committee deliberations, investors can generate forecasts that highlight potential market disruptions or opportunities. This approach not only provides a forward-looking perspective but also allows for real-time adjustments as new legislative information becomes available, enhancing decision-making precision.

To anticipate how legislation might sway market dynamics, consider the psychological and behavioral aspects of market participants. Legislative developments can often trigger emotional responses, leading to market overreactions. By studying behavioral finance theories, investors can develop strategies to capitalize on these fluctuations. For example, understanding that initial market reactions to a bill's passage might be overly exuberant or pessimistic allows for strategic entry or exit points. This approach requires a keen awareness of market sentiment and the ability to differentiate between short-lived fads and sustainable trends.

Another advanced technique involves scenario analysis, forecasting multiple legislative outcomes and their potential market implications. This method equips investors with a comprehensive risk assessment framework, allowing them to prepare for various eventualities. By constructing scenarios based on different legislative paths, such as a bill's passage, amendment, or rejection, investors can evaluate the impact on asset classes, industries, or individual stocks. This proactive approach not only mitigates risks but also uncovers hidden opportunities that might otherwise remain unnoticed in a single-outcome analysis.

Encouraging critical thought, one might ponder what role emerging technologies will play in the next legislative cycle and how these could reshape market landscapes. The integration of artificial intelligence in legislative processes, for instance, could accelerate decision-making and transparency, offering investors earlier access to crucial information. As the legislative environment evolves, staying attuned to these shifts enables a strategic advantage. By continuously refining analytical frameworks and remaining adaptable to change, investors can maintain a competitive edge, translating legislative complexities into tangible investment success.

As this chapter draws to a close, the intricate dance between infrastructure-related legislation and its economic implications comes into sharp focus. The ability to monitor and interpret legislative agendas across local, state, and federal levels is not just an academic exercise but a powerful tool for anticipating market trends and identifying investment opportunities. Understanding the policy pipeline and recognizing legislative deadlines as pivotal action points equips investors with a proactive stance, allowing them to align their strategies with the ebb and flow of governmental decision-making. This knowledge serves as a linchpin in the broader framework of infrastructure investment, enhancing one's capacity to foresee shifts in the landscape and capitalize on them. As we move forward, the insights gained here will serve as a foundation for exploring the multifaceted world of public-private partnerships and their role in infrastructure development. Reflect on the power of informed action: how might your investment strategy evolve when armed with the foresight that legislative tracking provides? This chapter encourages a continuous commitment to vigilance and adaptability, essential traits in the ever-evolving arena of infrastructure investment.

Chapter Eight

Early Warning Signals in Public Meetings

At the core of a city alive with movement and opportunity, a fascinating dance unfolds—one that holds the potential to reshape landscapes and economies alike. Imagine being able to discern the subtle cues that hint at tomorrow's urban transformation, much like a conductor interpreting the barely perceptible gestures of a maestro. This chapter takes you into the often overlooked yet fertile grounds of public meetings, where the seeds of future infrastructure projects are sown. These gatherings, frequently attended by local officials, planners, and community members, are treasure troves of information for those who know where to look and listen. They are the arenas where initial ideas are debated, budgets are tentatively earmarked, and the first glimmers of future opportunities are revealed.

For those willing to venture into the intricate world of public meetings, the rewards can be substantial. This chapter will guide you through the process of identifying which committees and boards warrant your attention, providing a gateway to the earliest possible insights into upcoming projects. You'll learn how to extract actionable intelligence from public discussions, transforming seemingly mundane details into crucial early warning signals. When a community member raises concerns about a proposed road extension or a board member hints at a new zoning initiative, these snippets can serve as the first whispers of change, offering you a valuable head start.

As you delve deeper, you'll discover the art of interpreting meeting minutes and leveraging public comment periods to your advantage. Building a network of contacts who are privy to insider information can further enhance your understanding of these proceedings. The skills you acquire here will not only refine your predictive framework but also embolden you to act with confidence. By the end of this chapter, you will be adept at reading the rhythm of public meetings, poised to seize opportunities before they become apparent to the untrained eye. The journey into this hidden world of public discourse promises not only to sharpen your acumen but also to fortify your strategic edge in the realm of infrastructure investment.

Identifying Key Committees and Boards to Monitor

A crucial element in uncovering hidden investment opportunities within government infrastructure projects is understanding the influential committees and boards that drive key decisions. These entities are the gatekeepers of information, often holding the power to steer project directions and outcomes long before plans reach the public eye. By identifying the right committees and boards to monitor, investors can gain an early edge, positioning themselves ahead of market trends. This strategic observation allows for the anticipation of policy shifts and project approvals, creating a roadmap for informed investment decisions. Recognizing the intricate tapestry of government bodies involved in infrastructure planning is akin to possessing a treasure map, where each committee and board meeting holds the potential to reveal the next significant project that could influence market dynamics.

As we navigate this landscape, evaluating board agendas becomes essential for distilling strategic investment insights. Each agenda item can serve as a breadcrumb, hinting at future development priorities and budget allocations.

Understanding the nuances of these agendas requires not just a surface-level glance but a deep dive into the context and implications of each discussion point. Furthermore, analyzing the membership dynamics within these committees offers another layer of foresight. The individuals who sit on these boards often bring with them distinct priorities and influences that can sway decision-making processes. By examining who holds sway within these meetings, investors can better predict outcomes and strategically align their investments with upcoming developments. This nuanced understanding transforms the seemingly mundane proceedings of committee meetings into a rich source of actionable intelligence.

Understanding the Role of Influential Committees in Infrastructure Decisions

Committees wield significant influence over the trajectory of infrastructure projects, and understanding their role can unlock a treasure trove of investment opportunities. These entities hold the reins of decision-making, setting priorities and allocating resources that shape the future of public works. Their power isn't merely administrative; it's strategic. They guide the approval process and can fast-track or stall projects based on their objectives and the political landscape. A savvy investor can identify which committees hold sway by examining their jurisdiction, historical impact on projects, and current political dynamics. This insight provides a foundation for predicting which projects will likely receive green lights, offering a roadmap for timely investments.

One effective strategy to decode these influential bodies is to scrutinize their meeting agendas. Agendas are more than mere lists of topics; they are strategic blueprints that reveal where the committee's attention and resources are directed. A discerning eye will spot patterns in agenda items that align with broader government priorities or public policy shifts. For instance, if a committee consistently prioritizes sustainable urban development, it may indicate forthcoming investments in green infrastructure. By aligning one's investment strategy with these trends, investors can position themselves advantageously ahead of public announcements.

The dynamics of committee membership also play a crucial role in decision outcomes. Membership is often a reflection of the current political climate, with appointees bringing their biases and priorities to the table. Understanding the background, expertise, and affiliations of committee members can provide clues about the committee's direction and potential biases. For example, a board dominated by members with ties to the transportation sector might prioritize road and transit projects. By anticipating these inclinations, investors can forecast which infrastructure initiatives are likely to gain momentum and prepare to capitalize on these insights.

Recent studies suggest that committees are increasingly integrating technology and data analytics into their decision-making processes. This trend offers an added layer of complexity and opportunity for investors. By monitoring how committees leverage data to inform their choices, one can gain foresight into not only what projects are favored but also the innovative solutions being prioritized. This forward-thinking approach allows investors to align their portfolio with cutting-edge developments, staying ahead of the curve in a rapidly evolving infrastructure landscape.

To extract actionable insights, one might consider engaging in scenario analysis, envisioning how different committee decisions could impact future infrastructure landscapes. By posing questions like, "What if this committee prioritizes renewable energy projects over traditional infrastructure?" investors can explore various outcomes and prepare adaptable strategies. This proactive approach enables investors to remain agile, ready to seize opportunities as they arise, and provides a robust framework for navigating the complexities of government project planning.

Evaluating Board Agendas for Strategic Investment Insights

A board agenda is a treasure trove for discerning investors, offering a window into the strategic priorities and imminent decisions of influential committees.

Understanding how to effectively evaluate these agendas can transform these documents from mundane listings into powerful predictors of forthcoming infrastructure developments. By examining agenda items, one can discern patterns and detect shifts in focus that may indicate upcoming projects or policy changes likely to impact investment landscapes. For instance, recurrent discussions around urban transit upgrades or green energy initiatives suggest potential areas for growth and opportunity. Beyond the surface, the inclusion of particular topics can signal deeper strategic alignments or changes in governance priorities, offering astute investors a lead on where to direct their attention and resources.

To gain strategic insights, it's essential to decode the subtle cues embedded within agenda structures. Look for the allocation of time to specific agenda items, as it often reflects the importance placed on these issues by the board. Extended deliberations on particular topics may indicate contentious debates or significant upcoming decisions, both of which could have profound implications for future infrastructure undertakings. Additionally, the presence of special sessions or workshops dedicated to particular themes can reveal emerging priorities or new directions in policy. For example, a sudden focus on cybersecurity in infrastructure projects could imply upcoming investments in digital resilience technologies, providing a fertile ground for early investment opportunities.

Advanced analytics can further enhance the process of agenda evaluation. Natural language processing (NLP) tools can assist in identifying key themes and sentiments from large volumes of textual data, streamlining the detection of strategic shifts in board priorities. By employing these technologies, investors can automate the analysis of meeting agendas and cross-reference them with other data sources to identify correlations and potential causations. This approach not only saves time but also increases the accuracy of predictions, allowing investors to act swiftly and confidently. As technology continues to evolve, staying abreast of these innovations and incorporating them into investment strategies can offer a significant edge in anticipating market movements.

Fostering connections with individuals familiar with board dynamics can provide additional layers of insight. Board members, administrative staff, or even attendees of these meetings often possess nuanced understandings of agenda items that are not immediately apparent from public documents. Cultivating these relationships can yield valuable context, enabling investors to interpret agenda items with greater depth and precision. By understanding the motivations and inclinations of those involved in decision-making processes, investors can better anticipate the outcomes and ramifications of board actions. Developing a network of informed contacts not only enriches one's analysis but also facilitates access to exclusive information that might otherwise remain obscure.

Evaluating board agendas is not merely about observing the present but also about anticipating the future. By critically engaging with these documents, investors can identify nascent trends and emerging themes before they become widely recognized. This foresight allows them to position themselves advantageously, capitalizing on opportunities that others may overlook. As infrastructure projects continue to evolve in complexity and scope, the ability to decode board agendas and derive actionable insights will remain a crucial skill for any investor seeking to stay ahead of the curve. Embracing a proactive and inquisitive approach, while continuously refining one's analytical toolkit, ensures that investors are well-equipped to navigate the ever-changing landscape of infrastructure investment.

Analyzing Membership Dynamics to Predict Decision Outcomes

Recognizing the intricate dynamics within committee and board memberships can significantly elevate one's strategic investment foresight. Each member brings unique expertise, biases, and affiliations that can influence decision-making processes. Scrutinizing these elements allows investors to anticipate potential outcomes of infrastructure projects. For instance, a board predominantly composed of members with backgrounds in environmental advocacy might prioritize sustainable development, while a committee with strong ties to the construction industry might lean towards rapid urban expansion. Understanding these nuances necessitates not only a study of professional backgrounds but also an analysis of previous voting patterns and public statements. This deeper comprehension equips investors to predict the trajectory of discussions and decisions, offering a strategic edge in anticipating market shifts.

A nuanced approach involves evaluating the interplay of power and influence within these groups. Power dynamics often dictate the direction of infrastructure planning, with certain members wielding more sway due to their seniority, expertise, or political clout. Recognizing these power centers can help forecast which proposals are likely to gain traction. Observing alliances and rivalries within the board can also provide valuable insights. For instance, if a highly influential member consistently aligns with a particular faction, this could signal the faction's growing influence on decision-making. Investors can leverage this information to adjust their strategies, aligning their investments with the anticipated outcomes of board decisions.

It is equally important to consider the external pressures that may affect board members. Political shifts, public opinion, and economic considerations can all impact how a member votes or champions specific initiatives. By staying informed about broader socio-political trends and understanding how these factors might sway decision-makers, investors can refine their predictions. For example, a surge in public demand for renewable energy might prompt previously reluctant board members to support green infrastructure projects. This adaptability in reading external factors and how they intersect with membership dynamics is crucial for staying ahead in the investment game.

Advanced investors often build comprehensive profiles of board members, combining publicly available information with insights gleaned from industry networks. This involves tracking career trajectories, affiliations, and even social media activity to gain a holistic view of each member's potential influence. Furthermore, engaging with professional circles and attending relevant industry events can provide firsthand insights into the priorities and inclinations of key figures. Such proactive networking not only enhances one's understanding of board dynamics but also opens avenues for collaboration or influence, presenting opportunities for strategic partnerships or advocacy.

As investors hone their ability to analyze membership dynamics, they should continually question and test their assumptions, fostering a mindset of critical inquiry. Are there emerging leaders within the board poised to shift the balance of power? How might recent appointments alter the decision-making landscape? By posing these thought-provoking questions and seeking diverse perspectives, investors can remain agile and responsive, ready to capitalize on the evolving landscape of infrastructure development. This proactive and informed approach ensures that they are not merely reacting to changes but are strategically positioned to anticipate and benefit from them.

How to Leverage Public Comment Periods

Public comment periods present a hidden treasure trove for investors willing to sift through the layers of public discourse to unearth valuable insights. At the heart of these seemingly mundane sessions lies a dynamic arena where community voices and government intentions intersect, revealing subtle hints of future developments. These gatherings are more than just platforms for civic engagement; they serve as early indicators of the direction in which local and regional projects might head. By tuning into the nuanced exchanges between stakeholders and officials, investors can glean information that might otherwise remain obscured in formal documents. This is where the art of listening becomes a strategic skill, allowing one to discern which voices hold sway and which emerging themes might signal shifts in policy or project priorities. As public comment periods unfold, they offer a window into the collective consciousness surrounding infrastructure projects, presenting astute observers with a unique opportunity to position themselves ahead of the curve.

Understanding the dynamics at play during these comment periods requires a keen ear for identifying the movers and shakers within the community—the key stakeholders whose opinions and interests often shape outcomes. Analyzing the feedback offered during these discussions can reveal patterns and sentiments that forecast policy shifts, providing a predictive edge. Engaging with these insights not only enhances one's ability to anticipate changes but also enriches the broader predictive framework outlined earlier in the book. As we navigate through the following subtopics, we'll explore how to pinpoint influential voices, decode the signals embedded in public discourse, and translate these into actionable investment strategies. This knowledge empowers investors to transform the abstract chatter of public meetings into tangible financial opportunities, solidifying their position in the competitive realm of infrastructure investment.

Identifying Key Stakeholders and Their Interests

Engaging with public comment periods in infrastructure planning requires an astute identification of key stakeholders and their interests. These stakeholders often include government officials, local businesses, community leaders, environmental groups, and private investors, each with distinct priorities that can significantly influence project outcomes. Recognizing who these players are and understanding their motivations is crucial for investors seeking to anticipate shifts in infrastructure projects. For instance, a local business association may lobby for improvements that enhance commercial accessibility, while environmental groups might push for sustainable practices, potentially altering project timelines or scopes. By mapping out the interests and power dynamics of these stakeholders, investors can gain a nuanced understanding of the likely trajectory of infrastructure plans, allowing them to position themselves advantageously.

To effectively identify stakeholders, investors should immerse themselves in the local context of each project. This involves attending public meetings, reviewing meeting minutes, and analyzing public records to discern the influential voices within the community. Advanced techniques such as network analysis can reveal connections between stakeholders, highlighting alliances or conflicts that might not be immediately obvious. Additionally, digital tools can assist in tracking social media discussions and news reports, offering insights into public sentiment and stakeholder priorities. By staying informed and engaged, investors can detect patterns and predict changes that might not yet be visible in official documents, providing them with a competitive edge.

Beyond merely identifying stakeholders, understanding their interests requires a deeper dive into their historical actions and stated objectives. This involves examining past projects they have influenced, public statements they have made, and any affiliations or partnerships that might affect their stance. For example, a construction company with a track record of supporting urban development projects may be a strong advocate for new infrastructure initiatives, while a community group with a history of opposing development could signal potential obstacles. By constructing a comprehensive profile of each stakeholder, investors can better anticipate how these interests might manifest in future planning decisions, enabling them to make informed investment choices.

An often-overlooked aspect of stakeholder analysis is the identification of emerging stakeholders—individuals or groups who may not yet wield significant influence but have the potential to do so. These might include new political figures, grassroots organizations, or industry disruptors. Keeping an eye on these emerging players can provide early warnings of shifts in the balance of power, allowing investors to adjust their strategies accordingly. For instance, a newly elected official with a strong infrastructure agenda could accelerate project timelines, while a growing activist group might introduce new regulatory hurdles. By staying vigilant and adaptable, investors can navigate the complex landscape of stakeholder interests with agility.

Investors should also consider the broader societal and economic trends that may impact stakeholder interests. For example, increasing awareness of climate change and sustainability is prompting many stakeholders to prioritize green infrastructure projects. Similarly, technological advancements are reshaping the priorities of both public and private entities, with smart infrastructure solutions gaining traction. By aligning their investment strategies with these overarching trends, investors can anticipate the evolving interests of stakeholders and position themselves to capitalize on future opportunities. This proactive approach not only enhances their ability to predict infrastructure developments but also ensures that their investments remain relevant and resilient in a rapidly changing world.

Analyzing Public Feedback for Investment Signals

In the vast arena of public meetings, the feedback offered during public comment periods often appears as a cacophony of voices. Yet, for the astute observer, this feedback holds a wealth of investment signals waiting to be unearthed. By attentively parsing these comments, one can discern patterns and trends that reveal public sentiment towards proposed infrastructure projects. This sentiment often precedes official decisions, providing a window into the potential trajectory of a project. A close examination of the language used by frequent commentators, especially those with vested interests or expertise, can yield insights into the undercurrents that might influence project outcomes. Recognizing these patterns involves more than just listening—it requires an analytical mindset that connects the dots between individual comments and the larger strategic picture.

Understanding the nuances of public feedback involves identifying key phrases and terms that suggest underlying concerns or support. These linguistic cues can indicate the level of resistance or enthusiasm a project might face, which can, in turn, affect its progress and the timing of its implementation. For instance, repeated mentions of environmental concerns might signal potential regulatory hurdles, while frequent expressions of economic benefit could imply favorable momentum. Sophisticated text analysis tools can assist investors in quantifying sentiment, transforming qualitative data into actionable insights. This approach not only sharpens an investor's predictive accuracy but also provides an edge over competitors who rely solely on official announcements and reports.

Beyond the immediate content of the comments, the context in which they are made is equally important. Public comment periods often coincide with critical junctures in the decision-making process, such as environmental reviews or budget allocations. By aligning feedback with these stages, investors can better anticipate shifts in project viability and timelines. For instance, a surge in public feedback during a budgetary review could indicate emerging concerns or support that might influence funding decisions. This contextual awareness allows investors to time their actions, whether by acquiring land, investing in related industries, or divesting from potentially troubled ventures.

Engaging with public feedback also involves recognizing the influence of stakeholder dynamics. Often, organized groups or influential individuals will attempt to steer public sentiment to align with their objectives. Understanding the motivations and strategies of these stakeholders can provide deeper insights into the likely success or failure of their advocacy efforts. By mapping out these relationships and their historical impact on similar projects, investors can develop a more nuanced understanding of the forces at play. This strategic foresight is invaluable in shaping investment decisions that are resilient to the volatile nature of public discourse.

Adopting a proactive approach to public feedback involves not just passive analysis but active participation. Engaging with the process by attending meetings, asking questions, or even contributing comments can provide firsthand insights and foster connections with key influencers. These interactions can enhance an investor's ability to interpret feedback with greater precision, turning public comment periods from a passive information source into a dynamic tool for strategic advantage. This proactive engagement, coupled with analytical rigor, equips investors to anticipate changes and capitalize on opportunities that others may overlook, transforming the cacophony of public discourse into a symphony of profitable insights.

Anticipating Policy Shifts Through Sentiment Trends

Public comment periods provide an invaluable opportunity for discerning investors to tap into the collective pulse of a community. These forums often reveal subtle sentiment trends that can foreshadow policy shifts before they are formally announced. By attentively listening to the voices of local stakeholders, one can glean insights into emerging priorities and concerns that might soon influence governmental decisions. For instance, a surge in comments advocating for sustainable infrastructure may indicate a forthcoming shift towards green projects. Such observations allow those with a keen eye to position themselves advantageously in anticipation of new regulations or funding allocations that prioritize environmental sustainability.

The analysis of sentiment trends during these comment periods requires a meticulous approach. Beyond simply tallying the number of comments for or against a proposal, investors should focus on the intensity and persuasiveness of the arguments presented. Patterns often emerge when examining the language used, emotional undertones, and the diversity of perspectives. For example, a unified demand for improved public transit solutions could reflect a growing public appetite for enhanced mobility options, signaling opportunities in related sectors. Identifying these patterns necessitates an understanding of linguistic cues and the ability to distinguish genuine grassroots movements from orchestrated campaigns.

Technological advancements have made it increasingly feasible to analyze sentiment trends on a larger scale. Natural language processing (NLP) tools, for instance, can decode the sentiment expressed in public comments, offering a quantitative assessment of public opinion. These tools can sift through thousands of comments, identifying common themes and detecting shifts in public mood over time. By employing such cutting-edge technology, investors can gain a more comprehensive understanding of community priorities, enabling them to anticipate policy adjustments with greater precision. This data-driven approach not only enhances predictive accuracy but also provides a competitive edge in the realm of infrastructure investment.

Incorporating sentiment analysis into one's investment strategy involves more than just technical prowess; it requires a nuanced understanding of the socio-political landscape. Investors should consider the historical context of public sentiments and the potential influence of external factors such as economic conditions, demographic changes, or technological advancements. Analyzing how these elements interact with public opinion can yield insights into the likelihood of policy shifts. For instance, in a region experiencing rapid population growth, public calls for expanded housing or transportation infrastructure might be particularly prescient. By connecting these dots, investors can develop a sophisticated framework for forecasting future policy directions.

To harness the full potential of sentiment trends, investors should actively engage with the communities they seek to understand. Attending public meetings, participating in discussions, and building relationships with local stakeholders can provide firsthand insights that complement automated sentiment analysis. This human element adds depth to the data, allowing investors to validate their interpretations and refine their strategies. By fostering these connections, investors can position themselves not just as observers but as informed participants in the evolving landscape of infrastructure development. This proactive approach enables them to capitalize on opportunities as they arise, turning public sentiment into a powerful tool for strategic investment.

Reading Between the Lines of Meeting Minutes

Starting with an overview of how public meetings can serve as a goldmine of information for those who know where to look, this section uncovers the art of deciphering the language hidden in the mundane. Imagine sitting in a dimly lit room, surrounded by a small group of individuals, each armed with their agendas and veiled intentions. The air is thick with jargon and procedural dialogue, but beneath the surface lies a treasure trove of insights waiting to be unearthed. These meetings, often open to the public yet overlooked, contain the seeds of future infrastructure projects. The nuances in conversation, the choice of words, and the subtle nods exchanged among stakeholders can reveal more than official documents ever will. This is the realm where astute investors can gain a distinct advantage, armed with the ability to read between the lines and anticipate the winds of change before they become gusts.

As we journey deeper into this topic, the focus shifts to identifying strategic language and coded terms that appear innocuous but can signify major developments on the horizon. These terms often act as signals, hinting at upcoming shifts in policy or priorities. Analyzing the interactions among stakeholders offers another layer of insight, as alliances and tensions play out in real-time, painting a vivid picture of potential outcomes. The financial discussions embedded in these meetings further provide clues about budgetary allocations and priorities, offering a glimpse into the fiscal roadmap of future projects. Together, these elements create a comprehensive framework for interpreting public meetings, transforming them from routine procedural gatherings into strategic intelligence hubs.

Identifying Strategic Language and Coded Terms in Meeting Minutes

Meeting minutes often serve as a treasure trove for those skilled in interpreting the nuanced language and coded terms used by officials. These documents may initially appear mundane, but a discerning eye can uncover strategic insights that precede public announcements. Words like "feasibility," "pilot," or "stakeholder consultation" can hint at nascent projects or shifts in policy direction. Similarly, seemingly innocuous references to "fiscal reassessment" or "prioritization review" might suggest impending budget reallocations or re-evaluations. By mastering the art of reading between the lines, investors can anticipate changes long before they are formally recognized, allowing them to position themselves advantageously.

Understanding the subtleties of language in meeting minutes involves recognizing patterns and recurring phrases that, although not explicit, often indicate significant developments. For instance, the consistent mention of "environmental impact assessments" may foreshadow infrastructure expansions or renovations. Additionally, phrases like "community engagement" or "public-private partnership exploration" can serve as precursors to major initiatives that require broad-based collaboration. By maintaining an updated lexicon of these strategic terms, astute investors can better predict which projects are likely to receive attention and resources, enabling them to make informed decisions.

The interactions between stakeholders, as recorded in meeting minutes, can also provide invaluable insights into potential project outcomes. Noting which parties are engaged in discussions and their respective stances can reveal underlying power dynamics and interests. For example, active participation from influential government agencies or private sector leaders might indicate a project's priority status. Conversely, noticeable absences or dissenting voices could signal challenges or delays. By analyzing these dynamics, investors can gauge the likelihood of project approval and allocate resources accordingly, minimizing risk while maximizing opportunity.

Financial discussions within meeting minutes often require a more sophisticated level of interpretation. Budgetary allocations and funding priorities might not always be explicitly stated, but key phrases and the context of discussions can offer clues. References to "reallocation of resources" or "funding realignment" could indicate shifts in financial focus, while detailed discussions on "cost-benefit analysis" might hint at projects nearing the execution stage. By honing the ability to decipher these financial nuances, investors can better forecast which sectors or projects will attract funding, allowing for strategic investment positioning.

For those eager to capitalize on these insights, it is crucial to cultivate a methodical approach to extracting and interpreting information from meeting minutes. Investing time in building a repertoire of strategic language and understanding its implications can lead to significant financial rewards. Furthermore, engaging in regular practice and cross-referencing findings with other public records or expert analyses can enhance one's predictive accuracy. This skillset, when combined with a robust network of informed contacts, forms a powerful toolkit for navigating the hidden yet lucrative world of government project planning.

Analyzing Stakeholder Interactions and Their Implications for Project Outcomes

Stakeholder interactions within public meetings can serve as a rich tapestry of insights that reveal underlying project dynamics and potential outcomes. Engaging with these interactions requires an astute ability to discern the nuances of communication, where the emphasis is placed not only on what is explicitly stated but also on what remains unsaid. Observing the mannerisms, tone, and emphasis of stakeholders during discussions can provide nuanced clues about their priorities and reservations. For instance, an unexpected shift in tone when discussing certain budgetary allocations may suggest underlying conflicts or hesitations that are not overtly articulated. By paying attention to these subtleties, investors can gain a deeper understanding of the project's potential trajectory and the likely hurdles it may encounter.

The composition of stakeholder groups often reflects the diversity of interests involved in a project, ranging from government officials and private sector representatives to community advocates and technical experts. Each participant brings a unique perspective and agenda, which can significantly influence the project's direction. By mapping out these relationships and understanding the power dynamics at play, investors can identify which stakeholders wield the most influence and how their interactions might shape project decisions. For example, a coalition between influential private companies and key government figures might expedite project approval processes, signaling a prime investment opportunity. Conversely, visible tension between community groups and policymakers could indicate potential delays or modifications, offering a different set of investment considerations.

Advanced insights can be drawn by analyzing patterns in stakeholder behavior over time. Historical data from past meetings can shed light on how similar interactions have previously influenced project outcomes. Investors can apply this knowledge to current scenarios, predicting how ongoing stakeholder dynamics might evolve. This form of predictive analysis is bolstered by staying informed about the latest research and trends in stakeholder engagement, which often highlight innovative strategies for conflict resolution and consensus-building. By leveraging such cutting-edge knowledge, investors can more accurately forecast the likelihood of a project's success and strategically position themselves to benefit from favorable outcomes.

Incorporating diverse perspectives is crucial for a holistic understanding of stakeholder interactions. While mainstream narratives often focus on the most vocal participants, it is equally important to consider the quieter voices that may represent significant yet underappreciated interests. Engaging with alternative viewpoints, such as those of environmental advocates or local community leaders, can unearth potential challenges that might not be immediately obvious. This comprehensive approach ensures that investors are not blindsided by overlooked factors that could impact project development. By fostering a dialogue with a broad spectrum of stakeholders, investors can preemptively address concerns, enhancing the viability and appeal of their investment strategies.

Actionable strategies emerge when investors translate these insights into practical steps. Building a network of contacts who attend these meetings regularly can provide access to firsthand information, fostering a deeper understanding of stakeholder dynamics. Encouraging open communication with these contacts can lead to timely updates on shifts in sentiment or focus areas. Additionally, investors can practice scenario planning, where they outline potential project trajectories based on observed interactions. This exercise not only sharpens predictive skills but also helps in crafting flexible investment plans that can adapt to changing circumstances. By continuously refining these strategies, investors can maintain a competitive edge, ensuring their actions are informed by the most relevant and comprehensive data available.

Deciphering Budgetary Allocations and Financial Prioritization from Discussion Highlights

Meeting minutes often serve as a goldmine of information for discerning investors keen on understanding budgetary allocations and financial prioritization within upcoming infrastructure projects. By closely examining these records, one can uncover the nuanced dynamics of financial decision-making processes. Stakeholders often communicate funding preferences through seemingly mundane discussions. For instance, repeated references to specific projects or initiatives can indicate a shift in budgetary focus, while seemingly inconsequential remarks might reveal underlying priorities. An attentive reader can identify these patterns and gauge the potential impact on investment opportunities.

The language and tone used during financial discussions can provide further insights into budgetary priorities. Strategic terms such as "priority funding," "critical infrastructure," or "emergency allocation" often hint at projects that may receive accelerated financial support. It's essential to analyze whether these terms are used consistently across multiple meetings, as this could signal a sustained commitment to certain projects. Such patterns may suggest a strategic pivot towards specific infrastructure enhancements, offering savvy investors a hint at where capital and resources might flow in the near future.

Analyzing the interactions and debates among stakeholders during financial discussions can yield valuable insights into the decision-making hierarchy and potential shifts in budget allocations. When key decision-makers express differing opinions or exhibit hesitation about approving certain financial plans, it can indicate underlying tensions or competing priorities. Understanding these dynamics enables investors to anticipate potential delays or accelerations in project timelines, allowing them to adjust their strategies accordingly. Being attuned to these subtleties can provide an edge in predicting which projects might gain traction and which might falter.

Deciphering budgetary allocations also requires understanding the broader economic and political context in which these decisions are made. Economic trends, policy changes, and public sentiment can all influence financial prioritization in infrastructure planning. For example, a government facing public pressure to address environmental concerns might prioritize sustainable infrastructure projects, redirecting funds from other areas. Staying informed about these external factors allows investors to predict shifts in financial focus and identify projects that align with both governmental priorities and market demand.

To translate these insights into actionable strategies, investors should develop a systematic approach to tracking and analyzing meeting minutes. This might involve creating a database of recurring themes, key phrases, and stakeholder positions over time. By maintaining an organized repository of insights gleaned from meeting minutes, investors can refine their predictive frameworks and enhance their capacity to spot lucrative opportunities early. This methodical approach, coupled with continuous monitoring of stakeholder behavior and financial language, ensures that investors remain at the forefront of infrastructure investment trends.

Building a Network of Insider Contacts

Building a network of insider contacts offers a rewarding yet complex avenue for uncovering early signals of forthcoming government infrastructure projects. This task, while challenging, is indispensable for those seeking to gain a competitive edge in the investment arena. The art of networking within this realm demands a strategic blend of skill, persistence, and ethical awareness. As you navigate this landscape, understanding how to effectively connect with key figures in government and industry becomes a powerful tool. These contacts can provide invaluable insights into the planning and execution of infrastructure projects, information that often remains hidden from public view until it's too late to capitalize on. The journey begins by pinpointing the right individuals who hold sway in decision-making processes or possess detailed knowledge of upcoming plans. Developing these relationships requires more than just exchanging business cards; it involves cultivating genuine, mutually beneficial connections that can lead to exclusive information and opportunities.

In the world of investment, access to timely, accurate data can mean the difference between success and missed opportunities. By weaving a web of relationships across professional networks and industry circles, investors can tap into a reservoir of insider knowledge that is both deep and broad. Each connection serves as a potential gateway to understanding the nuances of government infrastructure initiatives, from early planning stages to final approvals. Yet, as you build this network, ethical considerations must remain at the forefront. Navigating the fine line between gaining insight and breaching ethical boundaries is crucial. Approaching networking with integrity not only safeguards your reputation but also ensures that the information you gather is both legitimate and actionable. As these connections are nurtured and expanded, they become instrumental in forming a robust predictive framework, allowing for informed investment decisions well ahead of public announcements.

Leveraging Professional Networks to Access Key Government Contacts

Building a robust professional network is an essential strategy for gaining access to key government contacts, which can be a goldmine of information for those interested in predicting infrastructure developments. Harnessing these connections requires a nuanced understanding of both formal and informal networking opportunities. Many governmental and public sector professionals participate in industry conferences, workshops, and seminars. These events are invaluable for meeting influential figures who can provide insights into upcoming projects and priorities. Engaging with such gatherings demands more than just attendance; it requires active participation and intelligent dialogue, allowing you to stand out and be remembered among a sea of participants.

In today's digital age, social media platforms and online professional networks have become indispensable tools for establishing connections with government officials and industry experts. LinkedIn, for instance, offers unparalleled access to a global community of professionals, including those involved in governmental planning and infrastructure development. Joining groups and participating in discussions can facilitate introductions to individuals who possess the information you seek. Thoughtful engagement in these forums establishes you as a knowledgeable participant, increasing the likelihood that others will share valuable insights or direct you to relevant contacts.

Beyond digital platforms, cultivating relationships with intermediaries who already possess access to governmental circles can significantly expand your reach. These intermediaries might be consultants, lobbyists, or industry leaders who have established trust and credibility within governmental frameworks. Building rapport with such individuals involves offering genuine value in return, such as sharing your own expertise or insights. This reciprocal relationship can open doors to exclusive information about forthcoming public projects, which often remains concealed from the general public until late stages of planning.

Ethical considerations play a crucial role in developing these connections. While the aim is to gain insights into government plans, it's vital to navigate these relationships with integrity. Transparency about your intentions and adherence to legal and ethical standards will not only protect your reputation but also ensure long-term sustainability of your network. Ethical networking fosters trust, which is the foundation of any meaningful professional relationship. It's important to remember that respect for confidentiality and discretion is paramount in maintaining credibility among your contacts.

Critical thinking about the application of these networks can lead to actionable insights. For instance, consider how the knowledge gained from these contacts can be used to identify potential investment opportunities. Are there areas where government plans align with emerging technology sectors or urban development trends? Developing scenarios around these questions can guide strategic investment decisions. By continuously refining your approach and remaining adaptable to new information, you position yourself to capitalize on infrastructure developments long before they become apparent to the wider market.

Building Relationships with Industry Insiders for Exclusive Insights

Fostering alliances with industry insiders offers unparalleled access to insights that can significantly enhance one's ability to anticipate infrastructure developments. These relationships can be cultivated through participation in industry conferences, workshops, and networking events where professionals gather to discuss trends and projects. Engaging in thoughtful conversations and demonstrating genuine interest in the expertise of peers can lay the groundwork for lasting professional relationships. By actively participating in these circles, one can gain invaluable knowledge that is often not documented in public records, offering a competitive edge in predicting future opportunities.

Dialogue with industry experts often reveals unspoken nuances and unwritten rules that govern infrastructure planning. Insiders, such as engineers, project managers, and consultants, possess firsthand knowledge of timelines, technological advancements, and policy shifts that can influence project trajectories. By fostering trust and rapport with these individuals, one can access privileged information that goes beyond formal reports and announcements. A strategic approach involves identifying key players in relevant sectors and consistently engaging them in meaningful discussions, creating a two-way exchange of insights and information.

Navigating the landscape of insider information requires a nuanced understanding of ethical boundaries. It is crucial to maintain integrity while seeking insights, ensuring that all interactions adhere to legal and ethical standards. Transparency in intentions and a commitment to ethical networking can prevent conflicts of interest and maintain the credibility of one's investment strategies. By prioritizing mutual benefit and respecting professional boundaries, one can cultivate a network of insiders who are both willing and able to provide pivotal insights without compromising ethical standards.

In the fast-evolving realm of infrastructure, the ability to discern subtle shifts and emerging trends is invaluable. Building relationships with insiders enables a deeper understanding of the factors driving industry changes, such as innovative technologies or regulatory adjustments. These connections can illuminate the implications of broader economic or political developments on specific projects, offering a more comprehensive view of the landscape. By staying attuned to the intricate dynamics of the industry, one can better anticipate where and when to direct investments for maximum impact.

To capitalize on these relationships, consider integrating insights gained from industry insiders into a broader predictive framework. Use this privileged knowledge to enhance analyses of public documents, budgets, and planning signals. By connecting the dots between insider insights and public information, one can develop a refined strategy that anticipates not only what is likely to happen but also why and how it will unfold. This approach not only empowers more informed decision-making but also strengthens one's overall investment acumen in the infrastructure domain.

Navigating Ethical Considerations in Insider Networking

Establishing and maintaining ethical boundaries in insider networking is crucial for anyone seeking to leverage contacts in government infrastructure projects. Trustworthiness and integrity form the bedrock of effective networks, ensuring that information exchange remains within legal and moral confines. While cultivating relationships with key individuals can open doors to valuable insights, it is essential to navigate these interactions with a clear understanding of what constitutes ethical behavior. For instance, maintaining transparency in communication and avoiding any actions that might be perceived as coercive or manipulative is paramount. Upholding such standards not only safeguards your reputation but also fosters long-term professional relationships built on mutual respect and trust.

Engaging with professional networks requires a nuanced approach, where ethical considerations are not merely an afterthought but a guiding principle. As you seek insights from government insiders, it's important to recognize the fine line between legitimate information gathering and exploitation of privileged access. This involves adhering to relevant laws and regulations, such as those pertaining to lobbying or the handling of non-public information. For example, attending public forums and seeking information shared openly is acceptable, whereas pushing for confidential details that breach protocol is not. This distinction ensures that your actions remain within ethical boundaries, thereby preventing potential legal repercussions and safeguarding the integrity of your network.

Building alliances with industry insiders demands a strategy that is both respectful and reciprocal. In cultivating these relationships, consider the value you bring to the table, ensuring that interactions are mutually beneficial. This could involve sharing industry insights, offering consultation, or facilitating introductions to other valuable contacts. Such reciprocity not only strengthens your network but also reinforces an ethical framework where both parties gain from the relationship without crossing any moral lines. In this context, consider the role of empathy and understanding in these interactions, where recognizing and respecting the priorities and constraints of your contacts can enhance the quality and longevity of your professional connections.

While ethical networking offers paths to valuable information, it also demands vigilant self-awareness and continuous reflection. Assessing your motives and actions regularly can help maintain ethical standards. Consider scenarios where your decisions might impact your reputation or the trust of your contacts. Engaging in reflective practices, such as maintaining a journal of interactions or seeking feedback from peers, can help identify any potential ethical lapses and reinforce your commitment to integrity. This proactive approach ensures that your networking strategies align with both your personal values and the broader ethical standards of the industry.

As you develop your network, it's important to remain adaptable and responsive to the evolving landscape of government and industry regulations. Stay informed about changes in compliance requirements and best practices through continuous education and engagement with professional ethics seminars or workshops. This commitment to ongoing learning ensures that your networking activities remain informed and compliant, allowing you to capitalize on opportunities without jeopardizing your professional standing. By prioritizing ethical considerations and maintaining a vigilant approach to networking, you can turn insider contacts into a powerful, yet principled, tool for forecasting and capitalizing on future infrastructure developments.

Drawing insights from public meetings is a powerful tool in the investor's arsenal, offering a glimpse into the often obscured world of governmental planning. By identifying key committees and boards to monitor, investors can focus their attention on the most impactful discussions. Engaging proactively during public comment periods not only provides valuable insights but also establishes a presence in these critical dialogues. The ability to read between the lines of meeting minutes allows for the extraction of nuanced information that can signal future developments. Building a network of insider contacts enhances this process, offering direct access to firsthand perspectives and potentially undisclosed plans. Collectively, these strategies form a robust framework for predicting infrastructure trends, empowering investors to make informed decisions ahead of the curve. As we move forward, consider how these early warning signals can be integrated with other predictive tools discussed in the book, expanding your capacity to anticipate and capitalize on emerging opportunities. How will you apply these insights to refine your investment strategy and stay ahead in a rapidly evolving landscape?

Chapter Nine

Predicting Transit Corridors and Nodes

In the midst of a lively intersection, the steady rhythm of construction signals the arrival of a new transit line. This scene is not just a glimpse into the future of urban mobility but a potential goldmine for those who can read the signs. The expansion of transit corridors is more than just an infrastructure upgrade; it's a blueprint for economic transformation. Savvy investors recognize the hidden opportunities that transit developments bring, often leading to booming neighborhoods and surging property values long before the first train even arrives.

Throughout history, transit systems have been the arteries of urban growth, breathing life into once-overlooked areas and connecting them to the heartbeat of the city. By understanding the mechanics behind transit-oriented development, you can position yourself at the forefront of a lucrative wave of change. This chapter unravels the intricate dance of economics and logistics that drives these projects, revealing the subtle cues that hint at future transit expansions. These are the whispers of opportunity that, when detected early, can guide you to strategic investments with substantial returns.

In this exploration, you'll discover how to track the often-concealed plans of transit authorities, pinpointing the future hubs that will redefine urban landscapes. The potential ripple effects of these transit upgrades extend far beyond transportation, impacting real estate markets and community dynamics in profound ways. By the end of this chapter, you'll be equipped with the knowledge to not only decipher these developments but also harness their transformative power to bolster your investment strategy. As cities evolve, so too can your portfolio, flourishing alongside the new transit veins that promise to reshape tomorrow's cities.

The Economics of Transit-Oriented Development

In recent years, the concept of transit-oriented development (TOD) has rapidly transformed from a niche urban planning approach to a cornerstone of modern city design. This shift is not merely a trend but a reflection of profound changes in how cities and their inhabitants function. By integrating residential, commercial, and recreational spaces within walking distance of public transit, TOD aims to create vibrant, sustainable communities that thrive on accessibility and convenience. As cities grapple with challenges like congestion and pollution, the allure of transit-oriented living becomes more compelling. The strategic placement of transit corridors and nodes breathes new life into urban areas, catalyzing economic growth and reshaping the landscape of real estate investment. Understanding the dynamics of TOD is crucial for those eager to capitalize on the economic ripples it sends through both property markets and local economies.

Within this vibrant context, the value of land in transit zones often experiences a remarkable uplift, drawing attention from investors and developers alike. As transit nodes emerge, local businesses and communities undergo significant economic shifts, benefiting from increased foot traffic and enhanced accessibility. The promise of long-term investment returns in mixed-use developments becomes a tantalizing prospect, driven by the synergy between transit infrastructure and urban growth. This chapter will unravel the economic intricacies of transit-oriented development, offering insights into how land values change, businesses flourish, and investment potentials evolve in these dynamic areas. As we explore these themes, the transformative power of transit upgrades on real estate markets will become evident, revealing a landscape ripe with opportunities for the astute investor.

Analyzing Land Value Uplift in Transit Zones

Understanding the dynamics of land value uplift in transit zones offers a strategic vantage point for investors looking to capitalize on transit-oriented development. The introduction of new transit infrastructure often acts as a catalyst, significantly boosting the desirability and value of nearby properties. This phenomenon arises from improved accessibility and reduced travel times, which in turn attract a diverse range of residents and businesses. Investors can gain an edge by identifying areas poised for such uplift, focusing on regions where transit expansions are planned but not yet widely publicized. This foresight allows for strategic acquisitions before the broader market recognizes the potential, thus maximizing returns.

Research reveals that land value uplift is not uniform across all transit zones, necessitating a nuanced approach to analysis. Factors such as the existing urban fabric, demographic trends, and local policy frameworks play crucial roles in determining the extent of value appreciation. For instance, a study conducted in multiple metropolitan areas highlighted that neighborhoods with a strong mix of residential, commercial, and recreational amenities tend to experience more pronounced value increases. Investors should therefore assess the holistic ecosystem of a transit zone, considering how new transit access may integrate with and enhance existing amenities and infrastructure.

The ripple effects of transit-oriented development extend beyond mere property value increases, profoundly influencing local economies. As transit zones evolve, they often become magnets for economic activity, invigorating local businesses and energizing community life. This economic rejuvenation can manifest in various forms, from increased foot traffic for local retailers to a rise in employment opportunities as new businesses emerge. Investors should consider these broader economic impacts, recognizing that the success of transit-oriented investments often hinges on the vitality and resilience of the surrounding community. By fostering relationships with local stakeholders and understanding community dynamics, investors can better anticipate shifts in demand and align their strategies accordingly.

Advanced data analytics and geographic information systems (GIS) are instrumental tools for investors seeking to quantify and predict land value uplift in transit zones. These technologies enable a granular analysis of spatial data, offering insights into patterns and trends that may not be immediately apparent. By leveraging these tools, investors can model potential scenarios and visualize the future landscape of transit zones, aiding in informed decision-making. Additionally, recent advancements in machine learning algorithms provide the capability to process vast datasets, uncovering hidden correlations between transit developments and land value changes. Embracing these cutting-edge technologies equips investors with a formidable toolkit for navigating the complexities of transit-oriented investment.

Imagining future scenarios involving transit development invites investors to engage with thought-provoking questions that challenge conventional wisdom. What might the social fabric of a community look like once a transit hub becomes operational? How could shifts in land use policy impact the trajectory of land value uplift? By pondering these questions, investors can cultivate a forward-thinking mindset, refining their ability to anticipate and adapt to change. Actionable steps such as participating in public planning meetings, engaging with urban planners, and monitoring policy shifts provide practical pathways to staying ahead in the ever-evolving landscape of transit-oriented development. Through informed action and strategic foresight, investors can position themselves to not only profit but also contribute positively to the communities they invest in.

Assessing Economic Impact on Local Businesses and Communities

Transit-oriented development (TOD) has increasingly become a focal point in city planning, transforming how local businesses and communities interact with infrastructure enhancements. As transport nodes evolve, they act as catalysts for economic dynamism, presenting unique opportunities and challenges for the surrounding areas. Businesses often witness an uptick in foot traffic, driven by the increased accessibility that transit upgrades provide. A well-placed café, for instance, can flourish with the influx of commuters, while retail spaces may see a surge in demand as accessibility improves. However, it's crucial for investors and stakeholders to anticipate the nuanced shifts in consumer behavior and adapt business models accordingly to maximize the benefits of these infrastructural transformations.

Neighborhoods near transit corridors frequently experience a renaissance as improved connectivity attracts a diverse demographic, including young professionals and families seeking convenient urban living. This influx can stimulate local economies, fostering a vibrant community atmosphere. Yet, these changes can also lead to gentrification, shifting the cultural and socioeconomic fabric of the area. It becomes imperative for investors to recognize these patterns early, aligning their ventures to not only capitalize on rising property values but also contribute positively to community resilience. Engaging with local stakeholders, understanding community needs, and supporting inclusive growth can yield long-term benefits both economically and socially.

Understanding the economic ramifications of transit developments extends beyond immediate commercial gains. Longitudinal studies indicate that enhanced transit accessibility can lead to sustained economic uplift by attracting new businesses and encouraging existing ones to expand. The proximity to reliable transit options reduces transportation costs for employees and customers alike, further enhancing the appeal of these locales for business operations. Local governments often support such growth through incentives, creating a symbiotic relationship between public policy and private investment. Investors who remain attuned to these dynamics can position themselves strategically, aligning their investments with policy trends to harness maximum returns.

A forward-thinking approach entails not only recognizing the immediate economic impact but also forecasting the long-term evolution of transit-oriented zones. The introduction of innovative mobility solutions, such as electric buses or autonomous shuttles, can further revolutionize these areas. Investors should keep abreast of cutting-edge research and technological advancements in urban mobility, which can redefine the value propositions of transit zones. By anticipating these shifts, stakeholders can adapt investment strategies to align with future infrastructural paradigms, ensuring sustained relevance and profitability in an ever-evolving urban landscape.

Considering the ripple effect of transit enhancements, it becomes clear that the economic impact on local businesses and communities is multifaceted and dynamic. Investors and community leaders must engage in proactive planning and strategic foresight to navigate this complexity effectively. By fostering partnerships with municipal authorities, leveraging data analytics to predict trends, and committing to sustainable development practices, stakeholders can unlock the full potential of transit-oriented growth. This approach not only promises lucrative returns but also contributes to the creation of resilient, thriving communities where businesses and residents alike can prosper.

Evaluating Long-Term Investment Returns in Mixed-Use Developments

The prospect of investing in mixed-use developments that capitalize on transit-oriented growth presents a compelling opportunity for long-term investors. With urbanization accelerating and cities prioritizing sustainable transportation solutions, these mixed-use projects often become focal points of revitalization, creating vibrant communities that integrate residential, commercial, and recreational spaces. By understanding the unique dynamics of these developments, investors can position themselves to capture substantial returns over time. One key aspect is the synergy between transit accessibility and land use, which can significantly enhance property values and attract diverse tenant profiles. This blend of accessibility, convenience, and community appeal often results in higher occupancy rates and rental yields, which contribute to the overall financial viability of such investments.

Advanced insights into transit-oriented mixed-use developments reveal that these projects often serve as catalysts for broader economic activity, extending benefits beyond the immediate vicinity. For instance, enhanced connectivity attracts businesses seeking easy access for employees and customers, thus boosting local economies. Research indicates that commercial establishments in proximity to transit hubs experience increased foot traffic, translating into higher sales and revenue growth. Investors should consider the potential for positive externalities, such as improved infrastructure and public services, which can further enhance the attractiveness of these areas. Additionally, mixed-use developments often contribute to social sustainability by offering amenities that promote walkability and reduce car dependency, aligning with contemporary lifestyle preferences.

While the potential for long-term gains is substantial, investors must carefully evaluate risk factors associated with mixed-use developments. Market volatility, regulatory changes, and shifting demographic trends can impact project viability. A thorough due diligence process should include an analysis of local zoning laws, potential environmental concerns, and the financial health of development partners. Investors should also assess the adaptability of these projects to evolving market conditions, ensuring that they can withstand economic fluctuations and continue to meet consumer demands. Diversification within a mixed-use investment portfolio can mitigate these risks, offering a balanced approach that leverages multiple revenue streams while safeguarding against sector-specific downturns.

Recent trends in smart city initiatives provide another layer of opportunity for investors in transit-oriented developments. The integration of technology into urban planning is transforming how mixed-use projects are conceptualized and executed. Features such as energy-efficient buildings, smart utilities, and digital connectivity are increasingly becoming standard, enhancing the appeal of these developments to tech-savvy residents and businesses. Investors who recognize and incorporate these innovations can differentiate their offerings in the marketplace, potentially commanding premium rents and prices. Keeping abreast of technological advancements and their application in urban environments is essential for investors seeking to maximize returns in this dynamic field.

Engaging with the complexities of transit-oriented mixed-use developments requires both strategic foresight and a willingness to embrace novel concepts. Investors should consider scenarios where shifting urban policies favor increased density and mixed land use, prompting municipalities to offer incentives for such projects. Engaging with community stakeholders and understanding local priorities can offer valuable insights into future development plans, allowing investors to anticipate trends before they materialize fully. By fostering relationships with municipal planners and participating in public forums, investors can gain a competitive edge, positioning themselves as informed contributors to the sustainable growth of transit-oriented communities.

How to Track Transit Expansion Projects

Picture a world where urban landscapes are in constant flux, their evolution dictated by the invisible hand of transit expansion. In this dynamic environment, the key to unlocking future investment opportunities lies in understanding and anticipating the pathways of transit growth. As cities strive to accommodate burgeoning populations and reduce their carbon footprints, the expansion of transit corridors becomes not only a response to current demands but also a harbinger of economic opportunities. These projects, often outlined in complex governmental documents and detailed in transit authority reports, are a treasure trove for those with the acumen to decipher them. Recognizing the patterns and signals of transit development can transform seemingly mundane data into a powerful tool for predicting the next wave of urban growth, setting the stage for lucrative ventures and strategic investments.

The journey through the intricacies of transit expansion begins with harnessing the wealth of open data and insights found within transit authority reports. This information provides a foundation for understanding the scope and impact of upcoming projects. Next, the nuanced layers of environmental impact statements and community feedback offer a deeper, more localized perspective on potential developments, reflecting both the aspirations and concerns of affected communities. Monitoring legislative proposals and budget allocations completes this triad of investigation, revealing the political will and financial commitments behind transit projects. With these tools in hand, readers are equipped to navigate the complexities of governmental planning, turning what once seemed like an impenetrable web of information into a clear map of future opportunities.

Leveraging Open Data and Transit Authority Reports

Open data has transformed the landscape of transit planning, offering a treasure trove of information for discerning investors. By meticulously analyzing datasets released by transit authorities, one can uncover patterns and projections that hint at future expansion efforts. These datasets often include ridership statistics, service frequency, and maintenance schedules, which, when examined collectively, provide a nuanced picture of where expansions might be headed. For instance, a consistent uptick in passenger numbers on a particular line could signal the need for additional service or infrastructure upgrades. Pairing this with demographic trends and urban growth forecasts can sharpen an investor's ability to anticipate new transit projects long before they are officially announced.

Transit authority reports are another invaluable resource for those seeking to forecast transit expansion. These reports typically include strategic plans, performance reviews, and budget outlines, offering a window into future priorities and projects. By scrutinizing these documents, investors can gain insights into the political and financial underpinnings of transit decisions. A report detailing the allocation of funds for feasibility studies or preliminary engineering on a specific corridor, for example, could indicate impending developments. Additionally, understanding the language and terminology used in these reports is crucial, as it can reveal subtle hints about the likelihood and timing of proposed projects.

A growing trend in transit planning is the integration of advanced analytics and machine learning to model expansion scenarios. By leveraging these cutting-edge technologies, transit authorities can simulate various outcomes and adjust their strategies accordingly. Investors who stay abreast of these technological advancements can better interpret the implications of transit data and reports. For example, machine learning algorithms might identify underutilized routes with potential for redevelopment, offering early signals to savvy investors. Engaging with these technologies not only enhances predictive accuracy but also provides a competitive edge in identifying lucrative opportunities.

Taking a broader perspective, it's essential to consider the role of public sentiment and community involvement in shaping transit projects. Open data platforms often include community feedback and public meeting notes, which can influence the direction and scope of transit expansions. Investors who pay attention to these elements can detect grassroots support or opposition, which can significantly impact project timelines and outcomes. Understanding the local political climate and community priorities can therefore provide critical context for interpreting open data and transit authority reports, allowing for more informed investment decisions.

Reflecting on these insights, investors are encouraged to develop a systematic approach to tracking transit data and reports. This involves creating a framework for regular analysis and cross-referencing of various data sources, enabling the identification of emerging trends and opportunities. By establishing a routine that incorporates these practices, investors can position themselves to capitalize on transit expansions, enhancing their ability to make strategic, data-driven decisions. This proactive approach not only demystifies the complexities of transit planning but also empowers investors to act with confidence and foresight.

Analyzing Environmental Impact Statements and Community Feedback

Environmental Impact Statements (EIS) and community feedback represent pivotal resources for those aiming to anticipate transit expansion projects. An EIS provides a comprehensive analysis of the potential environmental consequences associated with proposed infrastructure developments. These documents, mandated by government regulations, offer an intricate understanding of a project's scope, potential challenges, and timelines. As they detail everything from anticipated traffic changes to ecological impacts, savvy investors gain an early glimpse into which areas might become future transit nodes. By methodically dissecting an EIS, one can identify not only the direct impacts outlined but also the broader implications for surrounding areas, including potential zoning changes and public sentiment.

Community feedback, often gathered during public consultations and hearings, serves as a real-time barometer for local sentiment towards transit projects. Engaging with this feedback provides a nuanced perspective on the community's priorities and concerns, which can significantly influence the progression and adaptation of transit projects. For instance, strong community opposition might delay or alter a planned expansion, while overwhelming support can expedite approval processes. Understanding these dynamics allows investors to better anticipate the feasibility and timing of projects. This insight is invaluable for anyone seeking to align their investment strategies with the anticipated outcomes of transit developments.

Incorporating both EIS and community feedback into one's analytical toolkit involves more than just passive observation. It requires active engagement with available data and reports, alongside an understanding of the socio-political landscape influencing these projects. Advanced investors might cross-reference EIS details with municipal zoning plans, seeking discrepancies or alignments that suggest forthcoming changes. This approach not only sharpens predictive accuracy but also positions investors to capitalize on opportunities that others might overlook, particularly in areas where policy shifts are likely to impact property valuations significantly.

The interplay between environmental assessments and public opinion often reveals underlying trends and emerging opportunities in transit-oriented development. For instance, a recurring theme in community feedback might highlight the demand for green spaces or affordable housing near transit hubs. Such insights can guide strategic investment in properties that align with these emerging community needs, potentially increasing both their desirability and value. Additionally, recognizing patterns in EIS reports across different projects can inform predictions about future transit corridors, enabling a proactive investment approach in areas primed for development.

When navigating these complex dimensions, it's crucial to remain adaptable and open to evolving narratives. While EIS documents and community feedback offer a wealth of information, they are aspects of a larger puzzle. Investors should remain vigilant, continuously updating their framework with new data and insights, ensuring their strategies remain aligned with the latest developments and community sentiment. This proactive approach not only mitigates risk but also enhances the potential for substantial returns in the dynamic landscape of transit-related investments. Encouraging critical thinking and adaptability, these insights empower readers to transform regulatory and community data into strategic action, ensuring they remain ahead in the ever-evolving field of infrastructure investment.

Monitoring Legislative Proposals and Budget Allocations

Navigating the intricate world of legislative proposals and budget allocations is akin to deciphering a complex puzzle, where each piece reveals significant insights into forthcoming transit projects. This subtopic unveils the art of interpreting the often-overlooked nuances within legislative documents, providing readers with the tools necessary to anticipate infrastructure expansions. Understanding the legislative process is critical, as it highlights the intentions and priorities of policymakers, offering a glimpse into future transit developments.

By scrutinizing these proposals, savvy investors can identify key trends and shifts in transit planning, positioning themselves ahead of market changes.

Diving into the specifics of budget allocations offers a wealth of information that goes beyond the numbers. Budget documents serve as a strategic blueprint, detailing the financial priorities of transit authorities and revealing where substantial investments will be made. By examining the allocations, investors can pinpoint which projects are likely to receive the necessary funding and support to move forward. This insight is invaluable for predicting the direction of transit growth, enabling readers to make informed decisions about potential investment opportunities. Moreover, understanding the budgetary process provides a framework for evaluating the feasibility and timeline of proposed projects, further refining investment strategies.

A critical approach involves the synthesis of legislative and budgetary information with broader economic and demographic data. This integration allows for a more comprehensive understanding of how transit projects align with regional growth patterns and policy objectives. By correlating these data points, readers can identify areas where transit investments are likely to spur economic development and urban revitalization. This holistic perspective not only enhances the accuracy of predictions but also equips investors with the foresight needed to capitalize on emerging transit corridors, turning legislative insights into tangible investment gains.

In addition to the technical analysis, actively engaging with the legislative process can yield unique advantages. Attending public hearings, engaging in community discussions, and networking with policymakers provide firsthand insights that are often not captured in official documents. This proactive involvement enables investors to gauge the political climate and community sentiment surrounding transit projects, offering additional layers of understanding. Such engagement can reveal potential obstacles or accelerators for project implementation, allowing for more nuanced investment strategies that account for both opportunities and risks.

Encouraging readers to adopt a forward-thinking mindset, this subtopic challenges conventional approaches to infrastructure investment. By leveraging legislative and budgetary insights, investors can shift from reactive to proactive strategies, identifying opportunities before they become widely recognized. The ability to anticipate transit developments not only enhances investment outcomes but also contributes to sustainable urban growth, aligning financial success with broader societal benefits. This subtopic lays the groundwork for a strategic, informed approach to infrastructure investing, empowering readers to seize opportunities that others might overlook.

Spotting Future Transit Hubs and Stations

Imagine a bustling cityscape where the hum of daily life is inextricably linked to the rhythm of its transit systems. In these urban jungles, transit hubs and stations serve as the lifelines, not merely connecting people to places but catalyzing entire ecosystems of opportunity. The advent of a new transit line or station can transform a sleepy neighborhood into a vibrant community hub, sparking a metamorphosis that attracts businesses, residents, and investors alike. The key to unlocking this potential lies in the ability to spot these future transit nodes before they materialize on the city map. It's a skill akin to peering into a crystal ball, but with the backing of data, insight, and a keen understanding of urban dynamics.

This chapter invites you to embark on a journey through the art and science of identifying these pivotal sites. We'll traverse the intricate tapestry of urban growth patterns and demographic shifts, offering a lens through which to view the subtle yet telling signs of impending transit developments. With an eye on policy changes and government priorities, we'll decode the often cryptic signals that hint at where the next transit hub might sprout. Finally, we'll explore the role of technological innovations in transportation planning, showcasing how these advancements can illuminate new pathways in infrastructure development. As we navigate these themes, you'll gain the foresight to anticipate the ripple effects of transit upgrades, positioning yourself to seize opportunities before they become apparent to the broader market.

Analyzing Urban Growth Patterns and Demographic Shifts

Urban growth patterns and demographic shifts offer insightful clues for predicting future transit hubs and stations. As cities expand and their populations evolve, infrastructure demands inevitably follow. Emerging urban centers often exhibit distinct patterns such as increased density in certain neighborhoods, shifts in population demographics, and economic diversification. These elements can signal the necessity for new transit solutions or enhancements to existing systems. By closely examining these trends, one can infer where transit authorities might focus their efforts next. For instance, a surge in young professionals moving into a previously residential area may indicate a future transit node, as this demographic often relies heavily on public transportation. This kind of pattern recognition is crucial in forecasting transit developments, enabling investors to make informed decisions ahead of the curve.

Recent advancements in data analytics have transformed the way urban growth is analyzed. Technologies that harness big data allow for nuanced insights into population movements and density changes. Real-time data from sources like mobile phone usage, social media activity, and GPS tracking provide an intricate map of how people interact with their urban environments. Such data can reveal undercurrents of change not immediately apparent through traditional methods. For example, a sustained increase in ride-sharing services in a particular district could presage a need for enhanced public transit options there. These advanced tools enhance the ability to predict where transit infrastructure is not only beneficial but essential, offering a strategic advantage to those who utilize them.

Demographic shifts not only inform where transit changes might occur but also how they might be structured. The aging population in many developed nations has prompted a reevaluation of transit needs, with an emphasis on accessibility and convenience. Meanwhile, younger generations prioritize sustainability and technology integration in public services. Understanding these preferences helps forecast transit developments that align with demographic expectations. An area with a burgeoning elderly population might see the introduction of more accessible transit options, while tech-savvy neighborhoods could be early adopters of smart transit solutions. Recognizing these nuances allows for a more precise anticipation of infrastructure projects, providing a roadmap for strategic investment opportunities.

Understanding policy changes and government priorities is equally vital in predicting transit hubs. Legislative shifts often reflect broader societal trends, and infrastructure policy is no exception. Governments respond to demographic changes by reallocating resources and adjusting priorities, often with long-term planning documents that offer glimpses into future transit projects. By meticulously studying these documents, one can discern which areas are likely to receive funding and attention. For instance, a government initiative focusing on reducing carbon emissions may prioritize mass transit options over road expansions, signaling potential growth in transit-oriented developments. Staying attuned to these policy directions provides invaluable context when analyzing demographic trends and urban growth.

Synthesizing knowledge of urban growth, demographic shifts, and policy directions offers a comprehensive framework for anticipating transit infrastructure evolution. By connecting these dots, one can identify not only where transit hubs are likely to emerge but also how they will be integrated into the broader urban fabric. This holistic view encourages investors to go beyond surface-level observation and engage with the underlying dynamics driving infrastructure changes. Encouraging a mindset of continuous exploration and critical analysis, this approach transforms complex data into actionable insights. By adopting this perspective, readers are empowered to capitalize on the hidden potential within urban landscapes, turning informed predictions into tangible investment success.

Deciphering Policy Changes and Government Priorities

Understanding the intricacies of policy shifts and government priorities is akin to decoding a complex puzzle, where each piece offers insight into potential future transit developments. Policy changes often act as harbingers of infrastructural evolution, guiding the course of urban planning and investment opportunities. Advanced research techniques allow investors to identify these shifts early, positioning themselves advantageously within the market. Legislative amendments, budget proposals, and strategic government documents reveal the underlying priorities that influence transit planning. By analyzing these documents, investors can discern patterns and anticipate where new transit hubs might surface, presenting lucrative opportunities for those with the foresight to act.

To comprehend policy changes effectively, one must adopt a holistic approach, integrating varied sources of information to form a cohesive understanding. Government priorities are frequently articulated through public statements, strategic planning documents, and funding allocations. Attention to these details can illuminate the government's commitment to expanding or enhancing transit networks. For instance, a sudden increase in funding for sustainable transportation or urban development initiatives often signifies impending growth in transit infrastructure. By cross-referencing these indications with current urban growth trends, investors can strategically position their investments to align with upcoming transit expansions.

Technological innovations are increasingly shaping transportation policy, offering new avenues for understanding government priorities. The rise of smart transportation systems and digital infrastructure has transformed how cities approach transit planning. Analyzing how governments integrate technology into their transportation frameworks can reveal future directions for transit development. Consider the implementation of intelligent traffic systems or the adoption of electric bus fleets; such initiatives often precede the establishment of new transit corridors. This technological lens provides investors with a nuanced understanding of potential transit hubs, allowing for more informed decision-making.

Policy shifts are not isolated phenomena; they ripple through communities, impacting real estate dynamics and urban landscapes. The anticipation of a new transit hub can lead to significant changes in property values and community development. Investors who understand these ripple effects can capitalize on opportunities to acquire undervalued properties before the market adjusts. Recognizing the interplay between policy changes and real estate trends is essential for developing a robust investment strategy. By predicting where transit-driven growth will occur, investors can secure assets that will appreciate in tandem with infrastructure projects, maximizing their returns over time.

Consider the implications of transit-oriented development policies, which prioritize the integration of residential and commercial spaces within transit nodes. These policies often reflect broader government objectives to enhance connectivity and reduce urban sprawl. By identifying areas designated for such development, investors can position themselves at the forefront of urban transformation. This strategic foresight requires a keen understanding of policy nuances, technological advancements, and market dynamics, enabling investors to not only predict but also influence the trajectory of urban growth. As complex as these dynamics may be, they offer a wealth of opportunity for those willing to navigate the intricacies of policy and infrastructure planning.

Leveraging Technological Innovations in Transportation Planning

Transportation planning has undergone a remarkable transformation, thanks to a wave of technological advancements that are reshaping how cities anticipate and implement transit solutions. One of the most exciting developments is the integration of big data analytics, which allows planners to interpret vast amounts of information from sources like mobile phone tracking, ride-sharing services, and social media activity. This data-driven approach offers unprecedented insights into commuter behavior, peak travel times, and underutilized routes, enabling more informed decisions about where to establish new transit hubs. By harnessing these insights, investors can identify potential growth areas before they gain widespread attention, positioning themselves advantageously in the market.

In addition to big data, geographic information systems (GIS) play a pivotal role in visualizing and analyzing spatial data, offering a detailed picture of urban landscapes. GIS can model various scenarios, such as population growth and land use changes, to predict future transit needs. With this technology, planners can simulate the impact of new stations or lines on surrounding areas, revealing opportunities for transit-oriented development. Investors equipped with GIS insights can anticipate shifts in real estate demand around proposed transit nodes, allowing them to make strategic decisions that capitalize on these changes. Such predictive capabilities are invaluable for identifying emerging markets and ensuring investments are well-timed.

Advanced transportation models, powered by machine learning and artificial intelligence, are also revolutionizing the forecasting of transit requirements. These models can process complex datasets to identify patterns and trends that traditional methods might overlook. For instance, AI can predict how modifications in public transport infrastructure will affect travel times, congestion, and accessibility. Investors who understand these models can better predict which areas will benefit most from transit improvements, thus enhancing their ability to select properties with the greatest potential for appreciation. Embracing these cutting-edge tools offers a competitive edge, turning raw data into actionable insights.

Beyond data analysis and modeling, the advent of smart technologies in transportation infrastructure itself is reshaping transit planning. Innovations such as autonomous vehicles and smart transit systems are gradually being incorporated into urban environments, altering the dynamics of transit corridors. These technologies promise to redefine accessibility, making previously undesirable areas more attractive. Investors who stay informed about these technological shifts can identify undervalued properties that stand to gain from changes in transportation accessibility. Such foresight is crucial for maximizing returns in an increasingly connected and automated world.

While technological innovations provide powerful tools for predicting transit developments, it is essential to adopt a holistic approach that considers economic, social, and environmental factors. This broader perspective ensures that predictions are grounded in reality, accounting for potential challenges and opportunities that technology alone cannot reveal. By integrating these diverse elements, investors can craft a comprehensive strategy that not only identifies promising transit hubs but also aligns with broader urban trends. This multifaceted approach fosters resilience in investment decisions, allowing investors to adapt to an ever-evolving landscape and maintain a competitive advantage.

The Ripple Effect of Transit Upgrades on Real Estate

In recent years, we've seen a surge in urban development projects that prioritize efficient transit systems as a catalyst for growth, blending mobility with enhanced living standards. The transformative influence of transit upgrades on real estate is profound, reshaping how cities expand and evolve. When a new transit line is announced or an existing network is upgraded, the surrounding areas often experience a flurry of activity as property values shift and demand fluctuates. Investors who can anticipate these changes stand to benefit significantly from what could be substantial returns. The strategic positioning of assets near transit corridors not only offers convenience but also has the power to redefine entire neighborhoods, making them more desirable and accessible.

This ripple effect extends beyond residential properties. It opens up strategic commercial development opportunities, inviting businesses to tap into the increased foot traffic and enhanced connectivity that transit upgrades bring. As transit hubs and stations emerge as focal points of activity, they become prime targets for retail, hospitality, and mixed-use developments. Meanwhile, long-term urban planning and zoning considerations come into play, as cities strive to balance growth with sustainability and livability. Recognizing these evolving dynamics allows investors to navigate the complexities of the real estate market with greater agility, aligning investment strategies with future urban landscapes. The ability to predict and leverage these shifts can transform a simple transaction into a cornerstone of a thriving portfolio.

Transformative Influence on Property Values and Demand

The landscape of property values and demand is profoundly reshaped by the introduction or enhancement of transit corridors. Historically, areas adjacent to new transit lines experience a surge in real estate interest as connectivity improvements translate into increased accessibility and reduced travel times. This transformation is not merely a matter of convenience; it's a catalyst for substantial economic shifts. Property near transit nodes often witnesses a notable appreciation in value, driven by both heightened demand and the perception of future growth. For investors, understanding these dynamics is essential, as it allows them to pinpoint areas primed for appreciation, offering a competitive edge in a fast-paced market.

As transit lines expand, the ripple effects extend beyond residential properties. Commercial real estate sees a parallel transformation, with businesses eager to capitalize on increased foot traffic and accessibility. This presents a fertile ground for strategic commercial development, where savvy investors can identify potential opportunities in retail, hospitality, and mixed-use spaces. The key is in recognizing nodes that will evolve into bustling hubs of activity, offering a diverse range of services and amenities. By assessing zoning changes and development incentives, investors can anticipate shifts in commercial demand and position themselves to benefit from the economic upsurge that accompanies transit enhancements.

The influence of transit upgrades goes beyond immediate property value changes, prompting a reevaluation of long-term urban planning and zoning strategies. Cities often respond to new transit developments by adjusting zoning regulations to accommodate higher density and mixed-use projects, fostering a vibrant urban environment. These modifications can dramatically alter the landscape, creating new opportunities for development and reshaping community dynamics. Investors who stay attuned to these regulatory shifts can strategically acquire parcels of land poised for rezoning, maximizing their investment potential as urban centers evolve.

Taking a broader perspective, one can observe the intricacies of how transit-oriented development fosters diverse communities and sustainable growth. By encouraging higher density living and reducing reliance on personal vehicles, these projects contribute to a more environmentally friendly urban footprint. They also support local economies by attracting a diverse workforce and encouraging a blend of residential, commercial, and recreational spaces. This holistic approach not only bolsters property values but also enriches the community fabric, creating vibrant neighborhoods that appeal to a wide array of demographics.

To harness these transformative influences, investors must adopt a proactive approach, continuously refining their strategies based on emerging data and trends. By leveraging Geographic Information Systems (GIS) and advanced data analytics, they can gain insights into transit patterns and demographic shifts, enabling them to make informed decisions. Engaging with local planners and attending public meetings can also provide invaluable foresight into upcoming projects. With these tools, investors are well-equipped to navigate the complexities of transit-driven real estate dynamics, turning potential challenges into lucrative opportunities.

Strategic Commercial Development Opportunities

Commercial development in proximity to transit upgrades offers a fertile ground for strategic investments, reshaping urban landscapes and catalyzing economic growth. As transit corridors evolve, they create fertile grounds for new business ecosystems, encouraging a symbiotic relationship between transport accessibility and commercial vitality. A well-placed retail establishment or office complex can thrive in these environments, benefiting from increased foot traffic and the enhanced connectivity that transit improvements bring. The strategic positioning of commercial ventures in transit-oriented areas not only capitalizes on the influx of commuters but also attracts a diverse range of businesses eager to tap into this vibrant market.

This transformative potential is particularly evident in regions undergoing significant transit enhancements, where previously underutilized parcels of land can become bustling commercial hubs. Developers with foresight recognize the value in acquiring properties before the completion of transit projects, positioning themselves advantageously to reap the benefits as these areas mature. This approach requires an astute understanding of zoning laws and urban planning trends, allowing investors to anticipate how cities might adapt their regulations to accommodate the burgeoning demand for commercial space. By aligning development strategies with local policy shifts, investors can effectively navigate the regulatory landscape and optimize their returns.

The integration of cutting-edge technologies, such as Geographic Information Systems (GIS), provides developers with powerful tools to identify promising sites for commercial development. GIS technology enables a granular analysis of demographic data, traffic patterns, and land use, offering insights that were previously inaccessible. This data-driven approach allows for precise targeting of investment opportunities, ensuring that new developments are not only viable but also ideally situated to capture market demand. Leveraging such advanced analytics aligns investment decisions with the nuanced realities of urban growth, providing a competitive edge in the pursuit of lucrative projects.

The economic ripple effect of transit upgrades extends beyond immediate commercial prospects, fostering long-term community engagement and resilience. Thoughtful commercial development can transform transit nodes into vibrant, mixed-use environments that foster social interaction and economic dynamism. By incorporating elements of sustainability and inclusivity into their projects, developers can contribute to the creation of spaces that resonate with the community, stimulating local economies and enhancing the overall quality of life. This holistic approach to development underscores the importance of aligning commercial objectives with broader societal goals, ensuring that growth is both profitable and sustainable.

Investors seeking to capitalize on transit-centric development opportunities should consider not only the immediate financial gains but also the enduring impacts of their ventures. This involves assessing potential risks, such as shifts in commuter patterns or changes in transit funding, and developing robust contingency plans to mitigate these challenges. By fostering partnerships with local governments and stakeholders, developers can gain valuable insights into future transit plans, ensuring that their projects remain aligned with evolving urban dynamics. Such strategic foresight is essential for navigating the complexities of transit-oriented development, empowering investors to maximize their impact while contributing to the broader urban tapestry.

Long-term Urban Planning and Zoning Considerations

Urban planning and zoning considerations have become pivotal factors in the evolving landscape of real estate, especially in the context of transit upgrades. As transit corridors and nodes expand, local governments often revisit zoning laws to accommodate increased population density and commercial activity. This proactive approach not only prepares the area for an influx of residents and businesses but also enhances the potential for sustained property value appreciation. For instance, cities like Portland and Denver have successfully integrated transit-oriented development by adjusting zoning codes to prioritize mixed-use developments around new transit stations. These changes encourage a seamless blend of residential, commercial, and recreational spaces, creating vibrant communities that attract diverse demographics and drive demand.

Incorporating cutting-edge urban planning practices, municipalities are increasingly turning to dynamic zoning, which offers more flexibility compared to traditional zoning models. This approach allows for adaptive land use strategies that can evolve alongside transit developments, accommodating the shifting needs of the community. By implementing form-based codes that focus on the physical form rather than the use of buildings, cities can foster aesthetically pleasing and functionally efficient neighborhoods. For investors, understanding these zoning innovations can provide a strategic advantage, as properties situated in areas anticipating such changes are likely to experience significant appreciation.

The integration of GIS technology in planning processes further enhances the precision with which urban planners can predict the impact of transit upgrades. By analyzing spatial data, planners can identify optimal locations for future development, taking into account variables such as population density, traffic patterns, and environmental factors. This data-driven approach aligns infrastructure projects with regional development goals, ensuring that transit expansions contribute to balanced urban growth. Investors who leverage GIS insights can pinpoint emerging hotspots, allowing them to make informed decisions that align with long-term urban planning trajectories.

The relationship between transit infrastructure and real estate is also influenced by policy shifts at the state and federal levels. In recent years, there has been a push towards sustainable urban development, with governments offering incentives for projects that promote reduced carbon footprints and energy efficiency. These incentives often lead to an uptick in green building projects near transit nodes, which in turn attract eco-conscious consumers and businesses. By staying abreast of policy trends and understanding their implications for zoning laws, investors can position themselves to capitalize on opportunities that align with broader environmental and economic objectives.

Ultimately, the ability to navigate the complexities of urban planning and zoning in the context of transit upgrades requires a nuanced understanding of both local and macroeconomic factors. Investors must not only keep an eye on legislative changes and technological advancements but also engage with community stakeholders to gauge sentiment and anticipate potential resistance. By adopting a holistic approach that considers diverse perspectives and scenarios, investors can develop a robust framework for identifying and seizing opportunities in the ever-changing real estate landscape. This strategic foresight transforms the unpredictability of urban development into a calculated pathway for investment success.

Mastering the art of predicting transit corridors and nodes opens a wealth of opportunities for savvy investors. By understanding the economics of transit-oriented development, tracking expansion projects, and identifying future hubs, readers gain a powerful edge in recognizing where transit upgrades will cause ripples in the real estate market. This knowledge not only enhances the ability to make informed investment decisions but also underscores the importance of strategic positioning in anticipation of public infrastructure improvements. As we turn our attention to the broader landscape of infrastructure investment, consider how this newfound insight into transit systems can be integrated into a comprehensive investment strategy. Reflect on the potential for transit developments to reshape urban environments and create lucrative opportunities. The tools and techniques discussed in this chapter are vital components of the larger toolkit for financial success in infrastructure investing, emphasizing the importance of ongoing research and vigilance as you navigate the intricate web of government planning and development.

Chapter Ten

The Power of FOIA and Public Records Requests

Imagine standing at the edge of a vast library, its shelves stretching endlessly into the horizon, each book a testament to untapped potential. This is the world of public records and the Freedom of Information Act (FOIA)—a treasure trove of knowledge waiting to be unlocked by those with the curiosity and tenacity to seek it. In the realm of infrastructure investments, these records hold secrets that can transform mere speculation into strategic foresight. This chapter invites you into this library, guiding you to the volumes that matter most, and showing you how to extract the insights that will set you apart.

Navigating the corridors of public records requires a keen eye and a strategic mind. Each document, each page, can reveal the heartbeat of government plans. Here, you'll learn not just how to request information, but how to pinpoint the documents that unveil the future. Challenges in accessing these records may seem like formidable barriers, but with the right approach, they become mere stepping stones. The art of leveraging public records lies in understanding their language, in seeing patterns where others see chaos, and in piecing together fragments to form a coherent narrative of opportunity.

As we delve deeper, the power of these records will become evident. They are not just tools for validation; they are instruments of confirmation, transforming predictions into concrete strategies. With this knowledge, you can refine your insights with precision, ensuring that your investment choices are both informed and effective. This chapter will equip you with the skills to turn the intricate dance of bureaucracy into a symphony of strategic advantage, preparing you to act decisively and confidently in the ever-evolving landscape of infrastructure investment.

How to File Effective Freedom of Information Act Requests

Picture a world where the hidden layers of government planning are no longer just the domain of insiders and bureaucrats but are accessible to those who know where to look and how to ask. This is the realm of the Freedom of Information Act (FOIA), a powerful tool that opens the door to the wealth of information held within government archives. For those eager to uncover the nuances of infrastructure projects long before they break ground, mastering the art of FOIA requests can be a game-changer. It transforms the seemingly impenetrable wall of government secrecy into a window of opportunity, where well-crafted inquiries can reveal the blueprints of future development. Yet, the path to navigating FOIA is not without its challenges. Precision, strategy, and an understanding of the system are essential to unlocking its full potential.

Crafting effective FOIA requests is an art form in itself. It requires precision and a keen eye for detail, ensuring that each request is not just heard, but acted upon efficiently. Just as an artist shapes clay with deliberate intent, so too must one shape their inquiries to extract the essence of what is needed without overwhelming the system or falling into the trap of ambiguity. But what happens when the response is less than satisfactory? Understanding the appeals process becomes crucial, turning potential roadblocks into stepping stones towards transparency. Each step, from submission to resolution, builds a foundation for accessing the vital information that can validate predictions and inform strategic investment decisions. As we explore these subtopics, the path to becoming an adept navigator of public records becomes clearer, equipping you to harness the power of FOIA with confidence and foresight.

Understanding the Scope and Limitations of FOIA Requests

Navigating the intricacies of the Freedom of Information Act (FOIA) is akin to unlocking a treasure trove of insights that can significantly influence investment strategies in the realm of infrastructure. FOIA requests serve as a gateway to accessing government-held information, yet understanding the scope and limitations of these requests is paramount. FOIA is designed to promote transparency, but not all information is readily accessible. Exemptions, such as those concerning national security, personal privacy, and proprietary business information, can restrict access. Being aware of these boundaries is crucial for setting realistic expectations and developing effective strategies to obtain the most pertinent information.

Crafting a successful FOIA request requires more than a basic understanding of its scope. Precision and specificity are your allies in this endeavor. A well-targeted request is more likely to yield valuable information, reducing the risk of receiving an overwhelming volume of irrelevant documents or facing delays. For instance, when seeking data on future infrastructure developments, pinpointing specific projects or timeframes can streamline the process. The art of constructing a request lies in striking a balance between being broad enough to capture essential information and narrow enough to avoid unnecessary detail.

The process of submitting a FOIA request can sometimes resemble a negotiation rather than a straightforward transaction. Agencies may initially deny or heavily redact documents, citing various exemptions. Here, the appeals process becomes a critical tool for overcoming these barriers. Understanding how to navigate this process requires both patience and persistence. It is essential to build a strong case by demonstrating the public interest in the requested information and challenging the validity of any exemptions cited. This approach not only enhances your chances of accessing the desired information but also reinforces the importance of transparency in public affairs.

Public records obtained through FOIA requests can serve as a robust foundation for validating predictions about government infrastructure projects. These documents can confirm or refute assumptions, providing a factual basis for investment decisions. Analyzing records such as meeting minutes, internal memos, or project proposals can reveal the underlying intentions and priorities of government agencies. This verification process is invaluable for reducing the uncertainty inherent in predictive investment strategies. It enables investors to make informed decisions based on concrete evidence rather than speculation or hearsay.

A deeper understanding of the FOIA mechanism encourages a proactive approach to information gathering, fostering a mindset that values diligence and foresight. By mastering the intricacies of FOIA requests, investors can transform potential obstacles into opportunities for gaining a competitive edge. The ability to decipher and utilize government documents not only enhances predictive accuracy but also empowers investors to engage with the broader landscape of infrastructure planning. This knowledge ultimately positions them to capitalize on emerging opportunities, guided by a well-informed perspective that transcends conventional investment paradigms.

Crafting Precise and Targeted Requests for Maximum Impact

Crafting a Freedom of Information Act (FOIA) request that yields valuable insights begins with a thorough understanding of the information landscape. Precision in wording and clarity of intent are the pillars upon which an effective request is built. Consider the vast array of documents available under FOIA; narrowing down your focus requires a strategic approach. Start by identifying the specific information pertinent to your investment interests, such as infrastructure project timelines or budget allocations. This specificity not only streamlines the request process but also minimizes the likelihood of receiving excessive or irrelevant data. An adeptly crafted request can transform a nebulous inquiry into a potent tool for uncovering untapped opportunities.

The art of assembling a precise FOIA request hinges on the ability to articulate the desired information succinctly yet comprehensively. Avoid broad or vague language that could lead to ambiguous results. Instead, employ well-defined parameters like project names, dates, and agencies involved, thereby enhancing the precision of the data retrieved. For instance, requesting "all documents related to transportation infrastructure improvements in 2024" is far too broad. A more refined approach would involve specifying the particular type of infrastructure, the geographic region, and the agency responsible, thus honing in on the exact data needed. This meticulous attention to detail not only increases the likelihood of a successful request but also strengthens the foundation for insightful analysis.

In navigating the landscape of FOIA requests, understanding the nuances of agency-specific protocols is paramount. Each government entity may have its own set of procedures and timelines for processing requests. Acquaint yourself with these variations to craft requests that align with the specific bureaucratic frameworks of the agencies involved. This knowledge not only expedites the process but also demonstrates a level of professionalism that can be advantageous if follow-up communication is required. Moreover, some agencies may provide guidance on how to structure requests for optimal efficiency, offering a roadmap for those seeking to refine their approach.

The pathway to extracting maximum value from a FOIA request is often riddled with potential roadblocks, such as delays or incomplete responses. Anticipate these challenges by preparing a strategy for addressing them. For instance, if an initial request is denied or heavily redacted, be prepared to utilize the appeals process as a means of obtaining the desired information. Mastery of this process involves understanding the legal grounds for appeals and crafting a compelling rationale that underscores the importance of the information sought. This proactive stance not only enhances the likelihood of success but also fortifies your ability to navigate future requests with greater confidence and efficacy.

To maximize the impact of your FOIA requests, consider how the information obtained can be seamlessly integrated into your broader predictive framework. Analyze the data within the context of existing trends, juxtaposing it against other intelligence gathered from government meetings or budget forecasts. This synthesis of information serves to validate predictions and refine investment strategies, transforming raw data into actionable insights. Engaging with the data critically and creatively can reveal hidden patterns or opportunities that would otherwise remain obscured. By honing the skill of crafting targeted FOIA requests, you not only enhance your ability to anticipate infrastructure developments but also position yourself to capitalize on them with greater precision and foresight.

Navigating the Appeals Process for Denied or Redacted Information

When faced with denied or redacted information from a Freedom of Information Act (FOIA) request, knowing how to navigate the appeals process can be a pivotal skill. The first step involves understanding the reasons behind the denial. Agencies are required to provide a justification, often citing exemptions like national security, privacy concerns, or internal deliberations. By dissecting these reasons, one can tailor an appeal that directly addresses and counters the agency's rationale. For instance, if a request is denied on privacy grounds, demonstrating a compelling public interest might persuade the agency to reconsider. This approach requires a nuanced understanding of both the agency's policies and the broader legal context surrounding FOIA.

Crafting a persuasive appeal involves more than just a rebuttal; it's an opportunity to refine the original request. A successful appeal often hinges on the ability to present a clear argument that emphasizes the public benefit of accessing the information. Highlighting previous cases where similar data was released can strengthen the appeal. Moreover, showcasing how the information aligns with the agency's mission or could enhance public understanding can tip the scales in favor of disclosure. This strategic framing not only increases the chances of success but also reinforces the requestor's commitment to transparency and accountability.

Timeliness is crucial in the appeals process. Most agencies have strict deadlines for filing appeals, typically within 30 days of the denial. Missing this window can result in the forfeiture of the right to appeal. Therefore, maintaining a meticulous record of all correspondence, including the initial request and the agency's response, becomes indispensable. This documentation serves as a foundation for the appeal, ensuring that the requestor can quickly and accurately respond to any further inquiries. Additionally, it demonstrates an organized and professional approach, which can positively influence the agency's perception of the appeal.

The appeals process often involves multiple layers of review within the agency. Understanding these internal hierarchies can be advantageous. Some agencies have specific officers designated to handle appeals, while others might route them through a legal department. Engaging with these officials in a constructive and respectful manner can open doors to informal negotiations that might resolve the issue without the need for a formal appeal. Establishing a rapport with agency personnel can not only facilitate the current request but also smooth the path for future inquiries.

Beyond the immediate goal of obtaining information, appealing a FOIA denial can have broader implications. Successfully challenging a denial sets a precedent that can benefit other requestors, contributing to a more transparent and accountable government. It also serves as a practical learning experience, equipping the requestor with insights and strategies that can be applied to subsequent requests. By mastering the appeals process, individuals not only enhance their ability to access valuable information but also reinforce the principles of open government, ultimately empowering communities and fostering informed public participation.

Identifying the Most Valuable Records to Request

One fascinating aspect of anticipating lucrative infrastructure investments lies in the strategic art of identifying the most valuable public records to request. The vast repository of government-held documents can be an investor's treasure trove, where each record holds potential clues about future developments. By skillfully navigating this maze, investors can uncover hidden gems that offer insights into upcoming infrastructure projects. The challenge, however, is knowing which records will yield the most significant returns on the effort spent accessing them. Successful investors must adopt a discerning eye, focusing on those records that provide the clearest window into governmental intentions and timelines.

This endeavor involves more than a mere paper chase; it's about understanding the interconnectedness of infrastructure projects and their broader implications. For instance, analyzing the projected impact of infrastructure initiatives on local economies can reveal potential growth areas ripe for investment. Evaluating the timing and scope of government contracts offers a glimpse into the strategic planning behind project rollouts, while prioritizing records aligned with policy trends can signal shifts in governmental focus and funding. Together, these steps form a cohesive strategy, transforming public records from static documents into dynamic tools that validate predictions and guide investment decisions.

Analyzing the Impact of Infrastructure Projects on Local Economies

When examining the impact of infrastructure projects on local economies, one must consider the intricate interplay of factors that catalyze economic transformation. Infrastructure projects serve as the backbone of economic development, directly influencing employment rates, business growth, and real estate values. As an investor, understanding these dynamics is crucial. Consider a new highway expansion; such a project can significantly reduce travel times, enhance connectivity, and attract businesses to previously inaccessible areas. This ripple effect often results in job creation and increased demand for local services, thereby stimulating economic vitality. By dissecting detailed project plans and environmental assessments, investors can identify areas poised for growth and make informed decisions on potential investments.

Advanced analytical techniques, such as input-output analysis and econometric modeling, offer valuable insights into the multifaceted economic impact of infrastructure projects. These methods allow for a nuanced understanding of how funds circulate within a community, revealing both direct and indirect effects. For instance, the construction phase of a project may boost local employment, while the long-term operational phase could enhance business efficiency and competitiveness. By leveraging these analytical tools, investors can quantify potential economic benefits and prioritize projects with the highest return on investment. This approach transcends traditional investment strategies, equipping investors with a robust framework for predicting economic trends and capitalizing on emerging opportunities.

Recent trends highlight the growing importance of sustainable infrastructure in shaping local economies. Projects that integrate green technologies or emphasize resilience against climate change not only address environmental concerns but also attract forward-thinking businesses and residents. In regions where sustainability is prioritized, investors may glean insights into future policy directions and community values, guiding their investment strategies accordingly. Analyzing project proposals and public consultations for sustainability indicators can unveil the long-term economic potential of these developments. By aligning investment decisions with societal trends, investors can position themselves at the forefront of progressive economic shifts, ensuring long-term profitability and relevance.

The socio-economic fabric of a community is another critical consideration when assessing the impact of infrastructure projects. Projects that enhance public transit, improve access to education, or expand healthcare facilities can significantly elevate the quality of life for residents, attracting a skilled workforce and fostering innovation. Investors should scrutinize demographic data and community needs assessments to identify projects that align with local priorities and offer sustainable growth opportunities. Engaging with community stakeholders and attending public forums can provide valuable perspectives, ensuring investment strategies resonate with local aspirations and contribute to the community's overall prosperity.

Thoughtful analysis of infrastructure impacts demands a strategic mindset, one that goes beyond conventional assessments. Investors are encouraged to ponder questions such as: How might a proposed project alter regional economic dynamics? What are the potential ripple effects on local industries and employment patterns? These inquiries not only illuminate potential pitfalls but also highlight untapped opportunities. By combining technical analysis with a keen understanding of socio-economic trends, investors can craft a predictive model that not only anticipates change but actively shapes it. This proactive approach empowers investors to transform foresight into tangible financial success, ensuring they remain agile and adaptive in an ever-evolving economic landscape.

Evaluating the Timing and Scope of Government Contracts

Evaluating the timing and scope of government contracts is both an art and a science, offering astute investors a window into forthcoming opportunities. Understanding the contract award process offers a profound advantage, as it grants insight into the future landscape of infrastructure developments. To gain a competitive edge, one must first grasp the various stages of contract development, from initial proposal to final award. This involves scrutinizing pre-solicitation notices and requests for proposals (RFPs) which, although often laden with technical jargon, reveal crucial details about project timelines and resources required. By decoding these documents, investors can anticipate which projects will be fast-tracked, which might face delays, and which are engineered for long-term growth.

In the realm of government contracts, timing is everything. By analyzing the cadence of contract announcements, savvy investors can align their strategies with the government's fiscal calendar and political cycles. The ebb and flow of contract issuance often coincide with budget approvals or political shifts, providing a predictive rhythm that can be ascertained through vigilant monitoring. Furthermore, the procurement process itself can be a goldmine of information. Understanding when certain contracts are likely to be renewed or when new initiatives are introduced can provide foresight into market dynamics and potential investment opportunities.

The scope of a government contract, meanwhile, offers a glimpse into the magnitude and impact of an infrastructure project. Contracts often specify the scale of work, geographical reach, and the technologies or materials to be employed, all of which can influence local economies and industry sectors. By dissecting these elements, investors can predict ripple effects that extend beyond the immediate project—impacting suppliers, labor markets, and ancillary businesses. Consider, for instance, a large-scale transportation project; the contract details may hint at not only the immediate construction needs but also long-term maintenance and technology upgrades, each representing distinct investment avenues.

To truly grasp the nuances of government contracting, it is essential to adopt a multifaceted approach. Recent studies have underscored the value of integrating data analytics with traditional contract analysis, thereby enhancing predictive accuracy. By employing advanced tools such as machine learning algorithms, investors can sift through vast amounts of public data to identify patterns and trends that might otherwise remain obscured. This quantitative approach, when combined with qualitative insights, forms a robust framework for evaluating government contracts—not just in terms of immediate opportunities, but also in predicting broader shifts within the infrastructure sector.

Encouraging a strategic mindset, investors should pose critical questions about the broader implications of specific contracts. What are the potential long-term benefits and risks associated with a particular project? How might changes in policy or technology impact the project's execution and subsequent investments? By engaging with these questions, investors can refine their foresight, ensuring they are not only reacting to current opportunities but proactively positioning themselves for future developments. By marrying this strategic foresight with actionable steps, such as establishing connections with key stakeholders or forming consortia with other investors, readers can effectively translate their insights into tangible investment success.

Prioritizing Records Based on Emerging Policy Trends

Navigating the labyrinth of public records requires an astute understanding of policy trends that can significantly impact infrastructure projects. Recognizing these trajectories is crucial for investors seeking to prioritize records that will yield the most insight. By anticipating which policy areas will gain traction, investors can strategically request documents that align with these developments. For instance, if a city council has recently shown interest in sustainable urban development, records related to green infrastructure and renewable energy projects may hold valuable insights. This proactive approach not only enhances the efficiency of records requests but also positions investors to capitalize on emerging areas of opportunity.

In the realm of infrastructure investment, timing is as pivotal as the insights themselves. Investors must remain attuned to policy shifts that signal imminent project launches or expansions. Legislative agendas, proposed bills, and regulatory changes are key indicators that can guide the prioritization of records. For example, if a new transportation bill is being debated, records pertaining to highway expansions or public transit improvements may become more relevant. Staying ahead of these policy curves enables investors to request records before these projects gain widespread attention, granting them a competitive edge.

The intricacies of governmental processes often require a nuanced understanding of how policies are formulated and implemented. This knowledge can be leveraged to identify which records will provide the most foresight into future developments. Considerations such as which departments are involved in a policy change, the stakeholders that may influence decision-making, and the historical context of similar initiatives can offer clues about which records to pursue. By dissecting these layers, investors can better predict the types of documents that will reveal substantive information about forthcoming projects.

To further refine their approach, investors should consider the broader geopolitical and economic landscape. Global trends such as the increasing focus on climate resilience or the push towards smart city technologies can have a cascading effect on local policies. Understanding these macro-level movements allows investors to anticipate how they might influence local infrastructure priorities and adjust their records requests accordingly. For instance, a global emphasis on digital infrastructure might prompt local governments to fast-track broadband expansion projects, making related records particularly valuable.

Engaging in a critical assessment of policy trends is not just about predicting which projects will materialize; it also involves understanding the potential obstacles and opportunities these projects might face. This includes assessing public sentiment, analyzing previous project outcomes, and considering the financial implications of new policies. Investors who can adeptly navigate these complexities will be better equipped to prioritize records that not only highlight potential investments but also elucidate the broader context in which these projects will unfold. This comprehensive lens ensures that investors are not merely reacting to changes but are actively shaping their strategies to align with future opportunities.

Overcoming Challenges in Public Records Access

Navigating the labyrinth of public records access can feel like an uphill battle, yet it's a journey that holds immense promise for those willing to persevere. At its heart, accessing these records is about unlocking doors to a treasure trove of information, often hidden in plain sight, that can transform your investment strategy. It's not just about filing requests; it's about understanding the nuances and complexities that come with prying open the vaults of governmental data. Every successful request brings you a step closer to insights that can validate predictions and illuminate paths to untapped opportunities. The process is akin to a strategic game of chess, where each move requires careful consideration and foresight.

As you embark on this quest, anticipate the hurdles of bureaucratic mazes and legal intricacies. These challenges, while daunting, are part of the process that sharpens your skills and resilience. Mastering the art of public records access means familiarizing yourself with the bureaucratic landscape and leveraging legal frameworks to dismantle barriers that stand in your way. It also involves developing a keen eye for detail, especially when interpreting redacted information, to ensure that even the most obscure data reveals its secrets. Each subtopic in this chapter will arm you with techniques to turn challenges into stepping stones, equipping you with the necessary tools to not only access but also interpret and utilize public records to your advantage.

Navigating Bureaucratic Complexities for Successful Requests

Mastering the art of navigating bureaucratic intricacies is essential for obtaining valuable public records. While the path to acquiring these documents may seem labyrinthine, understanding the nuances of institutional processes and the specific language used in requests can significantly enhance success rates. Start by identifying the correct governmental agency and department responsible for the records you seek. Each entity has its own protocols and personnel, so familiarity with these nuances can make a substantial difference. When submitting a request, precision in language is crucial; vague or overly broad requests often lead to delays or denials. Crafting a clear, concise, and specific request can expedite the process, ensuring that the request is processed efficiently and effectively.

In the realm of public records, persistence and patience are virtues. Bureaucracies are often slow-moving, and requests can get lost in the shuffle. Establish a follow-up system to gently remind the appropriate officials of your pending requests. Building a rapport with key contacts within the agency can also prove invaluable. These contacts can provide insights into the status of your request and may offer advice on how to refine it if necessary. Furthermore, understanding the typical timelines for request processing within each agency can help set realistic expectations and guide strategic planning.

As you navigate these complexities, consider the role of technology in streamlining your efforts. Digital platforms and online databases have become indispensable tools for accessing public records. Many agencies now provide electronic filing options, which can significantly reduce processing times. Additionally, online tracking systems allow requesters to monitor the progress of their submissions in real time. Leveraging these digital tools not only enhances efficiency but also provides a transparent view of the bureaucratic process, offering opportunities to identify and address potential bottlenecks.

Despite technological advances, obstacles such as fee structures and redaction policies often present challenges. Familiarize yourself with the cost implications of your requests, as some records require substantial fees for processing or duplication. Being aware of these potential costs ahead of time enables more strategic planning, allowing you to prioritize requests based on budget constraints. Redaction, while necessary for protecting sensitive information, can obscure critical details. Developing skills to interpret and work around redacted content, without compromising the integrity of the information, is an art in itself. Cultivating this skillset can transform seemingly incomplete data into actionable insights, keeping your predictive framework robust.

Consider the broader implications of your requests and the strategic insights they can provide. The data gleaned from public records can reveal patterns and trends that are not immediately apparent. Identifying these patterns requires a keen analytical eye and a willingness to think beyond conventional paradigms. Evaluating the context in which the records were created, the motivations behind their release, and their potential impact on future developments can provide a richer understanding of the information at hand. By approaching public records with a holistic perspective, not only can you overcome bureaucratic hurdles, but you can also unlock a treasure trove of strategic intelligence that informs and enhances your investment decisions.

Leveraging Legal Frameworks to Overcome Access Barriers

Navigating the labyrinth of public records access requires finesse and a keen understanding of the legal frameworks at play. The Freedom of Information Act (FOIA) and similar state-level statutes are powerful tools that can be harnessed to pry open the doors of governmental opacity. Mastering this process involves more than simply submitting a request; it demands familiarity with the nuances of the legislation, including the specific exemptions that agencies often cite to withhold information. By understanding the intricacies of these legal provisions, one can craft requests that strategically sidestep common barriers, thereby enhancing the likelihood of a successful outcome. This approach is not merely about gaining access but about doing so in a manner that minimizes delays and maximizes the yield of pertinent data.

An astute practitioner will recognize that the language and specificity of the request can significantly influence the response. Crafting a well-targeted request involves using precise terminology that aligns with the agency's record-keeping practices, thus reducing the chances of receiving a "no records found" reply. This requires a proactive stance, where one must research the agency's terminology and decision-making processes. Consider the case of a request for infrastructure project timelines: specifying the type of document, such as "project planning schedules" or "budget allocation reports," can streamline the retrieval process and enhance the relevance of the records obtained. This precision not only demonstrates a comprehensive understanding of the bureaucratic landscape but also respects the procedural constraints under which agencies operate.

In overcoming access barriers, one must also be prepared to engage in strategic negotiations. Agencies may initially deny or redact information, citing various exemptions. In these situations, understanding precedents in FOIA litigation can provide leverage. Familiarity with previous court decisions allows one to effectively challenge unwarranted withholdings or excessive redactions. By referencing these legal precedents in follow-up communications, requesters can assert their rights and compel agencies to reconsider their positions. This legal acumen turns what might initially seem like a rejection into an opportunity for advocacy, ultimately expanding access to critical information.

An often-overlooked aspect of utilizing legal frameworks is the potential for collaboration with legal experts or advocacy groups. These entities are frequently well-versed in the nuances of public records law and can provide invaluable assistance in navigating complex requests. By aligning oneself with organizations dedicated to transparency, individuals can benefit from collective expertise and experience, thereby enhancing their own capacity to penetrate bureaucratic defenses. This collaborative approach not only amplifies the strength of individual requests but also contributes to a broader culture of openness and accountability within government agencies.

The journey to access public records is not solely about acquiring information but about cultivating a mindset of persistence and adaptability. The legal landscape surrounding FOIA requests is dynamic, with changes influenced by legislative amendments, judicial interpretations, and evolving agency policies. Staying informed about these developments is crucial for anyone looking to maintain an edge in this field. By continuously refining one's strategy in response to these shifts, individuals can ensure they remain at the forefront of public records access, turning legal knowledge into actionable insights that fuel informed decision-making and strategic investment opportunities.

Advanced Techniques for Interpreting Redacted Information

Interpreting redacted information in public records is an art that requires a keen eye and a strategic approach. When faced with partially obscured documents, one can glean significant insights by focusing on the context and structure of the remaining visible data. The layout, headings, and any available metadata can offer clues about the content that lies beneath the redactions. Analyzing the frequency and pattern of redactions can reveal which sections are deemed sensitive, often hinting at areas of particular importance. By piecing together the fragmented information, a clearer picture can emerge, offering valuable data points that may validate or refine existing predictions about infrastructure initiatives.

A sophisticated understanding of language and legal terminology can further enhance the interpretation of redacted documents. Often, the language surrounding redacted sections can provide hints about the nature of the concealed information. Familiarity with common government jargon and document templates is invaluable, as it allows readers to anticipate the type of information that might be redacted based on the context provided by visible text. This interpretive skill can be honed by studying past examples of public records requests and understanding the types of information typically withheld, such as proprietary data or security-sensitive details. This knowledge empowers readers to make educated assumptions and informed decisions based on incomplete data.

The use of technology and data analysis tools can also play a significant role in deciphering redacted information. Text analysis software, for instance, can identify patterns and correlations within the visible portions of documents, suggesting underlying themes or connections. Machine learning algorithms could even be trained to predict the nature of redacted content by analyzing large datasets of similar documents. Additionally, Geographic Information Systems (GIS) can be employed to cross-reference visible data with other spatial information, revealing potential infrastructure developments. These technological approaches offer cutting-edge methods for extracting maximum value from seemingly sparse data, providing a competitive edge in the evaluation of public records.

In navigating the complexities of redacted information, collaboration and the sharing of insights with a community of like-minded individuals can be immensely beneficial. Engaging with forums or networks of experts in public records access and infrastructure planning can uncover diverse perspectives and interpretations that might not be immediately apparent. This collaborative approach can lead to the discovery of overlooked details or innovative strategies for interpreting redacted content. By fostering a community of shared knowledge, readers can enhance their understanding and improve their ability to predict infrastructure trends, turning challenges into opportunities for growth and learning.

Posing thought-provoking scenarios can further deepen understanding and application of these techniques. Consider a situation where a crucial infrastructure project is underway, but the relevant documents are heavily redacted. By applying advanced interpretation skills, one could potentially identify which companies or sectors are involved, assess the project's potential impact on local economies, and make strategic investment decisions. This scenario underscores the importance of honing one's skills in interpreting redacted information and highlights the tangible benefits that can be achieved by mastering this challenging yet rewarding aspect of public records analysis.

Using Public Records to Validate Predictions

To grasp the impact of public records in the realm of infrastructure investment, one must first appreciate their role as a vital compass in navigating government plans. Public records aren't just bureaucratic formalities; they are treasure troves of information that, when accessed and interpreted correctly, can transform an investor's approach from speculative to strategic. The ability to validate predictions through these documents offers a formidable advantage, grounding investment decisions in reality rather than conjecture. As such, public records serve not only as a confirmation tool but also as a mechanism to refine and enhance predictive models, providing a clearer view of where the winds of government planning might blow next.

Embedded within these records are insights that can significantly bolster the accuracy of investment forecasts. By skillfully leveraging historical data, investors can trace patterns and trends that have previously shaped the infrastructure landscape. Cross-referencing multiple sources further solidifies these insights, weaving a tapestry of information that supports or challenges initial predictions. Advanced analytical techniques then come into play, transforming raw data into actionable intelligence. These steps collectively empower investors to make informed decisions, reinforcing the idea that meticulous research and strategic use of public records can unlock the hidden opportunities of tomorrow's infrastructure projects.

Leveraging Historical Data to Assess Prediction Accuracy

In the realm of infrastructure investment, historical data offers a treasure trove of insights for evaluating the accuracy of predictions. A meticulous examination of past government projects can illuminate patterns and trends, offering a robust framework for predicting future developments. By analyzing historical records, investors can gauge the precision of previous forecasts, fine-tuning their methodologies for greater accuracy. For instance, examining the timeline and budget allocations of completed infrastructure projects can reveal deviations from initial plans, providing valuable lessons for anticipating similar variations in upcoming endeavors. This approach is not merely about validating past predictions but also about refining predictive models to enhance future foresight.

A sophisticated understanding of historical data allows investors to discern subtle signals that might otherwise go unnoticed. Consider the case of infrastructure projects that were delayed or altered due to unforeseen circumstances, such as regulatory changes or public opposition. These instances, documented in public records, can inform current predictive strategies by highlighting potential red flags. Investors armed with this knowledge can develop contingency plans, enabling them to navigate uncertainties with agility. Furthermore, identifying recurring patterns in public records, like common bottlenecks in project execution, can sharpen an investor's ability to anticipate potential hurdles and adapt their investment strategies accordingly.

Analyzing historical data is not solely about understanding past successes or failures; it also involves recognizing the nuanced interplay between various factors influencing infrastructure projects. By dissecting these interactions, investors can construct a more comprehensive predictive framework. For example, assessing how economic indicators, political shifts, or technological advancements influenced historical project outcomes can offer a multidimensional perspective on future investments. This holistic approach encourages investors to consider a broader array of variables when formulating their predictions, enriching their analytical toolkit with diverse insights that transcend conventional wisdom.

Advanced analytical techniques can further amplify the utility of historical data in honing prediction accuracy. Sophisticated statistical models and machine learning algorithms can unearth correlations and causal relationships buried within vast datasets, providing investors with a competitive edge. These cutting-edge tools can process complex data points at scale, identifying predictive signals that might elude traditional analysis methods. By harnessing the power of technology, investors can transform historical data from a static archive into a dynamic resource that actively informs their decision-making processes. This proactive engagement with data ensures that predictions are not only based on past occurrences but are also adaptable to future contingencies.

Envision a scenario where an investor uses historical data to validate their prediction about a forthcoming infrastructure project. They cross-reference their forecast with historical records, identifying discrepancies and refining their approach to better align with observed patterns. This iterative process bolsters confidence in their predictions, facilitating well-informed investment decisions. By consistently integrating historical data into their predictive framework, investors cultivate a proactive mindset, enabling them to anticipate changes and capitalize on emerging opportunities. The practice of leveraging historical data thus becomes an integral part of a dynamic investment strategy, empowering investors to navigate the complex landscape of infrastructure projects with foresight and precision.

Cross-Referencing Multiple Public Records for Confirmation

Unraveling the layers of public records can be akin to piecing together a complex puzzle, where each fragment of information holds potential insights into future infrastructure undertakings. The art of cross-referencing multiple public records lies in the meticulous alignment of these pieces to form a coherent narrative. For instance, permit applications, meeting transcripts, and environmental assessments, when examined in unison, can reveal the trajectory of a planned project. This synthesis not only bolsters the accuracy of predictions but also provides a more nuanced understanding of the project's implications. By comparing data across various documents, investors can discern patterns and inconsistencies that may signal either opportunities or potential pitfalls.

A prime example of harnessing this strategy is evident in the analysis of transportation infrastructure. When local government budgets outline funding allocations for road expansions, corresponding environmental impact reports may highlight the areas of development. Additionally, minutes from city planning meetings can shed light on community responses and anticipated timelines. Together, these documents create a tapestry of insights, allowing investors to predict not just the 'what' but also the 'when' and 'how' of infrastructure changes. This multi-faceted approach ensures that no single document is viewed in isolation, reducing the risk of misinterpretation and enhancing strategic decision-making.

The integration of public records also benefits from employing advanced analytical technologies. Machine learning algorithms, for example, can be utilized to identify correlations and anomalies across large datasets. By training models to recognize these patterns, investors can automate the process of cross-referencing, significantly enhancing efficiency and accuracy. This technological edge is particularly useful when dealing with voluminous records, enabling a focus on high-impact data points that may otherwise be overlooked. Such innovation underscores the value of blending human intuition with computational prowess to uncover actionable insights.

In the realm of infrastructure investment, the ability to validate predictions through diverse records provides a competitive advantage. Cross-referencing enables the confirmation of initial hypotheses, grounding them in verifiable facts. This approach not only mitigates risks but also cultivates confidence in the decisions made. Investors who master this technique find themselves better equipped to navigate the complexities of government planning, transforming uncertainty into opportunity. As public records become increasingly accessible, the skill to effectively cross-reference them becomes an indispensable asset.

While the process of cross-referencing may seem daunting, it opens doors to a deeper understanding of infrastructure dynamics. Readers are encouraged to cultivate a mindset of inquiry, questioning how disparate pieces of information might interconnect to reveal broader trends. By developing a robust framework for analysis, investors can turn the often overwhelming influx of public records into a strategic asset. The pursuit of cross-referencing not only enriches one's investment acumen but also serves as a testament to the power of informed, research-driven foresight in the ever-evolving landscape of infrastructure development.

Advanced Analytical Techniques for Integrating Public Record Insights

Harnessing advanced analytical techniques to integrate insights from public records can significantly elevate one's ability to predict infrastructure developments with precision. By employing sophisticated data analysis methods, investors can transform scattered and diverse pieces of information into coherent, actionable intelligence. One effective technique is data mining, which involves extracting patterns from large datasets. For instance, mining historical records of infrastructure spending can reveal trends and cycles that inform future project timing. Additionally, machine learning algorithms can be applied to predict outcomes based on historical data, offering a predictive edge that goes beyond conventional analysis. These tools enable investors to pinpoint potential investment opportunities with a high degree of accuracy, turning public records into a formidable asset in their predictive arsenal.

Cross-referencing information from multiple public records can further refine predictions and increase confidence in investment strategies. For example, juxtaposing data from environmental impact reports, zoning applications, and transportation planning documents can unveil hidden correlations and dependencies that might otherwise remain unnoticed. This multilayered approach allows for a deeper understanding of how various projects intersect and influence one another, providing a comprehensive picture of upcoming developments. By systematically cross-referencing diverse records, investors not only verify their predictions but also uncover additional insights that might not be apparent from a single source. This comprehensive validation process ensures that predictions are robust and grounded in reliable evidence.

Incorporating geospatial analysis into the interpretation of public records offers another advanced layer of insight. Geographic Information Systems (GIS) can visualize and analyze spatial relationships within infrastructure data, revealing patterns that are not immediately obvious through traditional methods. For instance, mapping out proposed infrastructure projects alongside demographic data can highlight underserved areas poised for development, presenting strategic investment opportunities. Moreover, GIS tools can simulate the potential impacts of infrastructure changes, enabling investors to anticipate and respond to shifts in property values or community dynamics. This spatial perspective enriches the predictive framework by integrating geographic context, ensuring a more nuanced understanding of how infrastructure developments will unfold.

While traditional records provide a wealth of information, integrating them with real-time data sources can enhance the timeliness and relevance of predictions. Sensor networks, satellite imagery, and even social media analytics can complement public records, providing up-to-date insights into current conditions and emerging trends. For instance, satellite data might reveal ongoing construction activities before they appear in official documents, offering an early indication of progress. By blending historical records with real-time data, investors can maintain a dynamic and responsive approach, adapting their strategies as new information emerges. This integration not only sharpens predictive accuracy but also positions investors to capitalize on developments ahead of the broader market.

Engaging with public records through advanced analytical techniques requires both creativity and critical thinking. Consider hypothetical scenarios that challenge conventional wisdom, prompting investors to question assumptions and explore alternative interpretations. What if a seemingly minor zoning change signals a larger, coordinated development effort? How might shifts in public sentiment, gleaned from social media trends, align with infrastructure plans? Encouraging such inquisitive exploration fosters a mindset that is open to diverse perspectives and unconventional insights. By cultivating this analytical agility, investors can transform public records from static documents into dynamic tools for strategic foresight, enabling them to seize opportunities and mitigate risks with confidence.

By harnessing the power of FOIA and public records requests, readers unlock a treasure trove of information that can significantly bolster their investment strategies. This chapter illuminated the practical steps for filing effective requests, helping to demystify the process and empowering readers to target the most valuable records. Navigating the challenges of accessing public records, while often daunting, provides a critical edge in validating predictions and refining investment decisions. Within the grander scope of the book, these techniques are pivotal, enhancing one's ability to anticipate and act on opportunities hidden within government plans. As you move forward, consider how this newfound knowledge can be woven into your predictive framework, transforming raw data into actionable insights. How will you leverage these skills to stay ahead in the competitive world of infrastructure investment? The journey continues, with each chapter building a more robust toolkit for uncovering and capitalizing on the potential of future projects.

Chapter Eleven

Building a System to Monitor Infrastructure Trends

Imagine a world where every significant infrastructure project is a puzzle piece waiting to be placed, a beacon for those who know where to look. Picture the thrill of piecing together these signals, gaining foresight into developments that will reshape communities and economies alike. This chapter invites you to step into that world, where the art of monitoring infrastructure trends becomes an invaluable skill. With the right tools and mindset, you can transform scattered information into a coherent vision of the future, positioning yourself ahead of the curve and ready to seize opportunities as they arise.

In this quest for clarity amidst complexity, we delve into the essential strategies and technologies that can transform how you perceive and interact with infrastructure data. The secrets lie in automating the tedious, leveraging platforms designed to streamline your research, and mastering the art of prioritizing the most crucial information. By understanding the nuances of these processes, you unlock the potential to see what others overlook, turning reams of data into a clear path toward strategic investments. The techniques discussed here are not just theoretical but practical steps that can be tailored to fit your unique investment goals.

As you continue, you'll discover how to craft a scalable workflow that not only accommodates your current needs but also adapts as new opportunities emerge. This is your chance to build a robust system that not only tracks trends but anticipates them, making your investment strategy both proactive and resilient. With each concept explored, you'll be better equipped to not only monitor but also capitalize on the evolving landscape of infrastructure developments. This chapter is your guide to mastering the dynamics of information flow, ensuring that as the world shifts, you move confidently with it, armed with insights others have yet to grasp.

Automating Document Tracking and Alerts

Experts have long debated the best ways to stay ahead in the investment world, but one truth remains: information is power. In the realm of infrastructure investing, where government plans can shift the landscape overnight, being the first to know is crucial. Imagine a system that tirelessly scans thousands of documents, distilling them into concise alerts tailored to your investment interests. This isn't just a futuristic dream—it's the reality of modern investment strategy. Harnessing the power of technology to automate the tracking of government documents transforms the tedious task of research into a streamlined process, freeing up valuable time to strategize and execute. By employing cutting-edge tools and platforms, investors can now receive real-time updates on pivotal developments, ensuring they never miss an opportunity.

This technological revolution extends beyond mere document tracking. It's about building a robust system that integrates multiple data sources, creating a comprehensive picture of emerging trends. The key lies in customizing these alert systems to filter out noise and zero in on the most investment-relevant information. As we explore the intricacies of automating document tracking and alerts, we'll uncover how artificial intelligence and data integration can be your silent partners, tirelessly working behind the scenes. These systems, when thoughtfully implemented, offer unparalleled efficiency and insight, setting the stage for informed decision-making. Transitioning into the subtopics, we will delve into the practicalities of leveraging AI for real-time analysis, blending data streams for thorough monitoring, and crafting alert systems with precision—all essential components of a successful infrastructure investment strategy.

Leveraging AI for Real-Time Document Analysis and Alerts

Artificial intelligence has revolutionized the way we approach document analysis, offering unprecedented capabilities for real-time monitoring and alert generation. By employing machine learning algorithms, investors can sift through vast amounts of government documents, budgets, and planning signals with remarkable speed and accuracy. These advanced systems can identify patterns, trends, and anomalies that would be nearly impossible for humans to detect manually. For instance, natural language processing (NLP) can interpret the nuances of legislative documents, extracting key points relevant to future infrastructure projects. This not only accelerates the research process but also enhances the precision of investment predictions by focusing on truly pertinent data.

Integrating AI into document tracking systems allows for the creation of sophisticated alert mechanisms that notify investors of critical developments as they happen. By combining AI with real-time data feeds, individuals can receive customized updates on infrastructure-related announcements, ensuring they are always a step ahead of market shifts. This dynamic approach to monitoring enables investors to respond swiftly to new information, capitalizing on opportunities before they become widely recognized. For example, a sudden allocation of funds to a transportation project in a particular region could trigger an alert for investors focused on real estate or construction sectors in that area, allowing them to make informed decisions promptly.

The versatility of AI-driven systems extends beyond simple alerts, as they can be tailored to prioritize data based on predefined criteria. Investors might choose to focus on specific types of projects, such as renewable energy or urban development, and customize their alert settings accordingly. By filtering information through AI, users can eliminate noise and concentrate on data that aligns with their strategic goals. This targeted approach not only streamlines the decision-making process but also empowers investors to allocate resources more effectively, ensuring their efforts are directed towards the most promising opportunities.

Implementing AI in document analysis also involves the integration of multi-source data streams, creating a comprehensive monitoring framework. By pulling data from a variety of governmental and non-governmental sources, such as public records, news outlets, and industry reports, investors can gain a holistic view of potential infrastructure projects. This convergence of data provides a richer context for decision-making, enabling investors to discern connections and correlations that might otherwise remain hidden. The ability to synthesize information from diverse origins is a powerful tool, transforming isolated data points into meaningful insights that inform strategic investment decisions.

As AI technology continues to evolve, the potential for real-time document analysis and alert systems will only expand, offering even more sophisticated tools for investors. The challenge lies in staying informed about the latest advancements and understanding how to harness these innovations effectively. By continually refining their AI systems and staying abreast of new developments, investors can maintain a competitive edge in the ever-changing landscape of infrastructure investment. This proactive approach not only maximizes the potential for financial gain but also encourages a culture of continuous learning and adaptation, essential qualities for success in a rapidly evolving market.

Integrating Multi-Source Data Streams for Comprehensive Monitoring

Harnessing the power of integrated data streams for comprehensive monitoring of infrastructure trends begins with embracing a holistic approach to information gathering. In the digital era, countless sources of data—from government websites and public records to industry reports and even social media—can provide valuable insights into upcoming infrastructure projects. To truly capitalize on this wealth of information, it is crucial to establish a seamless flow of data from multiple channels, ensuring that no potentially lucrative detail slips through the cracks. This involves setting up systems that can automatically collect and organize data from these diverse sources, creating a centralized hub of information that allows for real-time analysis and strategic decision-making.

A sophisticated approach to integrating multi-source data streams involves employing cutting-edge software and techniques that can efficiently handle large volumes of information. Data scraping tools, for instance, can extract pertinent details from a variety of online documents and platforms, while advanced APIs enable seamless communication between disparate data sources. By combining these tools, investors can construct a robust framework that not only gathers data but also cross-references it, identifying patterns, anomalies, and opportunities that might otherwise remain unnoticed. This integrated approach ensures that the insights generated are both comprehensive and nuanced, offering a competitive edge in the fast-paced world of infrastructure investment.

The integration of data streams is not merely a technical exercise; it also requires a strategic mindset to prioritize and filter the influx of information. With vast amounts of data at one's disposal, discerning relevant insights from noise becomes paramount. This calls for developing a refined filtering system that aligns with specific investment criteria. For example, by focusing on keywords, geographic regions, or specific agencies, investors can tailor their data streams to emphasize high-priority information, thereby enhancing the efficacy of their decision-making process. This strategic filtering not only streamlines the monitoring process but also ensures that resources are focused on the most promising investment opportunities.

In the realm of infrastructure monitoring, the ability to incorporate real-time updates and alerts into the data integration framework is a game changer. By setting up automated alerts that notify investors of significant developments or changes in data, they can respond swiftly to emerging opportunities. This proactive stance allows investors to stay ahead of the curve, capitalizing on trends before they become widely recognized. For instance, an alert about a new government policy or budget allocation can prompt immediate action, positioning an investor advantageously within the marketplace. These timely alerts transform raw data into actionable intelligence, empowering informed investment decisions that align with long-term strategic goals.

Encouraging a forward-thinking approach, consider the potential of collaborative data sharing and partnerships. By joining forces with other investors, analysts, or industry experts, one can enrich their data streams with insights from a variety of perspectives. This collaborative model not only enhances the quality and depth of information gathered but also fosters innovation and creativity in identifying investment opportunities. By opening up to diverse viewpoints, investors can challenge their assumptions, broaden their understanding of trends, and ultimately make more informed and strategic decisions. This shared intelligence approach underscores the importance of community and cooperation in navigating the complexities of infrastructure investment.

Customizing Alert Systems to Prioritize Investment-Relevant Information

Creating a customized alert system to identify investment-relevant information requires precision and foresight. In the realm of infrastructure investments, the ability to prioritize specific signals over others can be the difference between seizing a lucrative opportunity and missing it entirely. By tailoring alerts to focus on key indicators, such as changes in project funding, legislative adjustments, or shifts in public discourse, investors can streamline their decision-making process. Advanced algorithms and machine learning models offer the capability to filter through vast amounts of data, isolating the most pertinent pieces of information. These technologies enable the creation of a bespoke alert system that not only notifies investors of significant developments but also categorizes them according to potential impact, allowing for a quick and informed response.

Harnessing these tools involves more than just setting up generic alerts; it requires a deep understanding of what constitutes investment-relevant information. For instance, a sudden increase in budget allocation for a transportation project might signal impending construction contracts, thus offering a potential investment opportunity. Similarly, public opposition noted in meeting minutes could indicate project delays, affecting timelines and returns. By integrating historical data and predictive analytics, investors can fine-tune their alert systems to recognize patterns and anticipate future trends. This approach not only improves the relevance of alerts but also reduces the noise of irrelevant information, ensuring that the focus remains on actionable insights.

To enhance the effectiveness of alert systems, one must consider the integration of diverse data streams. These might include government reports, industry news, economic indicators, and social media sentiment. The synthesis of these sources provides a more comprehensive understanding of the factors influencing infrastructure projects. By employing Natural Language Processing (NLP) and sentiment analysis, investors can gauge public opinion and legislative language, capturing subtleties that might otherwise be overlooked. This multi-faceted approach ensures that the alert system is not just reactive but proactive, capable of discerning the underlying narratives that drive infrastructure developments.

Customizing alerts also involves setting specific thresholds and parameters that align with investment goals. This could mean focusing on projects within certain geographic regions or with particular funding levels. By defining these parameters, investors can tailor alerts to their unique strategic interests, ensuring that only the most relevant information reaches them. Furthermore, these systems can be adjusted over time, allowing for the dynamic adaptation of strategies as new trends emerge and investment priorities evolve. This adaptability is crucial in the ever-changing landscape of infrastructure investments, where timely and precise information is invaluable.

While technology plays a significant role, the human element remains indispensable in the process. Critical thinking and expert judgment are required to interpret the data and make informed decisions. Investors must continuously refine their alert systems based on feedback and results, questioning assumptions and adapting to new insights. This iterative process not only enhances the accuracy of the system but also deepens the investor's understanding of the intricate dynamics at play. By combining state-of-the-art technology with strategic human oversight, investors can develop a robust framework for monitoring infrastructure trends, positioning themselves to capitalize on opportunities with confidence and precision.

Tools and Platforms for Research Efficiency

Imagine a world where the complexity of infrastructure planning is no longer an obstacle but a treasure trove of opportunities waiting to be unlocked. In this digital age, the ability to efficiently sift through mountains of information can transform an ordinary investor into a savvy forecaster of future trends. This chapter peels back the layers on how technology can streamline research efforts, turning the daunting task of data collection into a strategic advantage. The power of advanced tools and platforms lies not just in their ability to gather data, but in their capacity to convert scattered pieces of information into a coherent, actionable narrative. By mastering these tools, you position yourself at the forefront of discovering untapped investment opportunities, well before they hit the mainstream.

In this exploration, we dive into the realm of big data analytics, artificial intelligence, and blockchain technology, illustrating how these cutting-edge platforms can be your allies in navigating the intricate web of government infrastructure plans. Big data analytics unlocks insights hidden in vast datasets, revealing patterns and trends that were once invisible. Meanwhile, AI and machine learning offer predictive capabilities, enabling you to anticipate shifts in government spending with remarkable precision. And with blockchain technology, data tracking becomes not only secure but transparent, ensuring the integrity and reliability of your research. Each of these subtopics serves as a cornerstone for building a robust and efficient research framework, transforming a deluge of information into a strategic asset for informed decision-making.

Leveraging Big Data Analytics for Infrastructure Intelligence

Harnessing the power of big data analytics offers a transformative approach to uncovering infrastructure intelligence, enabling savvy investors to anticipate government project trends with unprecedented precision. By analyzing vast datasets, one can discern patterns and correlations that are invisible to the naked eye, such as recurring themes in urban development plans or shifts in regional transportation priorities. These insights can be mined from a diverse array of sources, including public records, social media sentiment, and even satellite imagery. For instance, an uptick in social media discussions about traffic congestion in a particular area, when analyzed in conjunction with municipal planning documents, can signal upcoming investments in road expansions or public transit enhancements. This integration of multiple data streams provides a holistic view of infrastructure trends, granting investors a significant edge in decision-making.

The application of big data analytics in identifying infrastructure trends hinges on sophisticated algorithms capable of processing both structured and unstructured data. Natural language processing (NLP) plays a crucial role in extracting meaning from textual information found in government reports, news articles, and public comments. These algorithms can identify key phrases and sentiment, allowing for the prediction of future infrastructure initiatives. Moreover, advanced data visualization tools help distill complex datasets into intuitive graphics, enabling stakeholders to quickly grasp trends and make informed decisions. By engaging with these technologies, investors can transition from reactive to proactive, positioning themselves strategically to capitalize on forthcoming governmental undertakings.

A notable advancement in the field is the use of predictive analytics, which leverages historical data to forecast future infrastructure developments. Machine learning models are trained on past project data, budget allocations, and economic indicators to predict which types of infrastructure projects are likely to be prioritized. For instance, a machine learning model might analyze a decade's worth of data on highway repairs, economic growth, and public safety reports to forecast the next wave of government roadworks. This foresight allows investors to align their portfolios with anticipated government actions, maximizing return on investment. By constantly iterating on these models and incorporating fresh data, investors can maintain a dynamic and responsive strategy.

In addition, the concept of data democratization has emerged as a pivotal element in the landscape of big data analytics for infrastructure intelligence. By making data accessible and understandable to a broader audience, it dismantles barriers that traditionally favored large institutional investors. Open data initiatives and collaborative platforms empower individual investors with the same level of access to valuable information as their larger counterparts. This shift not only levels the playing field but also encourages diverse interpretations and strategies, fostering a more inclusive investment environment. By engaging with these tools, investors can contribute to a broader dialogue, enriching their understanding and enhancing their strategic frameworks.

In the realm of infrastructure investment, the ability to anticipate and adapt is paramount. By mastering big data analytics, investors can transform raw data into actionable intelligence, crafting strategies that are both innovative and informed. The key lies in embracing a mindset of continuous learning and adaptation, leveraging the latest technological advancements to stay ahead of the curve. This proactive approach not only enhances investment outcomes but also contributes to a more resilient and responsive infrastructure landscape. Through the thoughtful application of big data analytics, investors can unlock new opportunities and drive meaningful impact, aligning financial success with societal progress.

Utilizing AI and Machine Learning to Predict Government Spending Patterns

Unraveling the complexities of government spending patterns requires a sophisticated approach, and AI and machine learning offer an unprecedented advantage in this domain. These technologies enable investors to sift through vast amounts of fiscal data, discerning patterns and trends that might otherwise remain hidden. By deploying algorithms capable of learning from historical data, investors can anticipate future expenditure behaviors, identifying potential investment opportunities with remarkable accuracy. For instance, machine learning models can analyze past government spending to predict which sectors might receive increased funding. This foresight allows investors to position themselves strategically, optimizing their investment portfolios based on projected government priorities.

Harnessing these technological tools requires not only an understanding of AI and machine learning but also a keen insight into the nuances of government data. One must adeptly manipulate datasets that often reside in disparate formats and locations. This is where the integration of machine learning models can automate and streamline the data analysis process, transforming raw data into actionable intelligence. For example, natural language processing, a subset of AI, can be employed to review and interpret government documents, extracting relevant information about future infrastructure projects. By deploying such technologies, investors can maintain a vigilant eye on government announcements and adjust their strategies promptly, ensuring they remain at the forefront of emerging opportunities.

The predictive prowess of AI, when coupled with machine learning, extends beyond mere data analysis; it also encompasses pattern recognition and anomaly detection. These capabilities are crucial for identifying deviations in spending that could signify shifts in governmental priorities. By continuously monitoring such deviations, investors can stay informed about potential policy changes or new project launches. Consider the scenario where a sudden increase in permit approvals in a particular region is detected by a machine learning model—this could indicate an upcoming infrastructure boom, prompting timely investments. The ability to anticipate these shifts not only enhances investment readiness but also mitigates risks associated with unforeseen changes.

While the advantages of AI and machine learning are abundant, their implementation demands a thoughtful approach. Investors must navigate the challenges of model selection, data quality, and ethical considerations. Selecting the appropriate machine learning model is critical, as each model offers distinct capabilities suited to different types of data and analysis. Moreover, ensuring high-quality data is paramount, as the accuracy of AI predictions is directly tied to the caliber of the input data. Ethical considerations, such as data privacy and bias, must also be addressed to maintain the integrity and fairness of the analysis. By carefully managing these aspects, investors can leverage AI and machine learning responsibly, maximizing their potential while safeguarding against pitfalls.

In contemplating the integration of AI and machine learning into investment strategies, one must appreciate the dynamic nature of these technologies. They are not static tools but evolving systems that require continuous refinement and adaptation. Investors are encouraged to experiment with different models and approaches, learning from both successes and failures. Engaging with a community of like-minded individuals and experts can provide valuable insights and foster innovation. By staying informed about the latest advancements and trends, investors can ensure their strategies remain cutting-edge, continually enhancing their ability to predict and profit from government spending patterns. Such a proactive and informed approach not only enhances investment outcomes but also contributes to a deeper understanding of the intricate interplay between technology and public finance.

Integrating Blockchain for Transparent and Secure Data Tracking

Blockchain technology, with its decentralized and immutable nature, offers unparalleled opportunities for enhancing transparency and security in data tracking for infrastructure projects. By providing a tamper-proof ledger, blockchain ensures that all project-related data is recorded in a manner that is both transparent and resistant to unauthorized changes. This capability is particularly valuable in the context of government infrastructure plans, where maintaining the integrity of data is crucial. Blockchain's transparent framework allows stakeholders to verify the authenticity of information, fostering trust and accountability. This technology facilitates a comprehensive audit trail, making it easier to track the evolution of infrastructure projects from inception to completion.

Incorporating blockchain into infrastructure intelligence systems enables stakeholders to gain insights that were previously elusive. For instance, smart contracts can automate the execution of agreements by triggering specific actions when predefined conditions are met. This automation reduces the need for intermediaries, streamlining processes and decreasing the potential for human error. Imagine a scenario where payments to contractors are automatically released upon completion of project milestones, ensuring timely progress and reducing delays. Furthermore, blockchain can provide a secure platform for sharing sensitive information among relevant parties, mitigating the risk of data breaches and unauthorized access.

Recent advancements in blockchain technology have introduced innovative concepts such as interoperability and scalability, addressing previous limitations and expanding its applicability in complex infrastructure environments. Cross-chain compatibility allows different blockchain networks to communicate and share data seamlessly, enhancing the system's overall efficiency. This development is particularly beneficial for large-scale infrastructure projects that involve multiple agencies and jurisdictions. By utilizing blockchain's scalable architecture, these projects can handle increasing data volumes without compromising performance, ensuring that all relevant information is readily accessible and up-to-date.

Exploring diverse perspectives, some experts caution against over-reliance on blockchain due to its energy consumption and the need for regulatory frameworks to govern its implementation. These considerations highlight the importance of a balanced approach, where blockchain is integrated thoughtfully alongside traditional methods. By combining blockchain with other data management technologies, organizations can create a robust infrastructure intelligence system that capitalizes on the strengths of each approach. This hybrid model not only enhances transparency and security but also addresses scalability and environmental concerns, paving the way for sustainable infrastructure development.

Readers are encouraged to experiment with blockchain applications within their predictive frameworks, identifying opportunities to enhance data integrity and streamline processes. Setting up a pilot program to test blockchain's capabilities in a controlled environment can provide valuable insights into its potential benefits and limitations. By continuously evaluating and adapting their strategies, investors and stakeholders can harness the full potential of blockchain, transforming how they monitor and act upon infrastructure trends. This proactive approach not only optimizes investment decisions but also contributes to the broader goal of creating more efficient and transparent infrastructure systems.

How to Prioritize and Organize Data

At the core of successful investment in infrastructure projects lies the ability to prioritize and organize data effectively. In today's world, awash with a constant stream of information, discerning which pieces hold the most weight can be the key to unlocking profitable opportunities. The intriguing aspect of this endeavor is not merely collecting data but transforming it into a coherent narrative that predicts future trends. This is where the art of prioritization comes into play. By focusing on high-impact data sources, investors can construct a clearer picture of the infrastructure landscape, allowing them to anticipate developments before they become widely recognized. The process of data organization, therefore, is not just about efficiency but about creating a strategic edge in a competitive market.

As one navigates the intricate world of infrastructure investment, developing a scalable framework for data classification and retrieval becomes essential. Such a framework not only streamlines the research process but also enhances the ability to respond swiftly to emerging trends. It's an approach that combines advanced analytics with intuitive systems, enabling predictive prioritization of data. This chapter invites readers to explore how to build this framework, providing tools and insights to manage the influx of information effectively. As we delve into identifying the most impactful data sources and implementing sophisticated analytics, the journey towards mastering infrastructure trend monitoring becomes both a strategic endeavor and a rewarding pursuit.

Identifying High-Impact Data Sources for Infrastructure Projects

Navigating the vast landscape of infrastructure data requires a discerning eye for recognizing sources that yield high-impact information. Readers are encouraged to explore government databases, public records, and industry reports, which often harbor valuable insights into forthcoming projects. These repositories, though sometimes cumbersome to decode, can be treasure troves for those skilled in extracting pertinent details. Real estate filings, environmental assessments, and zoning changes are often overlooked but can signal the initial stages of significant developments. Identifying these sources involves understanding not only where to find them but also how to interpret the subtle cues they provide about upcoming infrastructure transformations.

Harnessing the potential of diverse data sources necessitates a strategic framework for classification and retrieval. A scalable system allows for efficient categorization of information based on relevance and potential impact. By employing metadata tagging and database management tools, investors can streamline their research process, ensuring that crucial data is readily accessible. This approach not only saves time but enhances the accuracy of predictions. For instance, prioritizing data from agencies with a history of timely project completions can improve the reliability of future forecasts. This structured methodology is vital for maintaining a clear focus amidst the deluge of available information.

Advanced analytics play a pivotal role in prioritizing data for predictive insights. Machine learning algorithms and data mining techniques can uncover patterns and correlations that might elude traditional analysis. By integrating these technologies, investors can forecast infrastructure trends with greater precision, adapting their strategies to emerging developments. Predictive analytics tools can, for example, identify areas with increasing public investment, allowing for timely positioning in markets poised for growth. This forward-thinking approach not only enhances decision-making but also secures a competitive edge in a rapidly evolving landscape.

Incorporating diverse perspectives enriches the data analysis process, offering a more comprehensive understanding of potential opportunities. Engaging with experts across various fields—such as urban planning, environmental science, and economics—can illuminate aspects of infrastructure projects that may not be immediately apparent. This interdisciplinary approach broadens the scope of data interpretation, ensuring that investment decisions are informed by a multitude of factors. By fostering a culture of collaborative inquiry, readers can refine their predictive models, aligning them more closely with real-world dynamics.

Thoughtful application of these insights leads to actionable steps for leveraging infrastructure data. Readers are encouraged to develop a personalized system for monitoring and responding to trends, tailored to their unique objectives and risk tolerance. This might involve setting up automated alerts for specific types of data releases or forming partnerships with local stakeholders to gain insider perspectives. By continuously refining their approach, readers can transform raw data into strategic advantages, positioning themselves to capitalize on infrastructure developments long before they become apparent to the broader market.

Developing a Scalable Framework for Data Classification and Retrieval

Establishing a robust framework for data classification and retrieval is a cornerstone of efficiently monitoring infrastructure trends. As infrastructure projects grow in complexity, the sheer volume and diversity of data sources can overwhelm even the most seasoned analysts. A scalable framework requires a methodical approach to discern which data streams hold genuine potential for yielding actionable insights. Identifying and categorizing these sources necessitates an understanding of how different data types interact and influence infrastructure projects. By focusing on relevance and potential impact, stakeholders can streamline their efforts, ensuring that critical information is not lost in the data deluge. For instance, prioritizing data from government budget allocations and environmental impact assessments can offer early signals of impending infrastructure developments.

To optimize data classification, advanced taxonomies should be employed, allowing for dynamic categorization that evolves with the scope of the project. This flexibility can be achieved through employing machine learning algorithms that learn and adapt to new patterns in data over time. By integrating artificial intelligence, the framework becomes a living system, continuously refining its classification processes based on new insights and trends. This adaptability not only enhances the precision of data retrieval but also ensures that the framework remains relevant in a rapidly changing landscape. The use of natural language processing can further refine this process by enabling the system to understand and categorize unstructured data from public meetings or legal documents with greater accuracy.

Retrieving data efficiently from this framework requires a synergistic blend of technology and strategic foresight. Leveraging cloud-based platforms ensures that data is not only accessible but also secure and scalable. These platforms offer the advantage of decentralization, allowing multiple stakeholders to access the same data sets without bottlenecks, thereby facilitating collaborative analysis. Furthermore, employing blockchain technology can enhance data integrity and security, providing a transparent trail that can be crucial in verifying the authenticity of data sources. Such technological advancements empower users to focus on analysis rather than being bogged down by logistical challenges.

The practical application of a scalable data framework extends beyond technology. A strategic mindset is crucial, wherein users are encouraged to think critically about the context and implications of the data they analyze. For instance, understanding the socio-economic impact of an infrastructure project can guide better prioritization of data sources. By engaging in scenario planning, stakeholders can simulate potential future developments using the classified data, thereby refining their predictive capabilities. This proactive approach not only aids in identifying opportunities but also equips stakeholders with the foresight to mitigate risks associated with infrastructure investments.

A comprehensive framework is incomplete without a mechanism for continuous feedback and improvement. Regular audits and evaluations of the system's performance can uncover areas for enhancement, ensuring that the framework remains aligned with organizational goals and industry standards. Encouraging a culture of innovation and openness to new methodologies can lead to transformative insights and efficiencies. By fostering an environment that values adaptability and foresight, organizations can stay ahead in the competitive landscape of infrastructure investment, turning data into a strategic asset that fuels sustainable growth.

Implementing Advanced Analytics for Predictive Prioritization of Data

Harnessing advanced analytics for the predictive prioritization of data is a transformative strategy that can significantly enhance the identification of lucrative infrastructure opportunities. By integrating machine learning algorithms and data modeling techniques, investors can sift through vast quantities of information to pinpoint the most impactful signals. These algorithms can be trained to recognize patterns and anomalies in government documents and planning data, offering insights that might be overlooked by traditional analysis methods. For instance, natural language processing can be employed to analyze meeting transcripts or legislative documents, highlighting phrases or topics that frequently correlate with forthcoming infrastructure projects. This approach not only saves time but also improves accuracy in forecasting which projects will likely garner investment interest.

Innovative platforms are emerging that facilitate this level of analysis, offering tools specifically designed for infrastructure trend monitoring. Platforms such as these provide dashboards that aggregate data from multiple sources, applying predictive analytics to forecast future developments. These systems can rank data based on predefined criteria, such as project size, budget allocation, or geographical impact, allowing investors to focus on the most promising prospects. For instance, an investor might prioritize a project with a large budget allocation and significant local economic impact, informed by algorithmic predictions about potential growth zones. By adopting these platforms, investors can maintain a strategic edge, accessing insights that are both timely and precise.

Creating a scalable framework for data prioritization involves establishing a robust classification system that categorizes information based on relevance and potential impact. This system should be dynamic, capable of evolving as new data becomes available and as analytical models are refined. Investors might consider developing a tiered classification approach, where data is ranked from high to low priority based on its potential to influence investment decisions. This ranking can be continuously updated as more information is gathered and analyzed, ensuring that the most critical data is always at the forefront of decision-making processes. A dynamic classification system not only helps in managing the influx of data but also ensures that the investment focus remains aligned with shifting market trends.

Implementing advanced analytics requires a foundation of strong data governance practices to ensure the integrity and reliability of the information being analyzed. Establishing clear protocols for data collection, storage, and processing is crucial, as is ensuring compliance with privacy regulations and ethical standards. Investors should consider collaborating with data scientists and IT professionals to develop secure and efficient data management systems. This collaboration can yield innovative solutions such as automated data cleansing tools or blockchain-based systems for enhanced data transparency. By prioritizing data governance, investors can ensure that their analytical insights are based on accurate and trustworthy information, enhancing their ability to predict and profit from infrastructure developments.

To apply these advanced analytical techniques effectively, consider the broader economic and political landscape that influences infrastructure planning. Analyzing data in isolation might yield limited insights; instead, consider how external factors like policy changes, economic shifts, or technological advancements could impact project viability. For example, an unexpected policy shift towards sustainable energy could suddenly increase the relevance of data pertaining to renewable energy infrastructure. Investors should remain agile, ready to adjust their data prioritization strategies in response to such changes. By embracing a holistic approach that considers both data-driven insights and external variables, investors can refine their predictive frameworks, enhancing their ability to identify and capitalize on infrastructure opportunities. This approach not only strengthens investment strategies but also equips investors to navigate the complex, ever-evolving landscape of infrastructure development.

Creating a Scalable Research Workflow

In the dynamic world of infrastructure investment, the ability to anticipate shifts and trends is a prized skill. Let's explore the heart of constructing a research workflow that not only adapts to the evolving landscape but can also scale with growing demands. This task, while intricate, is crucial for transforming raw data into actionable insights. The process involves weaving together various strands of information, from scattered government documents to the nuanced signals hidden within legislative changes. By establishing a robust system, investors can navigate this complexity with greater precision, ensuring they're always a step ahead of the curve. As we venture into this topic, envision a workflow that operates with the efficiency of a well-oiled machine, capable of sifting through vast amounts of information to extract the golden nuggets that signal opportunity.

The journey begins with designing automated systems that keep a watchful eye on government documents, ensuring nothing slips through the cracks. This is where automation plays a pivotal role, setting the stage for a seamless data collection process. As we delve deeper, the integration of machine learning becomes a game changer, enhancing predictive capabilities and offering insights that were previously out of reach. The final piece of the puzzle involves creating a collaborative platform that fosters real-time insight sharing, allowing investors to benefit from collective intelligence. These elements coalesce to form a scalable workflow, a powerful tool that equips investors to not only predict but also strategically act upon emerging trends in infrastructure development.

Designing Automated Data Collection Systems for Government Documents

Automated data collection systems have emerged as indispensable tools for efficiently tracking government documents related to infrastructure projects. By leveraging advanced technologies, these systems can meticulously sift through vast repositories of public records, identifying key documents that signal upcoming infrastructure developments. These systems not only streamline the gathering of information but also enhance accuracy by reducing the manual errors that can occur in traditional research methods. Consider the potential of web scraping technologies, which can be programmed to continuously monitor government websites for updates, extracting data from planning commissions, budget proposals, and legislative records. These automated systems act as a vigilant watchtower, alerting investors to pertinent developments as they happen, thus transforming a once tedious task into a seamless, automated process.

In the realm of automation, the integration of software such as RPA (Robotic Process Automation) can revolutionize how data is gathered and processed. This technology mimics human interaction with digital systems, allowing for the precise extraction of data from various formats, including PDFs and spreadsheets, which are commonly used in government documentation. RPA tools can be configured to recognize specific keywords or phrases, such as "infrastructure funding" or "transportation development," ensuring that only the most relevant information is captured. This level of specificity not only saves time but also enhances the quality of data collected, offering investors a refined dataset from which to draw insights. By harnessing the power of automation, readers can efficiently navigate the labyrinthine network of government documents, turning potential data overload into a strategic advantage.

Machine learning algorithms further augment the capability of automated systems, offering a sophisticated layer of analysis that transcends simple data collection. These algorithms can be trained to recognize patterns and trends within government documents that might elude the human eye. For instance, machine learning can identify correlations between budget allocations and subsequent project implementation timelines, providing predictive insights that are invaluable for investors. By continuously learning and adapting, such systems can refine their accuracy over time, ensuring that the most pertinent information is highlighted. This dynamic approach not only aids in understanding current infrastructure trends but also in forecasting future developments with greater precision.

Creating a scalable research workflow involves not just the collection of data, but also its organization and prioritization. Implementing tools like data visualization software can transform raw data into insightful graphs and charts, helping to elucidate complex information. By visualizing data, trends become more apparent, allowing investors to make informed decisions quickly. Furthermore, cloud-based platforms can facilitate collaboration among teams, enabling real-time sharing and updating of research findings. This fosters a collaborative environment where insights are continuously refined and expanded upon, enabling a more comprehensive understanding of infrastructural opportunities. Encouraging a culture of open communication and shared insights can significantly enhance the effectiveness of automated systems, as diverse perspectives converge to enrich the research process.

When constructing an automated data collection system, it is vital to ask critical questions that challenge existing paradigms and encourage innovation. What biases might the system inadvertently introduce, and how can these be mitigated? How can the system be adapted to respond to the dynamic nature of government policies and projects? By contemplating such questions, readers are prompted to not only apply the knowledge gained but also to push the boundaries of what is possible within automated research. Ensuring that these systems are not just reactionary, but also proactive, equips investors with a formidable toolset to anticipate and capitalize on emerging opportunities. As readers integrate these systems into their research methodologies, they position themselves at the forefront of infrastructure investment, poised to seize the financial benefits that lie in government project plans.

Integrating Machine Learning to Enhance Predictive Analysis

Harnessing the potential of machine learning for predictive analysis in infrastructure investment offers a transformative edge. Unlike traditional methods, machine learning algorithms can process vast datasets at remarkable speeds, uncovering patterns that might elude human analysts. These algorithms excel at identifying subtle correlations within government documents, such as budget allocations, project timelines, and legislative changes, which can signal impending infrastructure developments. By training these systems on historical data, investors can develop predictive models that anticipate government moves with unprecedented accuracy. This proactive approach allows investors to position themselves advantageously, turning data-driven insights into profitable opportunities long before these trends become widely recognized.

The integration of machine learning into your predictive framework necessitates a robust understanding of both the technology and the domain of infrastructure planning. It's crucial to select algorithms that align with your specific analytical needs. For example, decision trees and random forests offer interpretability, making them suitable for identifying which factors most influence infrastructure decisions. On the other hand, neural networks, while more complex, are adept at recognizing intricate, non-linear patterns in data that might signal emerging trends. With these tools, investors can develop a nuanced understanding of how various factors interact, allowing for more sophisticated forecasting.

Innovative applications of machine learning in this space extend beyond mere prediction. Consider the potential of natural language processing (NLP) to analyze textual data within government reports and public meeting transcripts. NLP can identify sentiment and keyword trends that might indicate shifts in policy or funding priorities. This layer of analysis adds depth to your predictive capabilities, allowing you to gauge the likelihood of project approval or identify emerging areas of governmental focus. By incorporating diverse machine learning techniques, investors can build a comprehensive, multi-faceted approach to prediction, enhancing their strategic decision-making.

Designing a machine learning system requires more than just technical expertise; it involves strategic integration into a broader investment framework. Ensure that your data collection processes feed seamlessly into your machine learning models, allowing for real-time updates and continuous learning. This dynamic approach helps maintain the relevance and accuracy of predictions as new information becomes available. Moreover, fostering a collaborative environment where insights are shared and refined can amplify the effectiveness of machine learning applications. By bringing together diverse perspectives and expertise, investors can enhance the robustness of their predictive models.

The journey towards integrating machine learning for predictive analysis in infrastructure investment is as much about mindset as it is about technology. Embracing a culture of curiosity and innovation encourages continuous exploration of new methodologies and techniques. Regularly revisiting and refining your models ensures they remain aligned with current trends and technological advancements. As readers embark on this path, they are invited to question established norms, explore unconventional approaches, and remain open to the transformative potential of machine learning. Through this proactive engagement, the horizon of investment opportunities expands, unlocking the hidden value within government project plans.

Developing a Collaborative Platform for Real-Time Insight Sharing

Constructing a collaborative platform for real-time insight sharing can significantly enhance the efficiency and accuracy of monitoring infrastructure trends. Such a platform acts as a dynamic hub where investors, analysts, and researchers can converge, exchange data, and refine their collective predictive models. Utilizing cloud-based technologies, these platforms facilitate seamless interaction and data sharing, enabling stakeholders to instantly access and contribute to a shared knowledge base. This collective intelligence becomes a powerful tool, allowing users to cross-verify findings, identify patterns more swiftly, and refine their strategies based on a broader spectrum of inputs. By adopting an open-source approach, contributors from diverse backgrounds can infuse the platform with a variety of perspectives, enriching the overall analysis and leading to more robust conclusions.

To optimize the platform's functionality, incorporating advanced analytics and visualization tools is essential. These tools can process vast amounts of data, transforming raw information into comprehensible insights. Machine learning algorithms, for instance, can identify subtle correlations that might be overlooked in traditional analyses, offering users predictive insights with higher accuracy. When paired with intuitive dashboards, these insights can be visualized in real-time, allowing users to quickly grasp complex trends and make informed decisions. Additionally, implementing customizable alerts and notifications ensures that users remain updated on the latest developments, enabling them to act promptly on emerging opportunities.

The architecture of this platform should prioritize scalability and flexibility to accommodate a growing user base and evolving technological advancements. Employing modular design principles enables the system to seamlessly integrate new tools and datasets, ensuring its long-term viability. By using APIs (Application Programming Interfaces), the platform can connect with various external data sources, enhancing its scope and enriching the analytical capabilities available to users. This interconnectedness allows for the continuous evolution of the platform, adapting to new challenges and opportunities as they arise. The integration of blockchain technology can further enhance data integrity, ensuring that all contributions are traceable and verifiable, which is vital for maintaining user trust.

Engaging users in the development and refinement of the platform fosters a sense of community and shared purpose. By encouraging participation through forums, webinars, and collaborative projects, users can contribute their expertise and insights, driving innovation and improvement. This participatory approach not only enhances the platform's capabilities but also cultivates an environment where users feel empowered and invested in the platform's success. Hosting regular hackathons or innovation challenges can also spur creativity, inviting novel solutions and ideas from a wide array of contributors.

Thoughtful consideration of user experience is pivotal in ensuring the platform's adoption and sustained use. Designing an intuitive and user-friendly interface lowers the barrier to entry, making it accessible to both seasoned professionals and newcomers. Providing comprehensive training resources and support ensures that all users can fully leverage the platform's capabilities. Moreover, by fostering a culture of continuous learning and adaptation, the platform can remain at the forefront of infrastructure trend analysis, consistently offering users a competitive edge in identifying and capitalizing on investment opportunities.

To encapsulate the key ideas explored, this chapter equips readers with a robust framework for effectively monitoring infrastructure trends. By automating document tracking and using cutting-edge research tools, investors can streamline their data-gathering processes, ensuring they stay informed without being overwhelmed by the sheer volume of information. Prioritizing and organizing data becomes an art form, allowing investors to discern significant patterns swiftly and accurately. The creation of a scalable research workflow not only enhances efficiency but also prepares investors to adapt as new projects and opportunities emerge. Mastery of these skills positions readers to capitalize on future infrastructure developments with precision and confidence. As the journey through this book continues, consider how these strategies can be integrated into a broader context of investment planning, transforming insights into actionable steps that can lead to substantial financial gains. Reflect on how refining your system can offer a competitive edge, and prepare to delve deeper into the next phase of transforming predictions into tangible investment outcomes.

Chapter Twelve

Executing Your Predictions for Maximum Profit

Picture a seasoned treasure hunter standing on the cusp of a vast, undiscovered landscape, map in hand, ready to uncover riches hidden just beneath the surface. This is where you find yourself now, armed with insights and strategies that hold the potential to transform your understanding of infrastructure investments into tangible wealth. The journey through the previous chapters has equipped you with the tools to decode the cryptic signals embedded in government plans and budgets, but the true adventure begins here. This chapter is your guide to translating predictions into profitable actions, ensuring that your foresight materializes into financial success.

Imagine the thrill of selecting the perfect property at precisely the right moment, akin to a chess master executing a well-planned move that secures victory. It's not merely about making a purchase; it's about aligning your investments with impending infrastructure developments that promise growth. Timing is critical, much like a surfer catching the perfect wave just as it crests. Here, the emphasis shifts from theory to practice, revealing how to strategically position yourself to capitalize on emerging opportunities before the broader market catches on. The focus is on seizing the moment, harnessing the momentum of anticipated changes to maximize gains.

Yet, as exhilarating as the prospect of profit may be, the seasoned investor knows that every opportunity carries its risks. Navigating the complexities of infrastructure-based investments demands astute risk management and a well-crafted exit strategy. Think of it as an artist knowing when to step back from the canvas, ensuring that the masterpiece they've created is both impactful and enduring. By mastering the art of risk and reward, you lay the groundwork not just for immediate success but for building long-term wealth. This chapter invites you to refine your approach, weaving together foresight and action into a cohesive strategy that sets you apart in the competitive landscape of infrastructure investing.

Selecting the Right Properties to Invest In

Envision a day when your keen insights into government project plans unlock the door to prime real estate opportunities. The landscape of infrastructure investment is not just about identifying where the next bridge or highway will be built; it requires a nuanced understanding of the surrounding environment to ensure maximum returns. This section reveals the art and science of selecting properties that align with both imminent infrastructure developments and broader economic trajectories. By weaving together demographic shifts and economic trends, you can pinpoint the locales where growth is set to explode, stepping ahead of the market and securing investments positioned for success.

As we explore this vital aspect of infrastructure-based investing, the focus will be on how to identify properties that promise not just short-term gains but also long-term value. Proximity to planned infrastructure is a key factor, yet it is just one piece of the puzzle. Regulatory and zoning considerations can dramatically alter the potential of a real estate venture, requiring careful scrutiny to avoid pitfalls. Each subtopic ahead will guide you through these complexities, offering strategies to transform predictions into smart, profitable property selections. With these tools in hand, you'll be ready to navigate the intricate dance of investment timing and risk management, setting the stage for enduring wealth creation.

Analyzing Demographic and Economic Trends for Property Selection

Identifying optimal properties for investment requires a nuanced understanding of demographic and economic indicators, which can serve as powerful predictors of future growth and demand. By scrutinizing population trends, investors can anticipate shifts that may influence property values. For instance, areas experiencing an influx of younger populations or a rise in household incomes often signal burgeoning opportunities, as these demographics typically drive demand for housing and services. Additionally, examining employment trends and industry growth within a region can provide insights into economic vitality. Cities or regions with burgeoning tech sectors, for example, may offer fertile ground for property investments due to the anticipated influx of high-income workers seeking residences and amenities.

The task of pinpointing the right properties also involves evaluating the synergy between demographic movements and planned infrastructure developments. Infrastructure improvements such as new transportation hubs or enhanced public service facilities often catalyze economic growth, creating ripple effects in the surrounding real estate market. Proximity to these developments can significantly enhance a property's value, as accessibility tends to attract both residents and businesses. Investors who can accurately forecast these developments and strategically position their investments stand to gain substantially. The anticipation of a new subway line or highway extension, for instance, can transform otherwise overlooked neighborhoods into thriving hubs of activity and commerce.

A comprehensive understanding of regulatory and zoning implications is equally crucial in assessing a property's investment potential. Changes in zoning laws or municipal regulations can drastically alter the landscape of an area, either enhancing or diminishing its attractiveness for development. Savvy investors pay close attention to local government plans that may signal shifts in zoning policies, such as the introduction of mixed-use zoning or increased building height limits, which can open up new avenues for development and increase property desirability. Conversely, areas facing stricter regulations may see stunted growth, underscoring the importance of staying informed and adaptable in one's investment strategy.

To maximize the potential of demographic and economic analyses, investors should employ a mix of traditional research and advanced technologies. Geographic Information Systems (GIS), for instance, offer sophisticated mapping and data analysis capabilities that can reveal hidden patterns and correlations between demographic shifts and economic indicators. By integrating these insights with qualitative research, such as community surveys or local business forecasts, investors can construct a robust framework for property selection that is both data-driven and contextually aware. This approach allows for a more informed and strategic investment process, ensuring that decisions are grounded in both empirical evidence and real-world conditions.

Engaging in critical reflection and strategic foresight is essential for leveraging demographic and economic trends effectively. Investors should consider posing probing questions that challenge conventional assumptions, such as: How might remote work trends alter residential demand in suburban versus urban areas? What impact could emerging industries have on local economies and, by extension, property values? By exploring these scenarios, investors can develop a more nuanced understanding of potential market shifts and prepare to adapt as conditions evolve. This proactive mindset, coupled with a rigorous analytical approach, equips investors to navigate the complexities of property selection with confidence and precision.

Evaluating Proximity to Planned Infrastructure Developments

Identifying properties near upcoming infrastructure projects presents a unique opportunity for savvy investors. Proximity to significant developments often correlates with increased property value and demand. Recognizing this potential requires a keen understanding of how infrastructure enhancements—such as new transit lines, highways, or public utilities—can transform a locality. Investors should seek areas where planned developments promise to improve connectivity, accessibility, or community amenities. These factors can elevate a neighborhood's desirability, attracting both residents and businesses. By focusing on the transformative impact of these projects, investors can identify areas poised for growth before changes become apparent in the broader market.

The strategic assessment of a property's proximity to planned infrastructure involves more than simply mapping its distance from the project site. It necessitates a nuanced understanding of the project's scale and scope. For instance, a new subway line might drastically alter commuting patterns and enhance local businesses, while a new highway interchange might offer better logistical access for industrial operations. Investors must evaluate the type of development and its anticipated influence on the surrounding environment. This analysis should include potential changes in traffic flow, noise levels, and local services, which may affect the attractiveness of the area to different types of buyers or tenants.

Advanced tools and technologies, such as Geographic Information Systems (GIS) and predictive analytics, can provide an edge in this evaluation. GIS allows investors to visualize spatial relationships and gain insights into how infrastructure projects will reshape urban dynamics. By incorporating demographic and economic data, these systems can forecast trends and identify potential hotspots for investment. Additionally, machine learning algorithms can analyze large datasets to predict which areas are likely to see the most significant growth. Investors equipped with these technologies can gain a competitive advantage, positioning themselves ahead of market trends.

Staying informed about the regulatory landscape is equally crucial. Infrastructure projects often come with changes to zoning laws or land-use regulations, which can significantly impact property values. Awareness of shifts in these regulations can help investors anticipate market fluctuations and adjust their strategies accordingly. Engaging with local planning authorities and participating in public forums can provide valuable insights into the regulatory environment and upcoming changes. This proactive approach ensures that investors are not caught off guard by unexpected shifts in policy or community sentiment that could alter the expected outcomes of their investments.

Imagining scenarios in which planned infrastructure developments do not proceed as expected is also vital for building robust investment strategies. Consider the implications of delays, budget cuts, or political opposition that may stall or alter project execution. Investors should prepare contingency plans and diversify their portfolios to mitigate such risks. By maintaining flexibility and adaptability, they can navigate uncertainties and capitalize on alternative opportunities that may arise. This strategic foresight, combined with an understanding of the interplay between infrastructure developments and property markets, empowers investors to make informed decisions that maximize their potential for profit.

Assessing Regulatory and Zoning Implications on Investment Potential

Understanding the regulatory and zoning implications on investment potential is pivotal when selecting properties near future infrastructure projects. Zoning laws dictate how land can be used, whether for residential, commercial, or industrial purposes, and can significantly impact property value. Zoning changes often precede infrastructure developments, offering a glimpse into future land use that can enhance or diminish an investment's attractiveness. For instance, the reclassification of a residential area to a mixed-use zone can signal an impending shift in local economic activity, potentially increasing property values as businesses and amenities move in. Investors should scrutinize zoning maps and local government meeting minutes to identify such trends, as these documents often reveal proposed changes long before they are enacted.

Regulatory frameworks present both challenges and opportunities for investors. Stringent regulations might initially appear as obstacles, but they can also create scarcity-driven value for properties already compliant with upcoming rules. For example, properties that meet new environmental standards before they are mandated can become more desirable, offering a competitive edge.

Investors should stay informed about proposed regulatory changes by subscribing to newsletters from relevant agencies or joining local business associations. This proactive approach enables investors to anticipate shifts that could affect property values, allowing them to position themselves advantageously within the market.

In addition to zoning and regulations, understanding the political landscape is crucial when evaluating investment potential. Infrastructure projects often require approvals from multiple government bodies, and political will can influence the speed and direction of these developments. Investors should pay attention to local elections and political agendas, as shifts in leadership can lead to changes in priorities and, subsequently, project timelines. Engaging with local stakeholders and attending public forums can provide insights into the political dynamics that could affect infrastructure projects, offering investors a more nuanced understanding of potential risks and opportunities.

Advanced analysis techniques, such as Geographic Information Systems (GIS), can further enhance an investor's ability to assess regulatory and zoning implications. GIS technology allows investors to visualize data spatially, providing a comprehensive view of how various factors, such as proximity to planned projects and zoning changes, intersect. By integrating GIS with demographic and economic data, investors can develop a sophisticated model of potential growth areas. This approach not only uncovers hidden opportunities but also helps investors mitigate risks by identifying areas that may be adversely affected by new developments or regulations.

Critical thinking and strategic foresight are essential in navigating the complexities of regulatory and zoning landscapes. Investors should continuously question assumptions and explore various scenarios to better understand potential outcomes. For instance, what might happen if a proposed zoning change is delayed or rejected? How would that impact the surrounding area and investment strategy? By considering such questions, investors can develop flexible plans that accommodate different possibilities. This proactive mindset, combined with thorough research and innovative tools, empowers investors to capitalize on opportunities while effectively managing risks, ensuring long-term success in infrastructure-based investments.

Timing Your Purchases for Optimal Gains

A historical perspective reveals that the timing of investments can be as crucial as the investments themselves. Throughout history, those who have mastered the art of timing have often reaped the greatest rewards, seizing opportunities that others overlook. Infrastructure projects, with their extended timelines and complex approval processes, present a unique landscape where timing becomes not just beneficial, but essential. Navigating this landscape requires a keen understanding of the ebbs and flows inherent in project lifecycles. This section unpacks the intricacies of timing, offering readers a roadmap to align their investment decisions with critical project milestones.

As government plans evolve from conception to completion, market signals begin to ripple outward, subtly indicating shifts in demand and opportunity. Recognizing and interpreting these signals is an art form in itself, one that can significantly enhance investment outcomes. Additionally, policy announcements serve as pivotal moments, often triggering market reactions that savvy investors can anticipate and capitalize on. By synchronizing investment decisions with these key developments, readers can position themselves at the forefront of emerging opportunities, maximizing potential gains while minimizing risks. The subsequent subtopics will delve into the specifics, guiding you through the nuanced process of timing your infrastructure investments for optimal returns.

Identifying Key Milestones in Project Lifecycles

Understanding the intricacies of project lifecycles is paramount for investors seeking to optimize their timing and maximize profits in infrastructure-based ventures. Project lifecycles often follow a series of predictable phases, each offering unique opportunities and risks. Recognizing these stages can provide investors with a roadmap to strategically enter the market. A project's initiation phase, for instance, frequently involves feasibility studies and environmental assessments, which can signal the project's seriousness and likelihood of advancement. Investors who discern these early signals can position themselves ahead of the curve, gaining a competitive edge over those who wait for formal announcements.

The transition from planning to execution is a pivotal milestone that often triggers market shifts. During this phase, projects secure permits and finalize funding, which can create ripples in local economies. Investors attuned to these developments can capitalize on the heightened demand for adjacent properties or services. For example, when a new highway project reaches the construction stage, nearby land values may escalate as developers anticipate increased accessibility and traffic flow. Savvy investors might acquire properties at this juncture, capitalizing on the upswing in demand before prices soar.

Monitoring project timelines also involves understanding the bureaucratic tempo, which can vary significantly between jurisdictions. Delays in approvals or funding reallocations are common hurdles that can stall projects, offering both challenges and openings for astute investors. By staying informed about governmental processes, investors can adjust their strategies accordingly, either by divesting early to avoid stagnation or by purchasing at a discount during a temporary lull. This nuanced approach requires a blend of patience and agility, positioning investors to benefit from both planned and unexpected developments.

Advancements in technology have introduced innovative tools for tracking project milestones in real-time. Geographic Information Systems (GIS), for instance, offer dynamic insights into spatial data, enabling investors to visualize how infrastructure projects might alter landscapes and influence property values. By integrating GIS with traditional market analysis, investors can refine their predictions, identifying not only when to invest but also where to focus their resources. This synergy of technology and strategy underscores a modern approach to infrastructure investment, where data-driven insights lead to informed decision-making.

Strategically timing investments requires a keen understanding of policy shifts and public sentiment. Policy announcements, such as new zoning laws or infrastructure grants, can act as catalysts, accelerating project timelines and influencing market dynamics. Investors who anticipate these changes can align their decisions with governmental priorities, ensuring their portfolios reflect emerging trends. This proactive stance not only maximizes financial returns but also contributes to sustainable economic growth, aligning individual gain with broader societal benefits. By weaving together these insights, investors can navigate the complexities of infrastructure lifecycles with precision, transforming foresight into tangible success.

Leveraging Market Signals to Anticipate Demand

Navigating the landscape of market signals to anticipate demand in infrastructure projects requires a keen eye for patterns that others might overlook. One effective approach is to scrutinize trends in local economic indicators, such as employment rates and commercial activity, which often precede shifts in demand for infrastructure. When businesses start expanding or relocating to a particular area, it signals an impending need for improved roads, utilities, and public transportation. Observing these subtle shifts with precision provides an edge, allowing investors to position themselves strategically before a wave of demand escalates property values.

In addition to economic indicators, technological advancements play a pivotal role in shaping future infrastructure needs. In recent years, the rise of smart cities has created a demand for digital infrastructure, including data centers and broadband networks. Investors who understand this trajectory can capitalize on the increasing need for technology-driven infrastructure. Analyzing government grants and incentives for tech adoption can reveal areas poised for digital transformation, offering investment opportunities in properties that will benefit from such developments. This foresight requires a blend of technical knowledge and market intuition, enabling investors to foresee and act upon the evolving needs of urban environments.

The interplay between policy changes and market conditions also offers valuable insights. Legislative trends, especially those focused on sustainability and environmental impact, are reshaping infrastructure priorities. For instance, as governments worldwide prioritize green infrastructure, demand for properties near renewable energy projects or low-carbon transit systems is likely to soar. By closely monitoring legislative sessions and public policy shifts, investors can align their strategies with future regulatory landscapes, thus anticipating where demand will surge next. This proactive approach emphasizes the importance of understanding not just current policy, but also the potential ripple effects of future regulatory actions.

While conventional wisdom might focus on immediate market trends, a more nuanced perspective involves understanding the cyclical nature of infrastructure investments. Recognizing how different stages of economic cycles affect infrastructure demand allows investors to time their acquisitions for maximum profitability. During economic downturns, for instance, governments often increase infrastructure spending to stimulate growth. Savvy investors can use this knowledge to acquire properties during low points in the cycle, anticipating their value will rise as infrastructure projects are announced and implemented. This cyclical understanding transforms market fluctuations into opportunities, rather than risks.

Questions of timing and demand prediction also invite a broader consideration of global influences. In a connected world, international trends can impact local infrastructure needs. For example, shifts in global trade routes might increase demand for logistics hubs in previously overlooked areas. By keeping an eye on international developments and considering their local implications, investors can identify opportunities that others might miss. This global perspective requires an openness to diverse information sources and a willingness to integrate complex data into a cohesive investment strategy, ultimately leading to well-informed and timely decisions that maximize returns.

Synchronizing Investment Decisions with Policy Announcements

Synchronizing investment decisions with policy announcements presents a strategic advantage for those adept at interpreting the implications of governmental communications. When governments unveil new policies, particularly those related to infrastructure development, the ripple effects can profoundly impact various sectors. Understanding the nuances of these policy changes allows investors to position themselves strategically ahead of market reactions. For instance, an announcement regarding increased funding for renewable energy infrastructure could signal a potential uptick in the value of related technologies and services. Investors who have honed their skills in reading the subtleties of policy language are better equipped to anticipate shifts in market behavior, thereby seizing opportunities that others might overlook.

The timing of investment decisions in relation to policy announcements is not merely about reacting to public statements; it involves a deep dive into the context and potential trajectory of these policies. A comprehensive analysis of the political landscape, stakeholder interests, and historical precedents can yield valuable insights. For example, tracing the evolution of a policy from proposal through to implementation can highlight critical junctures at which investment opportunities might arise. Coupled with an understanding of the legislative process, investors can estimate when policies are likely to transition from mere announcements to actionable plans, allowing them to time their market entries with precision.

In the realm of infrastructure investment, synchronizing with policy announcements necessitates an appreciation for the broader economic and social implications of these policies. Changes in infrastructure policy often aim to address specific societal needs or economic objectives, such as improving public transportation or enhancing digital connectivity. By aligning investments with policy goals that have widespread public and governmental support, investors can benefit from the momentum that these initiatives generate. This approach requires not only a keen understanding of policy details but also an ability to foresee how these changes might alter the competitive landscape, enabling investors to identify and capitalize on emerging trends.

Adopting a proactive stance involves more than just monitoring policy announcements; it requires a dynamic framework for evaluating the potential impacts of these policies on various asset classes. This might include assessing risks and opportunities within different sectors, regions, or even specific companies that stand to gain or lose from policy shifts. Advanced tools such as predictive analytics and scenario modeling can aid investors in crafting a robust investment strategy that aligns with anticipated policy outcomes. By employing such sophisticated methods, investors can mitigate risks associated with policy changes, ensuring their investment decisions are both informed and calculated.

Crafting an investment strategy that leverages policy announcements involves practical steps that investors can integrate into their decision-making process. One effective approach is maintaining a well-organized repository of policy documents, press releases, and related materials, enabling quick access and analysis. Regularly engaging with policy experts, industry stakeholders, and think tanks can provide additional layers of understanding and foresight. By fostering a network of knowledgeable contacts and resources, investors can stay abreast of policy developments, ensuring that their investment strategies remain agile and responsive to new information. This holistic approach, grounded in research and strategic foresight, empowers investors to navigate the complexities of policy-driven markets and maximize their financial gains.

Managing Risks in Infrastructure-Based Investments

In the vast landscape of infrastructure investments, managing risks becomes not just a task but an art form. The allure of government projects often clouds the inherent uncertainties that come with them. These projects, while potentially lucrative, are riddled with complexities that require a keen eye and strategic foresight to navigate. As we explore the nuances of risk management, it's essential to recognize that understanding the multifaceted risks involved is as crucial as predicting the projects themselves. Without a solid grasp of the potential pitfalls, even the most promising opportunities can quickly turn precarious. This exploration into risk management equips you with the insights needed to not only anticipate challenges but also to transform them into stepping stones for sustainable profits.

Navigating the world of infrastructure-based investments demands an intricate balance of awareness and strategy. As we journey into the specifics, we will dissect the regulatory and political risks that often lurk in the shadows of government projects. A thorough evaluation of financial and market risks will follow, uncovering the financial currents that can impact your investments. Finally, we'll construct a robust framework for comprehensive risk mitigation strategies, ensuring that your approach is both proactive and resilient. These elements, woven together, form a tapestry of knowledge that empowers you to execute your predictions with confidence and precision. With each insight, you refine your ability to manage risks and harness the full potential of infrastructure investments, steering your ventures toward maximum profit and enduring success.

Identifying Regulatory and Political Risks in Government Projects

Understanding regulatory and political risks in government projects is paramount for anyone looking to capitalize on infrastructure investments. These risks often stem from shifts in policy, changes in political leadership, or alterations in regulatory frameworks that can significantly impact project timelines and outcomes. For instance, a change in local government could lead to the reevaluation or cancellation of planned infrastructure projects, affecting stakeholders who have invested based on previous assumptions. One must vigilantly monitor legislative agendas and political climates to anticipate these changes, utilizing tools such as policy analysis and stakeholder mapping. By integrating these insights, investors can better navigate the uncertainty inherent in government projects and reduce their exposure to potential setbacks.

An astute investor recognizes the importance of examining the historical context and current trajectory of regulatory environments. This involves scrutinizing past government actions and current regulatory trends that may influence future infrastructure projects. For example, analyzing past government decisions regarding environmental regulations can provide insights into how future projects might be shaped. Additionally, understanding the nuances of zoning laws and land use regulations can illuminate potential hurdles or opportunities. By developing a comprehensive understanding of these elements, investors can position themselves to preemptively address challenges and capitalize on favorable regulatory conditions, thereby safeguarding their investments.

Political risks often manifest through changes in public opinion and the resulting shifts in policy priorities. Infrastructure projects that once enjoyed widespread support may face opposition due to evolving public sentiments or activist interventions. Investors should actively engage with community stakeholders and participate in public consultations to gauge the broader sentiment towards specific projects. By fostering relationships with key influencers and remaining attuned to public discourse, one can anticipate shifts in support and adjust investment strategies accordingly. This proactive approach not only mitigates risk but also positions investors to advocate for their interests in a constructive manner.

Advanced risk identification techniques involve utilizing cutting-edge technologies and data analytics. Geographic Information Systems (GIS) and big data analytics can reveal patterns and correlations that may not be immediately apparent through traditional analysis. For instance, GIS can help visualize the impact of proposed regulatory changes on land use, while big data analytics can identify trends in political campaign contributions that may signal shifting legislative priorities. By harnessing these technologies, investors can gain a competitive edge in discerning which projects are likely to succeed or face obstacles. Incorporating such tools into one's risk assessment framework ensures a more nuanced understanding of potential threats and opportunities.

The art of managing regulatory and political risks lies in developing a resilient strategy that accommodates the dynamic nature of these factors. Scenario planning is a valuable technique that allows investors to prepare for multiple outcomes by considering various political and regulatory developments. Crafting diverse scenarios helps in identifying potential risks and opportunities across different contexts, enabling investors to maintain flexibility in their approach. This strategic foresight, coupled with a robust network of industry contacts and a deep understanding of the political landscape, empowers investors to not only safeguard their interests but also exploit the evolving infrastructure landscape for sustained profitability.

Evaluating Financial and Market Risks in Infrastructure Investments

Investing in infrastructure projects requires a keen understanding of the financial and market risks that accompany such ventures. One of the primary challenges faced by investors is the variability in costs and returns associated with these large-scale undertakings. Factors such as raw material prices, labor costs, and technological advancements can significantly impact the financial landscape of a project. For instance, a sudden increase in steel prices can inflate construction costs, altering the investment's profitability. Astute investors continuously monitor market trends and economic indicators to anticipate these fluctuations, allowing them to make informed decisions that minimize financial exposure.

The volatility of financial markets also plays a crucial role in infrastructure investments. Economic downturns, shifts in interest rates, and currency fluctuations can all affect an investor's bottom line. A comprehensive understanding of macroeconomic conditions and their potential impact on financing options is essential. For example, a rise in interest rates may increase borrowing costs, thereby affecting the overall return on investment. By staying informed about global economic trends and employing hedging strategies to mitigate currency risks, investors can better safeguard their portfolios against market turbulence.

In addition to financial unpredictability, infrastructure investments are subject to market demand dynamics that can influence their success. Shifts in public and private sector demand for infrastructure services, such as transportation and energy, can affect the viability of projects. For instance, the growing emphasis on renewable energy sources has shifted market demand towards sustainable infrastructure solutions, creating new opportunities for forward-thinking investors. By aligning investment strategies with evolving market needs, investors can capitalize on emerging trends and position themselves for long-term gains.

A nuanced approach to evaluating financial and market risks also involves recognizing the potential for technological disruptions. Innovations in construction techniques, materials, or project management can drastically change the cost structure and timeline of infrastructure projects. Investors who remain abreast of technological advancements can identify opportunities to enhance efficiency and reduce costs. For example, the adoption of prefabrication techniques in construction can shorten project timelines and minimize labor expenses, thereby boosting profitability. By integrating technological foresight into risk assessment processes, investors can stay ahead of the curve and maximize returns.

To navigate these complex financial and market risks, a robust risk mitigation framework is indispensable. This involves diversifying investments across various projects and sectors to spread risk, as well as establishing contingency plans for unforeseen developments. Additionally, forging strategic partnerships with experienced industry players can provide valuable insights and resources that enhance risk management capabilities. Investors who adopt a proactive approach to risk assessment and mitigation are better equipped to weather uncertainties and achieve sustainable profits. By continuously refining their strategies and remaining adaptable to changing circumstances, they can transform potential risks into opportunities for growth and success.

Developing Comprehensive Risk Mitigation Strategies for Sustainable Profits

Planning and carrying out infrastructure investments requires a meticulous approach to risk mitigation strategies. At the forefront of sustainable profit is the ability to foresee potential challenges and design comprehensive plans to address them. This starts with a fine-tuned understanding of both the visible and latent risks embedded in infrastructure-based ventures. Rather than relying solely on traditional risk assessments, a more nuanced approach involves the integration of predictive analytics and machine learning to anticipate shifts in regulatory landscapes or market dynamics. By employing these advanced technological tools, investors can decode patterns that may signal emerging risks, enabling them to craft proactive strategies and maintain a competitive edge.

The intricacies of regulatory frameworks and political climates often pose significant threats to infrastructure investments. These can range from changes in zoning laws to policy shifts due to political turnover. A forward-thinking strategy involves not just tracking current regulations but also maintaining a pulse on political discourse and legislative forecasts. Engaging with local stakeholders and participating in public forums can provide valuable insights into future developments. This approach not only aids in preempting regulatory challenges but also positions investors to influence and adapt to political changes, ensuring that their investments remain viable and profitable.

Financial and market risks further compound the complexity of infrastructure projects. An adept risk mitigation strategy requires a multi-layered approach to financial analysis, encompassing both macroeconomic indicators and project-specific financial health. Employing scenario analysis and stress testing can uncover vulnerabilities in financial projections, allowing investors to develop contingency plans. Additionally, diversifying investments across various infrastructure sectors can buffer against market volatility, ensuring that a downturn in one area does not jeopardize the entire portfolio. This level of financial foresight is crucial for maintaining stability and achieving long-term success.

Crafting a comprehensive risk mitigation strategy also involves the strategic use of insurance and hedging mechanisms. These tools can safeguard against unforeseen events such as natural disasters or abrupt economic shifts. Innovative insurance products tailored to infrastructure investments, like parametric insurance, can offer more precise coverage tailored to specific risks. Meanwhile, financial instruments such as interest rate swaps and currency hedges can protect against the volatility of financial markets. By integrating these mechanisms into their risk management framework, investors can enhance the robustness of their strategy, ensuring resilience against a spectrum of potential disruptions.

Imagining alternate scenarios can deepen understanding and strengthen risk management strategies. Consider a situation where a major infrastructure project faces delays due to unforeseen environmental regulations. How would this impact timelines and budgets, and what measures could be in place to mitigate these effects? Engaging with such hypothetical situations encourages critical thinking and prepares investors for a wide array of challenges. By fostering a culture of proactive risk identification and management, investors can not only safeguard their investments but also unlock new opportunities for growth and innovation within the infrastructure sector.

Exit Strategies and Long-Term Wealth Creation

Imagine a future where your investment decisions not only yield immediate profits but also lay the groundwork for sustained wealth over decades. This is the promise of mastering exit strategies and long-term wealth creation in infrastructure investments. In the dynamic world of government projects, where variables shift and new opportunities arise with the turn of policy or the approval of a budget, the ability to craft a thoughtful exit strategy is paramount. It is not merely about knowing when to sell; it's about understanding how to maximize gains while safeguarding your financial future. The art of exiting gracefully, yet profitably, requires a blend of foresight, adaptability, and strategic acumen that can transform a simple investment into a legacy of prosperity.

At the heart of this approach lies the integration of diverse financial strategies tailored to ride the ebbs and flows of the market. Crafting adaptive exit plans allows you to respond effectively to market fluctuations, ensuring that your investments remain robust in the face of unexpected changes. Meanwhile, employing sophisticated tax strategies can significantly enhance the sustainability of your wealth, turning tax obligations into opportunities for growth. By embracing a diversified portfolio, you not only mitigate risks but also position yourself for long-term security, weaving together a financial tapestry resilient to the uncertainties of infrastructure investments. This chapter unfolds the nuances of these strategies, offering you the keys to unlock enduring wealth through informed and timely decisions.

Crafting Adaptive Exit Plans in Dynamic Markets

Navigating the unpredictable terrain of dynamic markets necessitates crafting adaptive exit strategies that are both nimble and robust. Understanding the fluidity of market conditions is paramount, as infrastructure investments can be influenced by shifts in government policies, technological advancements, and economic cycles. Investors must cultivate a mindset that is both strategic and flexible, allowing them to pivot efficiently in response to evolving circumstances. For instance, anticipating regulatory changes or technological disruptions can provide a competitive edge, enabling investors to adjust their exit strategies proactively rather than reactively. This foresight not only mitigates potential risks but also maximizes profit potential by aligning exit plans with market trends and shifts.

An adaptive exit plan involves continuous reassessment and realignment of investment goals with current market realities. By regularly analyzing market data and trends, investors can identify pivotal moments to exit or reallocate assets, ensuring that their portfolio remains aligned with both immediate and long-term objectives. This approach incorporates a blend of quantitative analysis and qualitative insights, allowing investors to discern patterns and signals that may not be immediately apparent. Integrating advanced analytics and machine learning tools can further enhance decision-making processes, providing deeper insights into market behaviors and potential turning points. By employing these innovative techniques, investors can refine their strategies, ensuring they are both informed and agile in their decision-making.

The emotional aspect of investing often leads to hesitation or impulsive decisions. To counteract this, establishing predefined criteria for exits, such as target returns or market conditions, can instill discipline and objectivity in the exit process. Crafting these criteria requires a nuanced understanding of one's risk tolerance and investment horizon, with a focus on balancing short-term gains against long-term wealth creation. Investors might consider scenario planning as a tool to visualize different market conditions and their potential impact on exit strategies. By simulating various scenarios, investors can test the resilience of their plans and make necessary adjustments, ensuring readiness for a range of outcomes.

Incorporating diverse perspectives in crafting exit strategies can also enrich the decision-making process. Engaging with industry experts, attending conferences, and participating in investor networks can provide fresh insights and challenge prevailing assumptions. This holistic approach encourages investors to step outside their echo chambers, considering alternative viewpoints that may reveal unseen opportunities or risks. By synthesizing these perspectives, investors can develop more comprehensive and adaptive exit strategies, enhancing their ability to navigate complex markets successfully.

Adapting exit strategies to dynamic markets is not a one-time task but an ongoing process that demands vigilance and responsiveness. Investors should regularly evaluate the effectiveness of their strategies, learning from past experiences to inform future decisions. This iterative process of reflection and adaptation fosters a culture of continuous improvement, empowering investors to not only respond to market changes but to anticipate them with greater accuracy. By embracing this proactive approach, investors position themselves to capitalize on emerging opportunities, ensuring their exit plans remain relevant and resilient in the face of ever-changing market dynamics.

Leveraging Tax Strategies for Sustainable Wealth Growth

Navigating the intricate landscape of tax strategies can be a powerful tool in crafting sustainable wealth growth through infrastructure investments. By judiciously applying advanced tax planning techniques, investors can enhance their returns and secure long-term financial stability. One sophisticated approach involves utilizing tax-deferred exchanges, such as the 1031 exchange in the United States. This strategy enables investors to defer capital gains tax by reinvesting proceeds from the sale of one property into another, thus preserving capital for further investment. Understanding the nuances of such exchanges, including timing and eligibility criteria, is essential for maximizing their benefits and aligning them with overall investment goals.

Furthermore, the strategic use of tax credits and incentives can play a pivotal role in optimizing returns. Governments often offer tax breaks for investments in specific types of infrastructure projects, such as renewable energy or low-income housing. By identifying and capitalizing on these opportunities, investors can significantly reduce their tax liabilities while supporting projects that contribute to broader societal goals. Researching and staying informed about available incentives, which can vary by jurisdiction and project type, is crucial for exploiting these advantages. Additionally, partnering with tax professionals who specialize in infrastructure investments can provide valuable insights and ensure compliance with complex regulatory requirements.

The dynamic nature of tax legislation demands a proactive approach to tax planning. Investors must remain vigilant and adaptable, ready to modify their strategies in response to legislative changes. For instance, shifts in tax policy can influence the attractiveness of certain investment vehicles or alter the benefits associated with specific tax deductions. By maintaining an agile mindset and regularly reviewing their tax strategies, investors can safeguard their wealth against unexpected changes and seize new opportunities as they arise. This forward-thinking approach not only mitigates risks but also positions investors to capitalize on emerging trends in the tax landscape.

Beyond traditional tax planning, innovative approaches such as tax-loss harvesting and income shifting can further enhance wealth growth. Tax-loss harvesting involves selling underperforming assets to offset taxable gains, thereby reducing overall tax liability. Meanwhile, income shifting entails distributing income among family members or entities in lower tax brackets, optimizing the family's collective tax position. These strategies, when executed with precision and foresight, can significantly augment an investor's financial portfolio.

However, they require a deep understanding of tax laws and careful planning to ensure they align with the investor's broader financial objectives.

Engaging with hypothetical scenarios can illuminate the potential impact of various tax strategies on investment outcomes. Consider an investor contemplating a series of infrastructure projects with varying tax implications. By projecting different tax scenarios, the investor can evaluate the long-term effects on their portfolio and make informed decisions. This exercise not only sharpens critical thinking skills but also reinforces the importance of integrating tax considerations into the broader investment strategy. In doing so, investors are better equipped to navigate the complexities of tax planning, ultimately fostering sustainable wealth growth and financial resilience in the ever-evolving landscape of infrastructure investments.

Integrating Diversified Portfolio Approaches for Long-Term Security

Diversifying a portfolio to secure long-term financial stability involves more than simply spreading investments across various asset classes. It requires a nuanced understanding of how different types of investments interact and respond to market conditions, especially those influenced by government infrastructure initiatives. The core of this approach lies in recognizing the multifaceted nature of infrastructure projects, which often impact sectors like real estate, technology, and energy. Integrating investments that are likely to benefit from these developments can enhance resilience and potential returns. For instance, investing in technology firms providing smart city solutions or renewable energy companies aligned with governmental priorities can offer substantial upside while balancing risk.

A sophisticated portfolio strategy also considers the geographical dispersion of investments. Infrastructure projects can vary significantly in scope and impact across regions, influenced by local policies, economic conditions, and demographic trends. An investor might examine regions with upcoming transportation hubs or urban revitalization plans, diversifying investments across municipalities to mitigate localized risk. This geographical diversification not only spreads exposure but also taps into unique growth opportunities inherent in varied local economies. Such a strategy demands a keen awareness of regional planning documents and an ability to synthesize disparate data sources to forecast where growth is likely to be most pronounced.

Incorporating diverse investment vehicles like real estate investment trusts (REITs), exchange-traded funds (ETFs) focusing on infrastructure, and direct property acquisitions is another layer of diversification. Each vehicle offers distinct advantages and risks. REITs provide liquidity and a relatively stable income stream, while ETFs offer exposure to infrastructure without the need for direct involvement in property management. Direct acquisitions, though requiring more hands-on management, allow for significant control and potential for value appreciation. Balancing these options requires careful analysis of one's risk tolerance, investment horizon, and financial goals, ensuring that the portfolio is aligned with both short-term objectives and long-term wealth creation.

Advanced diversification strategies also necessitate a forward-looking perspective, incorporating emerging technologies and innovative business models. The rise of smart infrastructure and the integration of IoT (Internet of Things) in public utilities exemplify areas where future growth is anticipated. Investors should consider how these technological advancements might shape infrastructure demand and create new market entrants worth considering. Keeping abreast of technological trends and regulatory changes enables investors to preemptively adjust their portfolios, capitalizing on innovation-driven growth while guarding against obsolescence.

Diversification, while a cornerstone of risk management, should not be static. Markets and infrastructural landscapes are dynamic, necessitating a continuous reassessment of portfolio composition. Investors benefit from periodically reviewing their holdings, ensuring alignment with evolving market conditions and personal financial goals. This iterative process involves not only tracking performance but also staying informed about policy shifts and technological advancements. By maintaining a proactive stance, investors can adapt to market changes, seize new opportunities, and safeguard their financial future.

As we reach the conclusion of this chapter, the journey of transforming predictions into profitable actions becomes clear. Selecting the right properties demands a keen eye for potential and alignment with projected infrastructure advancements. Timing your purchases is an art, necessitating a balance between market awareness and strategic foresight to maximize gains. Managing risks in infrastructure-based investments is essential, as it safeguards your ventures against uncertainties while enhancing resilience. Developing exit strategies fosters long-term wealth creation, allowing you to capitalize on your investments' growth and navigate the market's ebb and flow with confidence. Mastery of these elements not only strengthens your financial acumen but also reinforces the book's core message: that informed, research-driven decisions can unlock substantial opportunities. As you move forward, consider the broader landscape of infrastructure investments and the vast possibilities they hold. How will you leverage your newfound insights to carve your path in this dynamic realm? The tools and strategies discussed here are merely the beginning, inviting you to explore further and refine your approach in the chapters that follow.

Conclusion

Reflecting on the significant findings within "The Infrastructure Oracle: How to Profit from Hidden Government Project Plans," we recognize the transformative power of informed investing in infrastructure. The journey through these pages has illuminated how the discerning investor can decode the often opaque signals of government planning to uncover lucrative opportunities long before they enter the public domain. From understanding the lifecycle of projects to mastering the art of reading budgets and permits, this book has laid a comprehensive foundation for those eager to align their financial strategies with future developments.

The Competitive Advantage of Research-Driven Investing

At the heart of this book lies an unshakeable belief in the power of research-driven investing. By dissecting governmental processes and extracting critical insights from planning documents, readers are equipped with a formidable toolkit for gaining a competitive edge. Whether it's through identifying the early signs of public-private partnerships or utilizing Geographic Information Systems to map out potential growth areas, the advantage lies in staying ahead of the curve. This approach not only enhances one's ability to make informed decisions but also fosters a mindset attuned to the subtleties of economic forecasts and policy shifts. The infrastructure landscape is ever-evolving, and those who harness the skills outlined in these chapters are poised to capitalize on the hidden opportunities that others might overlook.

Staying Ahead of Market Trends and Innovations

Navigating the complexities of market trends and innovations requires a proactive and adaptive mindset. Throughout the book, we have explored how to stay vigilant and responsive to changes that shape the infrastructure sector. By closely monitoring legislative agendas, public meetings, and transit corridor developments, readers can anticipate shifts that may impact investment landscapes. It is this foresight that allows one to not only react to changes but to strategically position oneself to benefit from them. Innovations in technology and policy continue to redefine the boundaries of infrastructure, and those who remain informed and agile will find themselves at the forefront of new opportunities.

Continuing to Refine Your Predictive Framework

The journey does not end with the last page of this book; rather, it marks the beginning of a continuous process of learning and adaptation. As governmental processes and infrastructure needs evolve, so too must the predictive frameworks we employ. Embracing a mindset of perpetual refinement encourages readers to build upon the foundational knowledge acquired, integrating new tools and methodologies as they emerge. This iterative approach not only enhances one's predictive accuracy but also ensures resilience in the face of uncertainty. By cultivating a dynamic framework, investors can confidently navigate the complexities of infrastructure investments, adapting to new insights and refining strategies to stay ahead of the curve.

The path laid out in "The Infrastructure Oracle" is one of empowerment and opportunity. It invites readers to embrace a proactive approach, leveraging the detailed insights and strategies discussed to seize their place in the fast-moving world of infrastructure investment. The practical applications of this knowledge are vast, offering the means to identify and act upon emerging opportunities, manage risks, and craft exit strategies that maximize returns. As you embark on this journey, remember that the act of investing is not merely about financial gain—it is an engagement with the future, a commitment to understanding and shaping the spaces in which we live and work.

As we draw this exploration to a close, consider the broader implications of what has been discussed. The skills and insights gained here not only serve immediate financial interests but also contribute to a more informed and engaged civic life. By understanding the intricacies of government planning and infrastructure development, readers are better equipped to advocate for sustainable and equitable projects that benefit communities at large. This dual purpose—personal gain and public good—elevates the act of investing to a form of civic participation.

In closing, let this book be a call to action. Armed with the knowledge and strategies presented, you have the tools to navigate the complex world of infrastructure investment with confidence and foresight. As you apply these lessons, remember that the landscape is ever-changing, and staying informed is your greatest asset. The potential for growth and success is immense, and with the right approach, you can not only profit from hidden government project plans but also contribute to shaping the future of our built environment. Stay curious, stay engaged, and continue to refine your understanding as new opportunities unfold.

Resources

Books

1. "Infrastructure: A Guide to the Industrial Landscape" by Brian Hayes - This book offers an in-depth look at the physical infrastructure that supports modern society, providing context and understanding of the projects discussed in "The Infrastructure Oracle." Link to purchase

2. "Investing in Infrastructure: A Practical Guide to the Mechanics of Asset Class" by Barbara Weber, Hans Wilhelm Alfen - This book provides insights into the financial aspects of infrastructure investments, complementing the predictive focus of "The Infrastructure Oracle." Link to purchase

3. "The Black Swan: The Impact of the Highly Improbable" by Nassim Nicholas Taleb - While not specifically about infrastructure, this book offers a unique perspective on unpredictability and risk, which is valuable for understanding the uncertainties in infrastructure investments. Link to purchase

4. "Confessions of an Economic Hitman" by John Perkins - Provides an insider perspective on the intersection of economic policies, infrastructure projects, and international finance. Link to purchase

Websites

1. Planetizen - A comprehensive resource for urban planning and infrastructure news, offering articles, courses, and community discussions. Visit Planetizen

2. GovTrack.us - A civic tool to track federal legislation, providing updates on bills, and legislative trends relevant to infrastructure projects. Visit GovTrack

3. Infrastructure Investor - A website focused on infrastructure investment, offering insights, news, and analysis from industry experts. Visit Infrastructure Investor

4. Smart Cities Dive - This platform provides news and analysis on smart city initiatives, including infrastructure developments and public-private partnerships. Visit Smart Cities Dive

Expert Articles

1. "The Economics of Infrastructure Investment" by Lawrence Summers - An article discussing the economic impacts and benefits of infrastructure investments, offering a macroeconomic perspective. Read Article

2. "Public-Private Partnerships in Infrastructure: An Introduction" by Yescombe - An in-depth exploration of P3s, their structure, and their role in infrastructure development. Read Article

3. "Zoning and Land Use Planning" by William Fulton - This article provides insights into how zoning changes can impact infrastructure projects and urban development. Read Article

Tools

1. Google Earth Pro - This tool allows users to explore geographic data and visualize infrastructure development projects using satellite imagery. Download Google Earth Pro

2. ArcGIS Online - A cloud-based GIS tool for mapping and analyzing geographic data, essential for identifying infrastructure trends. Explore ArcGIS Online

3. Tableau - A data visualization tool that can be used to create dashboards and visualizations to track and predict infrastructure trends. Visit Tableau

Organizations

1. American Planning Association (APA) - Offers resources and networking opportunities for those interested in planning and infrastructure development. Visit APA

2. National Association of Home Builders (NAHB) - Provides insights into residential construction trends and their impact on infrastructure projects. Visit NAHB

3. Urban Land Institute (ULI) - A global network that provides leadership in the responsible use of land and in creating sustainable communities. Visit ULI

Communities

1. Reddit - Urban Planning Subreddit - An online community where

users discuss urban planning, infrastructure projects, and related topics. Visit Reddit Urban Planning

2. LinkedIn Groups - Infrastructure Investment Network - A professional group for networking and discussion on infrastructure investment trends and opportunities. Visit LinkedIn Group

These resources provide valuable insights and tools for further exploring the topics covered in "The Infrastructure Oracle," offering diverse perspectives and innovative approaches to infrastructure investment.

References

American Planning Association. (2020). The comprehensive plan: Sustainable, resilient, and equitable communities for the 21st century. American Planning Association.

Anderson, J. E. (2019). Public policymaking: An introduction. Cengage Learning.

Baldwin, R., Cave, M., & Lodge, M. (2012). Understanding regulation: Theory, strategy, and practice. Oxford University Press.

Bardach, E., & Patashnik, E. M. (2019). A practical guide for policy analysis: The eightfold path to more effective problem solving. CQ Press.

Baxter, R. (2016). Understanding GIS: An ArcGIS project workbook. Esri Press.

Bovens, M., Goodin, R. E., & Schillemans, T. (2014). The Oxford handbook of public accountability. Oxford University Press.

Bryson, J. M., Crosby, B. C., & Bloomberg, L. (2015). Public value and public administration. Georgetown University Press.

Burchell, R. W., & Listokin, D. (2018). The fiscal impact handbook: Estimating local costs and revenues of land development. Routledge.

Cervero, R. (2018). Transit-oriented development in the United States: Experiences, challenges, and prospects. Transportation Research Board.

Clark, G. L., Gertler, M. S., & Feldman, M. P. (2018). The Oxford handbook of economic geography. Oxford University Press.

Dye, T. R. (2017). Understanding public policy. Pearson.

Flyvbjerg, B. (2014). Mega-projects and risk: An anatomy of ambition. Cambridge University Press.

Friedmann, J. (2019). Planning in the public domain: From knowledge to action. Princeton University Press.

Glaeser, E. L. (2011). Triumph of the city: How our greatest invention makes us richer, smarter, greener, healthier, and happier. Penguin Press.

Henderson, J. V. (2014). Urban development: Theory, fact, and illusion. Oxford University Press.

Hodge, G. A., Greve, C., & Boardman, A. E. (2010). International handbook on public-private partnerships. Edward Elgar Publishing.

Innes, J. E., & Booher, D. E. (2010). Planning with complexity: An introduction to collaborative rationality for public policy. Routledge.

Katz, B., & Bradley, J. (2013). The metropolitan revolution: How cities and metros are fixing our broken politics and fragile economy. Brookings Institution Press.

Krumholz, N., & Forester, J. (2017). Making equity planning work: Leadership in the public sector. Temple University Press.

Lindblom, C. E., & Woodhouse, E. J. (1993). The policy-making process. Prentice Hall.

Mazzucato, M. (2018). The entrepreneurial state: Debunking public vs. private sector myths. Penguin Books.

Meyer, M. D., & Miller, E. J. (2013). Urban transportation planning: A decision-oriented approach. McGraw-Hill Education.

Moore, M. H. (1995). Creating public value: Strategic management in government. Harvard University Press.

Ostrom, E. (2015). Governing the commons: The evolution of institutions for collective action. Cambridge University Press.

Peters, G. B. (2018). The politics of bureaucracy: An introduction to comparative public administration. Routledge.

Popper, F. J. (1988). Understanding American land use regulation since 1970. Journal of the American Planning Association, 54(3), 291-301.

Pressman, J. L., & Wildavsky, A. B. (1984). Implementation: How great expectations in Washington are dashed in Oakland. University of California Press.

Rittel, H. W. J., & Webber, M. M. (1973). Dilemmas in a general theory of planning. Policy Sciences, 4(2), 155-169.

Rosenbloom, D. H. (2014). Public administration: Understanding management, politics, and law in the public sector. McGraw-Hill Education.

Savas, E. S. (2000). Privatization and public-private partnerships. Chatham House Publishers.

Sclar, E. D. (2000). You don't always get what you pay for: The economics of privatization. Cornell University Press.

Scott, J. C. (1998). Seeing like a state: How certain schemes to improve the human condition have failed. Yale University Press.

Stone, C. N. (1989). Regime politics: Governing Atlanta, 1946-1988. University Press of Kansas.

Vogel, D. (2018). California greenin': How the Golden State became an environmental leader. Princeton University Press.

Walker, R. M., & Andrews, R. (2015). Local government management and performance: A review of evidence. Journal of Public Administration Research and Theory, 25(1), 101-133.

Weimer, D. L., & Vining, A. R. (2017). Policy analysis: Concepts and practice. Routledge.

Yaro, R. D., & Hiss, T. (1996). A region at risk: The third regional plan for the New York-New Jersey-Connecticut metropolitan area. Island Press.

Thank You for Reading – Realty Insider

A Final Word from Realty Insider

Thank you for taking this first step into the closely guarded world of institutional real estate investing. The tactical knowledge and hidden market mechanisms revealed in this book represent just a fraction of the sophisticated strategies that major property empires use to build massive wealth. **Your journey into these protected realms of real estate mastery has only begun.**

We invite you to join our exclusive community of tactically empowered investors at **RealtyInsider.io.** Here, we continue to expose new profit frameworks, decode hidden market signals, and reveal insider strategies as we systematically break down the artificial barriers between institutional knowledge and independent investors. **Our digital knowledge vault provides continuous tactical updates** as we uncover new market opportunities and winning strategies.

Your experiences strengthen our mission. Consider sharing your implementation success by leaving a review **on Amazon**. Your feedback helps us refine our approach to exposing these closely held secrets and encourages others to break free from traditional real estate limitations.

Love this book? Leave a quick review wherever you bought it! Your feedback helps more readers discover valuable insights.

Remember, true wealth creation requires more than just knowing the basics – it requires understanding how to make opportunities untouchable. **We look forward to continuing this journey together as we reveal more sophisticated strategies from the world's most successful property empires.**

Visit **RealtyInsider.io/tactical-access** to claim your free Property Insider's Arsenal and join our movement to expose real estate's hidden wealth-building mechanisms.

Market Knowledge. Real Wealth.

RealtyInsider.io

Insider Preview

Prepare for Your Next Real Estate Advantage with Insider Knowledge

Thank you for reading **[Book Title Here]**! To complement your learning, we've included exclusive previews from three of our companion guides—each designed to give you a strategic edge in real estate investing.

- ***The Pattern Seekers: Hidden Market Signals That Predict Real Estate Opportunities*** – Learn how to spot unconventional indicators—like zoning changes, business permits, and migration patterns—to anticipate real estate trends before they happen.

- ***The Demographic Detective: Hidden Profits in Population Shift Patterns*** – Master the art of predicting population migration trends, identifying emerging neighborhoods, and leveraging demographic data to uncover high-profit opportunities.

Insider Preview from The Pattern Seekers: Hidden Market Signals That Predict Real Estate Opportunities

Real estate winners spot opportunities before they hit the headlines. This book reveals how to track unconventional indicators that signal where the next profitable real estate markets will emerge.

Here's a glimpse into the strategies you'll master:

- **Zoning Changes and the Ripple Effect** – Discover how new zoning laws create hidden investment pockets before developers move in.

- **Business Permits as a Growth Indicator** – Learn to decode business permit applications to identify areas on the verge of economic expansion.

- **Retail Expansion and Property Value Trends** – See how corporate retail expansion forecasts where property values will rise.

- **Infrastructure Projects and Real Estate Booms** – Uncover the direct correlation between public works projects and rising home prices.

- **Migration Patterns and Population Growth** – Learn how demographic trends shape real estate demand long before mainstream investors react.

With real-world case studies and data-backed methodologies, **The Pattern Seekers** will teach you how to outmaneuver competitors and invest with precision.

Insider Preview from The Demographic Detective: Hidden Profits in Population Shift Patterns

Population shifts drive real estate profits. But by the time these trends show up in traditional reports, it's too late. This book teaches you how to track and predict migration trends before they shape the market.

Here's what you'll uncover:

- **The Science of Predicting Migration Trends** – Learn how to analyze data-driven movement patterns and economic drivers shaping new real estate opportunities.

- **Spotting the Early Movers** – Identify the first waves of artists, professionals, and businesses signaling urban revitalization.

- **Housing Affordability as a Predictor** – Discover how affordability gaps in major cities push buyers and renters into new markets before trends become obvious.

- **Infrastructure and Its Ripple Effects** – Explore the relationship between public projects, transportation hubs, and booming housing markets.

- **Remote Work & The Suburban Renaissance** – See how remote work is fueling new migration patterns from urban centers to high-growth suburban and exurban areas.

- **Retiree Migration & International Investment** – Learn where aging populations and foreign buyers are concentrating wealth in real estate.

With a blend of demographic insights, economic forecasting, and real estate strategy, **The Demographic Detective** will show you how to turn population shifts into investment wins.

Want to Keep Gaining an Edge?

- **Get the Full Books Now** to unlock exclusive strategies, case studies, and investment roadmaps.
- **Join the Realty Insider Community** for real-time investment insights and networking.
- **Access our Investor Toolkit** with zoning trackers, legislative updates, and data tools.

Take the Next Step – Visit RealtyInsider.io to continue your real estate journey today!

FINAL ACCESS ALERT

Realty Insider

Elite Real Estate Intelligence Now Released The hidden market mechanisms you've just discovered are merely the surface. Continue your journey into the closely guarded world of institutional property investing with the complete Property Insider's Arsenal – available FREE for a limited time.

This restricted tactical package includes five comprehensive guides revealing:

- Hidden market indicators that predict neighborhood transformations
- Off-market acquisition strategies used by property empires
- Value acceleration tactics that force rapid appreciation
- Risk elimination protocols used by institutional investors
- Psychological triggers that win negotiations against any competitor

→ Visit ***RealtyInsider.io/tactical-access*** now before these strategies become restricted.

"The secrets of institutional real estate wealth are finally being exposed. Master them while you still can."

Also By Realty Insider

What's Next?

Exciting projects are underway! Realty Insider is continuously developing new titles and resources that delve deeper into market cycles, financial mastery, and predictive analytics for real estate. Stay tuned for more insights to empower your investment journey.

Explore More Titles from Realty Insider

- **The Infrastructure Oracle**:
  Discover how to analyze government budgets, monitor zoning changes, and track transit-oriented developments to identify profitable opportunities.

- **The Demographic Detective**:
  Learn to predict profitable migration patterns and uncover neighborhood transformations before they hit the mainstream radar.

- **The Regulatory Goldmine**:

Leverage real estate laws and policy changes to unlock profit opportunities hidden in plain sight.

- **The Arbitrage Hunter**:
  Spot regional pricing mismatches to identify lucrative opportunities and maximize profits.

- **The Value Whisperer**:
  Uncover the science behind property appreciation to strategically build long-term wealth.

- **The Value Accelerator**:
  Transform underperforming properties into high-yield investments using proven value-add strategies.

Stay Connected:

Visit RealtyInsider.io to explore expert resources, innovative tools, and actionable strategies that will help you succeed in your real estate journey. Thank you for being part of our mission to unlock the potential of the real estate market and build a prosperous future!

Enjoyed This Book?

Your feedback is invaluable! Please leave a review wherever you buy your books. Your feedback helps other readers and supports independent authors.

Market Knowledge. Real Wealth.

RealtyInsider.io

The Realty Insider Mission

THE REALTY INSIDER MISSION

The real estate industry's most powerful profit mechanisms have remained hidden for too long. Behind the complex contracts of institutional investors, within the protected playbooks of property empires, and inside the guarded strategies of billion-dollar portfolios lies a treasure trove of sophisticated real estate tactics – methods deliberately obscured from independent investors through artificial complexity and industry gatekeeping. RealtyInsider exists to expose these secrets.

Through unprecedented access to industry whistleblowers, exhaustive analysis of institutional success patterns, and deep investigation into hidden market mechanisms, we reveal the closely guarded methods that consistently create real estate fortunes. Our mission isn't simply to educate – it's to expose the exact frameworks, triggers, and tactical advantages that major property empires use to build their wealth.

What makes our approach revolutionary is our ability to decode the unwritten rules of institutional real estate success. By analyzing thousands of profitable transactions, market patterns, and wealth-building strategies employed by successful property empires, we uncover the subtle signals and hidden principles that separate extraordinary profits from ordinary returns. These aren't theoretical concepts – they're battle-tested tactics that have proven effective across every market condition and property cycle.

Our tactical library spans the entire spectrum of real estate wealth creation. We expose hidden market indicators that predict neighborhood transformations before they happen, sophisticated value-add strategies typically reserved for institutional investors, and protected profit-maximization methods used by property empires. We reveal negotiation psychology that wins against higher bidders, off-market acquisition techniques unknown to most investors, and advanced portfolio optimization frameworks used by billion-dollar funds.

Through our revolutionary intelligence synthesis system, we transform thousands of hours of institutional analysis into clear, actionable strategies that readers can implement immediately. Each guide we publish breaks down another barrier between insider knowledge and independent investors, systematically dismantling the artificial ceiling that has historically limited individual real estate success.

The implications of our work extend far beyond publishing. We're creating a new model for real estate empowerment – one where the sophisticated strategies and insights previously reserved for institutional investors become accessible to independent wealth builders. Our global community of tactically empowered investors shares insights, refines strategies, and collaborates to expose new opportunities, creating an ever-expanding arsenal of practical knowledge about how real estate fortunes are built.

When you understand the hidden mechanisms we expose, you transform from a passive market participant into someone who can see and exploit the true drivers of property wealth. This is the transformation we ignite with every guide we publish – not just sharing market information but fundamentally changing how people approach real estate investing.

Join us in this historic movement as we continue to expose the barriers between institutional knowledge and independent investors. The secrets of real estate wealth creation are finally being revealed. The artificial limitations on individual success are being systematically dismantled. And the sophisticated strategies that have driven property empires for generations are now accessible to those bold enough to implement them.

Because true wealth creation requires more than just knowing the basics – it requires knowing how to make opportunities untouchable.

Market Knowledge. Real Wealth.

RealtyInsider.io

www.ingramcontent.com/pod-product-compliance
Lightning Source LLC
LaVergne TN
LVHW052243200926
848481LV00002B/255
* 9 7 9 8 2 2 7 4 1 6 6 1 2 *